Integrating RTI Cognitive Neuropsychology:

A SCIENTIFIC APPROACH TO READING

Steven G. Feifer, D.Ed.   Douglas A. Della Toffalo, Ph.D

Tier II
...eted small group
...ic interventions and
...tives classroom
...nagement

Dete...
e...

...r III
...oblem solving;
...zed academic
...ehavioral

Foreword by James B. Hale, Ph.D

Integrating RTI With Cognitive Neuropsychology: A Scientific Approach to Reading
by Steven G. Feifer and Douglas A. Della Toffalo

Published by School Neuropsych Press, LLC
PO Box 413
Middletown, MD 21769
Snpress@frederickmd.com

Cover designed by Octavo Designs in Frederick, Maryland.

ISBN # 978-0-9703337-3-5

Printed in the United States of America by
Signature Book Printing, Inc. www.sbpbooks.com

ACKNOWLEDGMENTS

Writing is a labor of love, though this book was written with more perspiration than sheer inspiration. The field of school psychology is fraught with controversy over the age-old questions as to what exactly constitutes a learning disability and what represent the best data collection measures to assist children in being successful in school. Clearly, a point of critical mass was reached over the past few years stemming from decades of frustration surrounding the over-reliance of intelligence test scores to determine disabilities in children. The passage of IDEA 2004 was a landmark decision in terms of removing the shackles of finite scores and senseless cut points, and allowing professional educators to use their own judgment and their own data collection methods to determine if a child possesses a learning disability. Hence, the birth of RTI has taken shape, though many remain a bit skeptical and confused regarding the best way to implement this newfound technique. Still, a breath of fresh air has blown through the corridors of our schools as professional educators can finally focus on prevention measures, and not just wait for a child to fail before considering an educational intervention. Nevertheless, the pendulum seems to have shifted a bit too far to overcorrect many years of psychometric miscues in classifying children for special education services based upon intelligence test scores. Today, there is clearly a national movement to eliminate all psychometric testing in the educational arena, and to rely solely upon curriculum-based measurement techniques to make educationally relevant decisions about children. What has become lost in the endless debate over the best means to assess academic prowess in our children is that utilizing multiple data collection measures from multiple sources integrating multiple methodologies seems to be the most balanced and sensible way to address the complicated educational needs of today's youth.

This book was written in the hope of reflecting a more balanced perspective on the most efficient means to assist struggling readers in our schools. The intent was to integrate the wonderful tenets of a response-to-intervention model within the framework of cognitive neuroscience. Both approaches demand that scientific rigor be used to make any relevant educational decision on children, and both approaches need to be applauded. Much of the impetus behind this manuscript also stemmed from the many participants who have attended my workshops over the years and have expressed such an overwhelming desire to go deeper in their assessments and to go deeper with intervention options. This book clearly would have stalled on the editor's desk had it not been for my co-author, Dr. Douglas A. Della Toffalo, who dove in mid-project and navigated through the milieu of text in such a timely fashion. His contributions on both the RTI side and cognitive neuropsychology side were invaluable. It is also imperative to thank my friend and colleague, Dr. George McCloskey, for providing such outstanding consultative comments to direct the flow of thoughts and reshape my own thinking in so many ways. Clearly, much gratitude goes to the brilliant work of Dr. James B. Hale who has published so extensively on this topic. Thank goodness Lesley Carter was available to provide such efficient editorial services, as well as tone down my act when I stepped out of bounds on a few comments throughout the text. Of course, the terrific work of Mark Burrier at Octavo Designs continues to be both highly professional and highly creative in designing the layout and cover design of the book. I also want to thank my good friend and fellow presentation partner, Ron Sudano, for the countless dinners and late night talks, as well as providing me with the necessary sense of balance on this topic. Much appreciation also goes to Dr. Daniel Miller, who continues to be a champion of school neuropsychology, and has successfully expanded a national training model for school neuropsychology across the country. I cannot express my gratitude enough for entrusting me to be a part of the program. Also, thanks again to Linda Wood at Signature Printing for always being so agreeable when up against my timelines. Certainly, a special thanks to my family for providing me with the emotional support needed to tackle the rigors of creating a manuscript. Lastly, thanks to you, the reader for taking time out of your busy schedule to peruse this manuscript in hopes of finding that special nugget that may actually make a difference in the life of a child. That, my friend, is my greatest inspiration.

Dr. Steven G. Feifer

DEDICATION

To my beloved wife Darci and three children for putting up with my many obsessions which include an insatiable need to write. In addition, to my students and many colleagues I have encountered throughout the country who continue to inspire me to fight the good fight in this all too polarized profession, thanks! - SGF

With thanks to my colleagues, friends, and especially my family; without your inspiration and unwavering support, this would not have been possible. - DDT

Table of Contents

| Steven G. Feifer, D.Ed.   Douglas A. Della Toffalo, Ph.D

Table of Contents

| Steven G. Feifer, D.Ed.   Douglas A. Della Toffalo, Ph.D

FOREWORD

It is an exciting time to be a psychologist practicing in the schools. The changes brought forth by the most recent rendition of IDEA seem dramatic and unprecedented—suggesting we are at a pivotal point in history—with the future shaped by you and others deeply committed to serving children in the schools. Although these changes seem daunting to many, especially those who adhere to traditional models of practice, they offer an incredible opportunity as we forge new practice models that will better serve children with and without disabilities. Both the seasoned practitioner and novice student alike should encourage and embrace the new ideas and methods put forth by others, yet temper our thirst for change with the reality that evidence-based practice must guide our ideologies, conversations, debates, and decisions about the future of our fields.

Change has never been easy or comfortable. We know that novelty, complexity, and ambiguity can lead to dissonance, discord, and negative affect. To overcome these disquieting experiences, we seek definitive answers to our questions—we look for confirming evidence to support our restructured beliefs and may ignore incongruent or competing information. We may rally behind the predominant view of our colleagues or the works of scholars we respect, dismissing other perspectives as irrelevant, shortsighted, or obstacles to change. Social psychology taught us about these basic characteristics of human nature, but sometimes we forget what this field taught us several decades ago.

The education field seems to be particularly vulnerable to this phenomenon. We have a tendency to be fervent advocates of the latest trend or fad, yet quickly divorce ourselves from that position when it falls out of favor. As a result, we may become adamant and possibly dogmatic supporters of positions. These positions may or may not have sufficient empirical support or widespread social or political acceptance. Only one thing stands in the way of this naturally-occurring phenomenon—the voice of reason and logic dictated by scientific evidence. No political or social dogma should trump scientific evidence, yet in the "soft" sciences of education and psychology, evidence is seldom explicit or definitive. Despite individual, community, and societal pressures for conformity, we must regularly re-evaluate our beliefs and practices, and remain steadfastly committed to growth and development as a profession.

What does science say about response-to-intervention (RTI) as an approach for serving all children with diverse needs? Unfortunately, the science of RTI is in its infancy, and many questions about implementation remain. Preliminary findings are quite good, especially in the areas of word reading and reading fluency, and the literature is bolstered by complementary methods such as curriculum-based measurement, applied behavior analysis, and single subject methodologies. Another reason RTI has gained such widespread appeal is that traditional practice models (i.e., ability-achievement discrepancy) have been largely ineffective in meeting the needs of children. Identification is not always accurate using this approach and it does little to inform intervention— which is exactly what children with learning or behavior problems need.

Despite its rise to prominence, many questions about RTI remain, with empirical support still too limited for widespread adoption as the sole method of serving all children or determining disability status. Even among those who advocate RTI methods, there is much debate over whether RTI is best represented by the standardized RTI approach, the problem-solving RTI approach, or a combination of both methods at different tiers. Even then, RTI does not appear to be sufficient for specific learning disability diagnosis. Only a comprehensive evaluation of cognitive and neuropsychological processes combined with RTI can meet the IDEA SLD definitional requirements and method for SLD determination—a position lucidly argued in this book. The comprehensive evaluation methods touted in this book are reasoned, thorough, and sensitive to a variety of reading difficulties, but to be truly useful in daily practice they must have sufficient ecological and treatment validity as well.

Although this book provides readers with critical information regarding RTI, its greatest asset is its focus on the cognitive and clinical neuropsychology of reading and reading disability. Seldom addressed in RTI positions is the explosion of knowledge gained in these fields in the last 20 years. We knew virtually nothing about the brain and very little about measurement of cognitive and neuropsychological processes when James Ysseldyke first attempted aptitude-treatment interaction (ATI) in the early 1970's. We knew preciously little of the infamous "black box" brain when Lee Cronbach advocated experimental over correlational methods in his purported disavowal of ATI's. This archival "evidence" is often used to support fervent RTI advocates claim that psychological testing has no relevance for children with disabilities. Yet the science of brain-behavior relationships, and their measurement, has grown exponentially since that time. No area of psychology has witnessed such phenomenal growth in recent times as the areas of cognitive neuroscience and neuropsychology. Although this information is neither easy nor readily accessible, this book attempts to bring this knowledge to the forefront for practitioners, with authors determined to display its relevance for understanding reading competency and disability. What is clear from this presentation is that there are many types of reading disability, and that no one method of assessment or intervention can meet the diverse needs of this heterogeneous and enigmatic population.

The schism between RTI and cognitive/neuropsychological assessment advocates leads to different types of evidence, with different positions seemingly supported by their respective data. These positions, perspectives, and data can be used to drive some practitioners apart, while others may be brought together. It is this latter aspiration that apparently fueled the scholarship of this book—the authors professing a sincere desire to provide ideas and methods designed to bridge differences in our field. Rather than stoking tension and struggle among disparate factions, this book is designed to address scientific fact and fiction in a meaningful and illuminating way, presenting readers with a clearer picture of the strengths and limitations of these positions. This not only helps readers gain a realistic appraisal of the RTI and cognitive/neuropsychological assessment camps, but it also provides the impetus for individual and system-level changes so drastically needed in education today. This book does so by encouraging practitioners and scholars alike to work together to develop balanced practice models that incorporate the best tenets of multiple positions.

As the science of RTI and cognitive neuropsychology continue to mature, a plethora of evidence and positions among its advocates will too. Similar to what we see in measurement, more extreme positions will be discarded for more moderate ones. If practitioners and scholars alike endorse perspectives such as those espoused in this book—perspectives that draw upon multiple lines of scientific evidence—philosophical chasms will be bridged, and reasoned positions and practices will replace naïve, dogmatic ones. With the release of the final regulations for IDEA, the door is open for new ideas, practices, and promises. Combined with others in the fledgling fields of RTI and school neuropsychology, this book will serve as a foundation for understanding individual differences in reading competency, and provide several relevant tools designed to foster best practices in reading assessment and intervention for years to come.

James B. Hale, Ph.D.
Philadelphia College of Osteopathic Medicine

CHAPTER 1

Cognitive Neuropsychology and Five Dirty Words

In the early 1970's, during an unprecedented tide of social and cultural change, comedian George Carlin launched into the classic routine of seven dirty words that were absolutely forbidden on public television. This hilarious skit estimated that among the 900,000 to one million words in the English language, just seven remain taboo and utterly offensive. As George Carlin often said, "Those are the words that will infect your soul, curve your spine, and keep the country from winning the war." While it probably is not appropriate to list each of these words, Carlin (1997) further explored the illogical patterns of words, and found that even appropriate words, if paired together, can be equally offensive. The ridiculousness of an oxymoron, so prevalent in our discourse, remains equally offensive especially if accepted as truths. It's as though certain phrases and slogans become so embedded and woven into the fabric of our cultural dialect that the illogical semantics of these phrases are free to prosper. Some of the classic oxymorons that are given a semantic "free pass" are included in Table 1-1:

Table 1-1

Favorite Oxymorons

(Carlin, 1997)

Assistant supervisor	Partial cease-fire
New tradition	Limited lifetime guarantee
Plastic glass	Live recording
Uninvited guest	Original copy
Authentic reproduction	Peace force

The educational community is not immune to using words that are similar to the above *"semantic nonsense"* in describing learning and behavioral issues with children. While some individuals would be patently offended by George Carlin's initial sketch of the seven dirty words not allowed to air on public television, children are also being patently offended and in many cases educationally harmed by misguided attempts to describe learning and behavior using words and phrases of similar semantic frivolity. In fact, there are five rather perplexing phrases often used not only to describe children, but also to craft educational policy decisions. Perhaps the scientific rigors inherent in the discipline of cognitive neuropsychology can help dissect these phrases to their hollow core, and by doing so, cast a new light on learning through an examination of brain-behavioral relationships. With the advent of the Response to Intervention (RTI) movement, the door has finally swung open for science to permeate the boundaries of educational policy making by exposing fraudulent ideas, theories, and ridiculous adages that are often common practice in schools. Let's begin with the single most harmful phrase echoed in the halls of public schools: *"over-achievement"*.

I. OVER-ACHIEVEMENT: Ricky was referred for a psycho-educational evaluation due to difficulty keeping pace with the 3rd grade curriculum. His teacher indicated that Ricky was a well mannered student with an excellent work ethic, but he simply struggled with reading and written language types of skills. Ricky was reported as reading on approximately a 2nd grade level, despite coming to school early each day for extra assistance. The school-based assessment team was summoned to complete an evaluation on Ricky to determine if a learning disability was hindering his educational progress. An eligibility meeting was later convened to discuss the results of Ricky's assessment. The school psychologist began the meeting by reporting that Ricky was administered the *Wechsler Intelligence Scale for Children (WISC-IV)*, and had a Full Scale IQ score of <u>86</u>, which was in the *Below Average* range of functioning. The school psychologist indicated that most students who had general intellectual abilities in this range were slower paced learners, and had difficulty keeping pace with the academic curriculum. There were no other tests administered by the school psychologist, outside of a few behavior rating scales, and there were no specific recommendations offered as well. Next, the special education teacher reported the results of the educational assessment using the *Woodcock-Johnson Tests of Achievement (WJIII)*. She indicated that Ricky's Broad Reading Score was a <u>92</u>, Broad Math Score a <u>101</u>, and Broad Written Language Score a <u>94</u>. The special education teacher explained that all of these scores were in the Average range of functioning, and were actually higher than expected given Ricky's Full Scale IQ of <u>86</u>. Therefore, Ricky did not qualify for special education services, or for that matter, any other services the school had to offer.

When queried by Ricky's mother as to why he continued to have so much difficulty keeping pace in class, the special education teacher merely shrugged her sagging shoulders and replied that Ricky was an over-achiever. When queried by Ricky's mother about specific scores such as percentile ranks, *Relative Performance Index (RPI)* indexes, and grade equivalent scores that were also on the data sheet, the special education teacher tensed her jaw squarely and indicated those scores served no bearing when determining a discrepancy between ability and academic achievement. When queried by Ricky's mother for an explanation as to what an RPI score even means, the special education teacher seemed aghast and a bit flustered, and bellowed that they were irrelevant scores generated by the computer. When queried by Ricky's mother as to how Ricky could score in the *Average* range on the *WJIII* test of reading, yet still be well below grade level, the building administrator chimed in by replying *Average* means a wide range of performance. Finally, Ricky's mother looked at the school psychologist squarely in the eye, and unwaveringly asked what does it mean to *over-achieve?* The school psychologist explained rather frankly that an IQ score measured innate intellectual ability, and Ricky was surpassing this ability score in his academic work. Therefore, his academic achievement scores in reading, math, and written language were markedly higher than he was capable of achieving, when compared to his Full Scale IQ score. With a look of bewilderment, puzzlement, and sheer astonishment from Ricky's mother, the meeting was quickly adjourned and she was hustled out of the conference room so the next meeting of illogical twists and paradoxical turns could begin on time. Farfetched? Not likely; this happens each and every day in all of our schools.

This rather straightforward vignette is unfortunately very common, as most educators tend to use a *discrepancy paradigm* as the lens to view academic learning. Therefore, if students happen to be performing (achieving) commensurate with their ability (IQ), then no disability is present. Conversely, if there is a numerical discrepancy between IQ and achievement, then an educational disability must be present. There are numerous grandiose and markedly illogical assumptions inherent in this paradigm, not the least of which is that IQ represents an innate, inflexible score which remains uninfluenced by academic experience, and accurately encompasses the wide array of skills and abilities representative of human cognitive functioning. These common fallacies regarding the misinterpretation of intelligence tests will be discussed in the next section. For now, let's examine the rationale behind this particular educational policy decision. Certainly, an argument can be made for the statistical imprecision of comparing scores from one norm group *(WISC-IV)* against another *(WJIII)*, or the sheer ignorance of discarding the *RPI* score as a means to comprehend subject mastery, or the fact that Ricky's classroom curriculum had little to do with the skills being measured by the *WJIII*. However, the relative absurdity of the phrase over-achiever remains the fundamental problem in this scenario, and defies any logical discussion of academic functioning. Here is where cognitive neuropsychology needs to be utilized to foster a better explanation of Ricky's academic strengths and weaknesses.

According to Baron (2004), intelligence test measures do not always measure adaptive and flexible decision making, abstract reasoning skills, planning and organizational skills, or regulating social and emotional behavior. This cluster of *managerial* behaviors that allow human beings to perform at an optimal level when confronted with a goal-directed problem solving task has been conceptualized under one overarching construct termed executive functioning. Baron (2004) defined *executive functioning* skills in the flowing manner:

"Executive functioning skills are the metacognitive capacities that allow an individual to perceive stimuli from the environment, respond adaptively, flexibly change directions, anticipate future goals, consider consequences, and respond in an integrated or common-sense way, utilizing all of these capacities to serve a common purposive goal."

Weingartner (2000) noted that although executive functioning is often treated as one multifaceted phenomenon, perhaps it would be more useful to consider the component parts separately. In other words, executive functioning skills are really a collection of directive processes that cue the use of other cognitive abilities to execute a strategically planned and organized task. Baron (2004) depicted what some of these cognitive processes may entail:

Table 1-2

Executive Functioning Attributes

(Baron, 2004)

Shifting cognitive sets	Working memory skills
Hypothesis generation	Task initiation
Creative problem solving	Inhibiting distractions
Abstract reasoning	Behavioral self control
Planning skills	Mental flexibility
Organizational skills	Attentional Control
Goal setting skills	Anticipation
Fluency skills	Adaptive responses

Certainly, the question must be asked as to why human cognition needs a supervisory control mechanism, as most higher level problem solving tasks are often conceived as being tests of intelligence. Barkley (2001) noted the evolutionary significance of executive functioning skills may have been to generate sequential mind scripts that allowed human beings to better adapt to their social environment. For instance, as human beings and their ancestors learned to live in groups, it became a great adaptive advantage to master the benefits of social exchange through skills such as the inhibition of pre-potent responses *(internalization of emotion)*, hindsight and forethought *(working memory)*, and by inventing new sequences of social exchange such as bargaining *(reconstitution)*. All of these attributes were deemed necessary for survival within the spirit of social reciprocity. In addition, the privatization of language was deemed necessary to delay pre-potent emotional responses for the purpose of attaining much larger social goals. Therefore, the fundamental purpose of executive functioning skills may have been to create a shift in the sources of control of behavior from the external to the internal, from social others to the self, and from control by the moment to control by time and the future (Barkley, 2001). Hence, this strategy of maximizing long-term outcomes over immediate needs may have offered an environmental advantage that allowed human beings to adapt more readily to their newfound social environment.

Nevertheless, an important distinction needs to be made. Most tests of intelligence do not include executive control processes as a distinct content domain. In other words, IQ tests are constructed so the examiner serves as the executive control board during test taking. The examiner tells the child what to do when, cues attention and performance, often motivates the child to put forth their best effort, allocates time on task as dictated by the testing manual, explicitly gives and repeats directions, and self monitors performance. As a result, intelligence test scores do not accurately reflect a child's executive control capacities. Hence, the correlations between most executive functioning measures and tests of generalized intelligence tend to be rather low (Barkley, 2001). In a nutshell, intelligence tests measure reasoning processes, executive functioning tests measure performance processes.

Now, let's turn our attention back to Ricky. His overall IQ was in the *Below Average* range of functioning; therefore, a better explanation of his supposed over-achievement was that Ricky had strong executive functioning skills. In reality, there really is no such thing as over-achievement, as Ricky was basically applying his core intelligence in a highly effective manner in the pursuit of a goal directed task. Consequently, students with marginal levels of cognition can clearly perform above their purported ability level should they also possess well endowed executive functioning skills. As Baron (2004) noted, high intelligence is not a guarantee of flexible thinking, while lower intelligence does not dismiss the possibility of good common sense coupled with creative and adaptive thinking. Ricky had been described by his teacher as a resourceful and well mannered student who always put forth his best effort. It is highly probable that Ricky may have had a learning disability, though disabilities are often hidden through the myopic paradigm of ability-achievement discrepancies. Executive functioning skills may be the single most important cognitive construct often overlooked in most psychological assessments. With respect to reading skills, executive functioning and working memory skills play a pivotal role in reading comprehension by allowing students to selectively choose salient information from the text, stitch together the new information with previously read material, and effectively store the information in a semantic manner to allow for effective recall. The precise role of executive functioning and reading comprehension will be further explored in Chapter Six.

2. POTENTIAL: As the great philosopher and highly popular cartoon character Charlie Brown once noted, "A kid's greatest burden is his potential." Since the inception of intelligence tests, there have been disparate views about how to precisely measure such an elusive trait as human cognitive functioning. For instance, some theorists have advocated that intelligence is a single, unitary construct (Spearman) while others have argued that intelligence is comprised of multiple constructs (Gardner, Sternberg). There have been theorists who have argued that fixed intelligence test scores are outstanding predictors of success in life (Jensen) while others see little relative utility in the measure (Reschly, Ysseldyke). There are some who argue for the importance of recognizing both global measures of ability as well as specific measures of ability (Elliott, Kaufman) and those who see intelligence being encompassed within more of a hierarchical structure (Carroll, Horn, Woodcock). While the debate rages about how to best encapsulate and measure human cognitive functioning, there is certainly agreement among most practitioners that IQ scores are overemphasized in the public school setting. Consequently, the misinterpretation of intelligence test scores has led to inappropriate identification of minority students as having mental retardation, fueled the highly flawed *ability-achievement* discrepancy model, and has basically rendered school psychologists impotent in making individual intervention decisions (Hale & Fiorello, 2004). However, the most degrading aspect of utilizing one numeric value to represent the wide spectrum of human cognitive abilities has been the notion that intelligence is merely a synonym for a student's *potential*.

In reality, the evolution of intelligence testing remains in its infancy in capturing the cortical complexity and realm of possibilities that human cognitive functioning may take. The disciplines of neurology, psychology, education, and medicine, all of which have devoted countless time and energy toward the study of brain functioning, have begun to converge toward an amalgam or hybrid field known as cognitive neuropsychology. Clearly, the fundamental goal for researchers in cognitive neuropsychology is to explore the development and expression of the nearly 100 billion neurons that comprise the human brain. This staggering volume of neurons resonates louder when one considers that to individually count each neuron, one per second, would take some 32 million years. Simply put, neuropsychological research has focused on the neural networks and underlying anatomical circuitry that makes up specific cognitive constructs crucial to the learning process. These constructs include aspects of cognition such as attention, memory, language, processing speed, and graphomotor functioning. In fact, Kaufman (1994) has stressed that intelligence testing should be interpreted within a conceptual model around given cognitive constructs, no matter the test of choice. Therefore, the emphasis should not revolve around the measurement of *intelligence* per se, but rather on the measurement of *cognition*, which refers to the underlying constructs necessary to perform a given task.

Furthermore, Hale and Fiorello (2004) argued that full scale scores of intelligence should not be interpreted for at least 80% of children due to significant factor or subtest variability. In addition, intelligence test scores are intimately related to prior educational opportunities and previous academic experiences, and are not direct measures of ability. For years, Sattler (1988) has promoted six misconceptions about equating intelligence test scores with a child's *potential*:

Table 1-3

Common Misconceptions About Intelligence Tests

(Sattler, 1988)

1. Intelligence tests measure innate intelligence.

2. Intelligence tests measure intellectual capacity or potential.

3. IQ scores are fixed, immutable, and never change.

4. Intelligence tests provide perfectly reliable scores.

5. Intelligence tests provide all we need to know about a child's intelligence.

6. IQs obtained from a variety of tests are interchangeable.

In summary, Ricky's case illustrates the critical importance of evaluating the underlying cognitive constructs that serve as the building blocks for academic performance. With respect to reading, this includes measuring Ricky's overall phonological awareness and phonological processing skills (Chapter Three), measuring Ricky's orthographic processing and reading fluency skills (Chapter Four), and assessing executive functioning capacities critical to reading comprehension (Chapter Six). Furthermore, the school-based assessment should have discussed previous reading interventions charting and monitoring Ricky's response to these interventions over time. Simply writing Ricky off as being a slower paced learner due to his Full Scale IQ score being in the *Below Average* range represents a very misguided and skewed understanding of the true nature of cognition and reading. It also promotes the continued belief that intelligence is tantamount to *potential* in the academic arena. Unfortunately, most state regulations still rely on the *discrepancy model* of analysis in determining reading disabilities in children, despite the reauthorization of IDEA in 2004.

3. DISCREPANCY: Until the reauthorization of the *Individuals with Disabilities Act* in the final month of 2004, 48 out of 50 states were required to identify learning disorders in children by certifying a significant discrepancy between a student's intelligence, and scores from a nationally normed test of reading achievement. Nevertheless, just 20 states actually had parameters to assist school teams in mandating the magnitude of the discrepancy. Shame on *those* 20 states for mandating such a "cookbook" methodology in determining a disability! The notion that human intellectual prowess can be quantified and packaged in a singular monolithic value is to assume that intelligence is fixed and not fluid, innate and not experiential. This paradigm has clearly forced psychologists into the awkward role of choosing a test score that best reflects a student's *intellectual potential* for comparison purposes. Therefore, the richness and subtleness of current research tools such as the *WISC IV, Stanford-Binet V,* and *Woodcock-Johnson III*, which place more emphasis on selected aspects of cognition instead of misleading Full Scale scores, tend to be lost. Clearly, defining a learning disability requires some clinical interpretation by professionals who truly comprehend the neurocognitive demands of a given cognitive task, coupled with the learning strengths and weaknesses of the child.

According to Reschly (2003), the average IQ of a child with a learning disability is *87.1*, which is nearly 1 standard deviation below the mean of 100. In most states that over-rely on discrepancy formulas or artificially contrived "cut points" between ability and achievement, there is often a minimum of a 15 point discrepancy needed to qualify for special education services. Therefore, children need to score *2* standard deviations below the mean of 100 on a nationally normed referenced test of reading to receive services. This equates to most elementary aged children needing to score below *70* on a specific reading measure to create enough of a discrepancy from an IQ score of *87*. Since the average age at which children qualify for special education services as a learning disabled student is 9 years old (Shaywitz, 1998), discrepancy models clearly promote a "wait-to-fail" policy, as students require years of academic futility and years of academic failure in order to attain such a low achievement score. Feifer and DeFina (2000) list ten reasons why utilizing a discrepancy model as the sole identification for a learning disability is not only invalid, but frankly, harmful for children as well.

Table 1-4

10 Pitfalls of Aptitude/Achievement Discrepancy Models

(Feifer & DeFina, 2000)

1. There is no universal agreement on what the discrepancy should be.

2. It remains unclear as to which IQ score should be used to establish a discrepancy.

3. A discrepancy model of reading disabilities precludes early identification.

4. Intelligence is more a predictor of school success, and not necessarily a predictor of successful reading.

5. There is little evidence to suggest that poor readers on the lower end of the reading distribution differ in their educational needs from individuals classified as dyslexic.

6. It is illogical to utilize just one method to calculate a learning disability when research from the neuropsychological literature has documented numerous subtypes of reading disabilities.

7. Discrepancy models are not developmentally sensitive toward different stages of reading at different age groups.

8. A discrepancy model promotes a "wait and fail" policy forcing intervention to come after the fact.

9. Discrepancy formulas often do not detect subtle neurological variations such as organization and attention problems, poor memory and retrieval skills, and dyspraxias or dysphasias. In other words, they are too simplistic and generate little information for the development of IEP goals and objectives.

10. Discrepancy formulas are often used as a political means to regulate funding for special education.

4. LAZY: Traditional school psychologists as well as most educators have been somewhat remiss to acknowledge that social behavior, is in part, a brain function, and therefore subject to similar learning pitfalls to other cognitively oriented skills (Lezak, 1995). It is hardly uncommon to attribute student underachievement to a lack of effort, poor motivation, or just flat out academic laziness. The term *lazy* is often ascribed as a moral or value judgment tantamount to a character flaw within the child. Perhaps among all of the possible reputations a student may earn, "lazy" tends to be the most damaging. Why? Simply put, there tends to be resistance in providing any further academic remediations for students deemed "too lazy to read", as most interventions involve behavioristic approaches to increase academic motivation. According to Cicerone (2002), public school systems tend to use behavioral paradigms as an intervention for students with virtually any social, emotional, or behavioral concerns. The methodology of *behaviorism* involves the creation of behavioral plans, which seek to modulate the behavior of children by rewarding pro-social behaviors assumed to be related to educational success. Therefore, the ability to stay on task, complete assignments in a timely manner, stay in one's seat, refrain from calling out, and a variety of other disparate skills are isolated, measured, analyzed, and rewarded to ensure successful classroom behavior. As Cicerone (2002) noted, the goal of behaviorism is to induce task specific performance, as opposed to the internalization of self-regulatory processes. In other words, some children may demonstrate more desired behaviors in the artificial contextual environment of the classroom, but rarely can internalize these behaviors to guide and regulate their functioning in other environmental settings.

In the neuropsychology literature, the term *conation* is used to encompass the connection of knowledge and affect to behavior, and refers to the personal, intentional, planful, deliberate, and goal-oriented aspect of motivation (Huitt, 1999). Bagozzi (1992) proposed that utilizing overt behavioral plans as a means to predict behavioral tendencies often fail because the concept of conation tends to be omitted. In essence, helping students develop intentional and intrinsic motivation of behavior in a self-directed manner remains an indispensable and vital aspect of the learning process. Therefore, behavioral modification plans, star charts, functional behavioral assessments, and other extrinsic reward methods may not be nearly as effective in establishing more volitional components of behavior, such as teacher praise, parental recognition, or simply making reading fun. J.K. Rowling, author of the *Harry Potter* series that has sold more than 250 million books, has amazingly created a world so entertainingly imaginative and utterly suspenseful, that Play Station 2, Game-Boys, Nintendo, and iPods cannot compete for the after school attention of many children. However, most students with reading disabilities fail to see the entertainment aspect of reading, as the process of reading is so utterly laborious for them. In effect, it becomes increasingly problematic to maintain a persistent pattern of effort on any task that is so inherently difficult. Therefore, educators need to carefully determine the underlying premises for a lack of effort with respect to reading.

A second possible factor underscoring difficulty with task initiation, or what some educators deem as being "lazy," goes back to the discussion on executive functioning skills. The strategic aims and aspirations of all learners tend to be exposed by the cognitive construct of *executive functioning*. What some teachers would refer to as lazy students may in fact be children who are poor strategic learners and therefore require extra guidance and assistance with virtually any academic task. Once student inertia is set in motion, these children perform relatively well. From a brain-behavioral standpoint, the key anatomical region responsible for task initiation, maintaining a persistent pattern of effort, resistance to distractions, and plotting a general strategy or course of action when actively engaged in a problem solving task lies within the *dorsolateral* region of the *prefrontal cortex*.

The *prefrontal cortex* is comprised of three main areas, each of which plays a vital role in the modulation of attention to achieve a purposeful goal. The first region is termed the *dorsolateral circuit*, and helps to organize a behavioral response to an actual problem solving task (Chow & Cummings, 1999). Interestingly, damage to this brain region often results in a *psuedo-depressive* personality that is characterized by apathy, depressed cognitions, an inability to plan, and a genuine lack of desire or motivational drive. In other words, task initiation is a fundamental attribute of the dorsolateral prefrontal cortex. Specific cognitive attributes may include poor organization and planning skills, poor memory search strategies, and poor cognitive set shifting when engaged in two or more tasks. Specific behavioral manifestations may include a complete withdrawal from school, as well as little interest in the planning and pursuit of positive academic or interpersonal goals (Morgan & Lilienfield, 2000).

The second region of the prefrontal cortex that houses executive functioning types of skills is the *orbitofrontal cortex*, which helps to mediate empathetic, civil, and socially appropriate behaviors (Chow & Cummings, 1999). Deficits in this region produce an almost *pseudo-psychopathic* personality characterized by a jocular attitude, disinhibition, extreme self-indulgence, and inappropriate sexual humor (Morgan & Lilienfeld, 2000). There is an overwhelming need for immediate gratification, with deficits often resulting in poor attention and time-management skills, similar to attention-deficit-disorder. However, most areas of cognitive functioning remain in tact. Specific behavioral manifestations include poor regulation of emotions, irritability, mood disorders, antisocial behaviors, and an inability to self monitor and regulate emotional functioning (Chow & Cummings, 1999). According to Blair (2004), the reason for these emotional pitfalls lies in the neural architecture of the orbitofrontal cortex, which has rich subcortical connections with the limbic system, a key emotional center of the brain.

The third region of the prefrontal cortex that plays a vital role with *executive functioning* skills is the *anterior cingulate cortex*. This particular brain region supplies a multitude of functions linking attention capabilities with that of a given cognitive task, as well as maintaining task motivation. According to Carter (1998), the anterior cingulate helps the brain divert its conscious energies either toward internal cognitive events, or to external cognitive stimuli. A helpful analogy is that of an *attention general* in the brain making an executive decision as to which events require conscious attention, and which will be overlooked. Certainly, impairment in this region can produce a wide variety of unusual emotional responses, including apathy and poor motivation, as well as an inability to appreciate and interpret emotions (LeDoux, 1996). Figure 1-1 illustrates the major subdivisions of the prefrontal cortex.

In summary, it is crucial for educators and psychologists to be aware that some aspects of "laziness" may indeed be related to executive functioning deficits. In fact, all three regions of the prefrontal cortex contributes to various aspects of executive functioning, and ultimately, task initiation and motivation. Effort is the by-product of a multitude of factors, albeit driven by biological factors, emotional factors, and environmental circumstances. Nevertheless, successful reading requires a price, and that price is the ability to repetitively practice this complex skill until it becomes effortless, automatic, and hopefully, just plain fun.

Figure 1-1

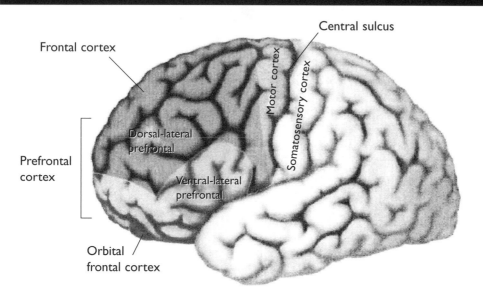

Subdivisions of the Prefrontal Cortex

Central sulcus

Frontal cortex

Motor cortex

Somatosensory cortex

Dorsal-lateral prefrontal

Ventral-lateral prefrontal

Prefrontal cortex

Orbital frontal cortex

(5) MANIPULATIVE: Both the structure of the brain and the function of the mind have an innate capacity to seek homeostasis, to achieve a sense of self-regulation and stability in order to optimize functioning. Take for example bipolar disorder, and the rapid cycling of moods between episodes of mania interspersed with bouts of depression. According to Siegel (2006), this emotional instability often becomes cognitively interpreted as a stable feature of one's make-up, as if the brain were desperately attempting to retain a pattern of stability in the midst of emotional chaos. For most children, the daunting task of imposing some set of emotional structure or stability within the social milieu and interpersonal exchanges of a public school setting can be rather overwhelming. Consequently, children often respond best to an external set of structures or rule-governed environment whereby tasks and activities are predictable, can be anticipated, and have clear and distinct boundaries. As Barkley (2001) noted, effective school performance requires, in part, successful social and emotional management through a myriad of emotional challenges, where frustration and anger must be tempered for the pursuit of goal attainment. Perhaps this is why a new breed of educational curriculum, one that invokes a healthy school climate by promoting character education programs, peer mediation techniques, bullying prevention methods, and conflict resolution scenarios has now permeated the boundaries of public education.

Certainly, not all children respond to class rules, comply with behavioral paradigms, or demonstrate respect for authority figures in their class setting. While some educators may cast moral dispersions on these students, and attribute behavioral dysfunction to a lack of moral values and flawed character development, there may also be a core biological cause triggering such behavior. According to Kraly (2006), behavioral dysfunction may reflect disturbances in brain processes that allow a person to detect, interpret, and respond emotionally to the outside world around them. Siegel (1999) reiterated that a part of the frontal lobes, namely the *orbitofrontal cortex* (see Figure 11), is not only responsible for the regulation of emotional behavior, but also is an organizational component of the mind that provides flexibility and adaptability to the world around us. In fact, when the *orbitofrontal cortex* is damaged, or in some cases fails to develop properly due to overwhelmingly negative early attachment experiences, children may become stuck in a state of constantly feeling threatened, and automatically respond to stimuli in an aggressive or maladaptive fashion (Siegel, 1999).

Rolls (1997) surmised that the *orbitofrontal cortex* is responsible for the rapid learning and execution of a behavioral response based upon reward contingencies in the environment. It stands to reason that children brought up in households with inconsistent parenting, turbulence and violence, or unpredictable reinforcement contingencies may be at risk for reactive aggression due to an inability of the orbitofrontal cortex to effectively modulate reward valences in fear-based learning circuits. In other words, what is often castigated as manipulative and noncompliant behavior in school may simply be the brain's overarching quest to achieve some sort of balance in a world where reinforcement contingencies are often unpredictable and overwhelmingly negative.

Certainly, behavioral *manipulation* is a complex phenomenon, with many learning paradigms, neural systems, temperamental attributes, and environmental stimuli all contributing to the subsequent behavioral output of a student. However, the term "manipulation" is often used to describe a child bent on altering the response contingencies in a class setting in his or her favor. Therefore, trying to "outsmart" a behavior plan, or only putting forth effort during situations that benefit the student, or constantly blaming others for behavioral transgressions in class, may be due to a misguided orbitofrontal cortex attempting to make a higher-level decision while simultaneously fueled by emotional feelings engendered from previous experiences (Dolan, 1999). With respect to reading, no intervention, remediation, strategy, or technique will be effective until a positive, warm, and unguarded relationship can be established. Students who appear to be manipulating the system and putting forth little effort, may in fact be crying out for help in their own way. This help can take the form of emotional assistance or academic support, but nonetheless should be viewed not as a character assassination of the student, but rather a plea for an emotional bond to be created before the implementation of any academic assistance.

CHAPTER 2

Overview of Response to Intervention (RTI)

Response to Intervention (RTI) is a phrase that has sparked a national movement, redefined educational policy, and most importantly has come to represent a long-awaited alternative method in determining a student's eligibility for special education services. The 2004 reauthorization of the Individuals with Disabilities Education Act (IDEA 2004) represented a paradigm shift, as schools were no longer required to utilize the long standing *discrepancy model* in order to determine whether or not a student was eligible for special education services. This was an especially important federal legislative decision primarily affecting those students with a learning disability. The discrepancy model has been the long-standing method that school systems have used to qualify students for special education services. It basically involved assessing academic achievement in one or more major curricular areas such as reading, math, or written language, and determining whether or not the student's achievement was significantly discrepant from their overall intelligence. In other words, the discrepancy model sought to measure whether or not a student was achieving at a level commensurate with their cognitive functioning.   Throughout the years, there have been numerous shortcomings identified in the discrepancy model, including the statistical impreciseness of using cut-off scores from two different normative samples (e.g., *Wechsler Intelligence tests* vs. *Woodcock-Johnson Tests of Academic Achievement*), the over-reliance on a Full Scale IQ score in an attempt to capture the dynamic properties of one's reasoning skills (Hale & Fiorello, 2004), and the lack of agreement on the magnitude of the discrepancy at various ages and grades (Feifer & DeFina, 2000). Perhaps the most notable shortcoming of the discrepancy model was that it resulted in a 'wait-to-fail' scenario in which a student must display a level of failure to acquire skills that reaches a particular threshold of severity, or significance, in order to qualify for special educational services. This was especially at odds with the National Reading Panel's (2000) conclusion highlighting the importance of early interventions services for children with reading difficulties.

Subsequent to the 2004 reauthorization of IDEA, states are no longer allowed to *require* school districts to consider a discrepancy between IQ and achievement as being a necessary condition to identify students as having a learning disability. Among the many provisions in this bill, states were finally allowed to opt out of using a discrepancy model to identify reading disabilities, and replace it by using a Response to Intervention (RTI) model.   In other words, rather than comparing a student's level of academic achievement with their purported intelligence, school districts were given the flexibility to craft a policy in which students who do not respond to evidence based early reading programs may be considered eligible for special education services. Furthermore, the law also required districts with significant over-identification of minority students to consider eliminating IQ testing and establish procedures to reduce disproportional representation of minorities in special education.

RTI is not new. It has been in use primarily as a school-wide prevention program within various districts for several decades. What is new, however, is RTI's explicit support in federal special education law as a viable alternative to less effective traditional models of determining student eligibility for special education services (Canter, 2006). RTI refers to an expansive array of procedures that can be used to determine eligibility and need for special education services within a problem-solving model that emphasizes scientifically-validated instructional approaches. RTI has enjoyed considerable support, especially from organizations such as the National Association of School Psychologists (NASP), because it circumvents many of the shortcomings of the traditional discrepancy model.   Additionally, RTI emphasizes the use of evidence based approaches to instruction in hopes of eliminating academic problems that are frequently due to deficient curricula or poor instructional methodologies.   In other words, RTI provides a framework for instruction and progress monitoring that prioritizes sound instructional practices for *all* students, not just those with disabilities. RTI also incorporates the well-established benefits of pre-referral intervention strategies meant to ensure that, when poor student progress is observed, it is addressed as early as possible and through the least intrusive means possible.

KEY LEARNING POINT	RTI is not new. It has been in use primarily as a school-wide prevention program within various districts for several decades. What is new, however, is RTI's explicit support in federal special education law as a viable alternative to less effective traditional models of determining student eligibility for special education services (Canter, 2006).

As described by McCook (2006): *"One of the fundamental tenets of an RTI model is to not look at a 'within child' issue until you can document that your core curriculum and instruction are sufficiently sound for the vast majority of students."*

Educational Underpinnings of RTI

Certainly, there are many different variations, critical components, and subtle nuances embedded within most versions of RTI. Nevertheless, McCook (2006) described six critical components that must be addressed in the application of any RTI model, which include the following:

Table 2-1

Six Components of an Effective RTI Model

1. ***Universal Screening*** - must be conducted with *all* students at least 3 times per year, ideally in fall, winter, and spring beginning in kindergarten.

2. ***Baseline Data*** - must be gathered for *all* students using curriculum based data in order to monitor individual and group response-to-instruction.

3. ***Measurable Terms*** - must be used to define problem areas for both individual students and groups of students.

4. ***Accountability Plan*** - must be developed once problems have been identified and interventions have been selected. The plan should specify critical features used to monitor intervention fidelity including the type, duration, intensity, setting, and parties responsible for each intervention component.

5. ***Progress Monitoring Plan*** - must address how, when, and where intervention results will be measured, recorded, and reviewed.

6. ***Data Based Decision-Making*** - involves the ongoing analysis of progress monitoring data to drive future instructional or intervention decisions for entire school populations, smaller instructional groups, and individual students who are at risk.

The Tiered Aspect of RTI Models

RTI models specifically identify *tiers* of intervention corresponding to increasing levels of support and assistance for students manifesting learning or behavioral problems. Once again, different models vary in the number of tiers that they delineate, though most are centered around a structural format consisting of three or four tiers. The first three tiers in nearly all RTI models are remarkably similar, and tend to be based upon an initial tier (Tier 1) that is actually more *prevention* than *intervention*. In fact, Tier 1 basically consists of a high quality and evidence based curriculum and general instructional methods for all students in *any* given educational setting. In Tier 1, performance data is generally gathered at least 3 times per year (usually in September,

January, and April), thereby providing an overall barometer of student progress being made by all students in both regular and special education settings. This periodic school-wide snapshot of progress allows for decisions to be made regarding the efficacy of the general curriculum and instructional methods based upon the obtained performance data. Figure 3-1 is a graphic representation of a 4-tier model developed by the Heartland Area Education Association (2002).

Figure 2-1

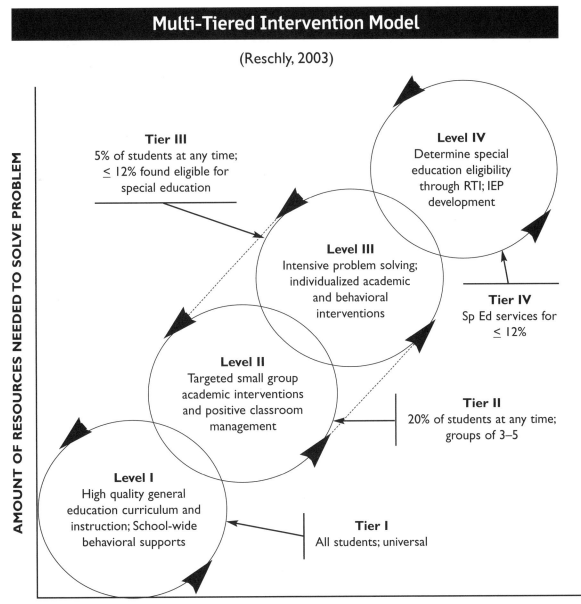

Figure adapted from Heartland AEA Program Manual, 2002).

Table 2-2

Critical Features of Tier 1 Instruction

1. Tier I is done within the regular classroom in whole-group format.

2. Tier I uses a scientifically-validated core curriculum series and materials.

3. Tier I focuses on bringing large percentages of students to acceptable proficiency.

4. Tier I is driven by system-wide performance data—if too few students make adequate progress, then the core curriculum needs to be changed.

5. Tier I employs ongoing assessment of student progress to screen for individuals who are in need of more intensive interventions.

6. Tier I is delivered in tandem with effective teaching principles including high academic engaged time, high success rates, direct and supervised teaching, scaffolded instruction, differentiated instruction, opportunities for re-teaching material, and strategic and explicit instruction.

7. Tier I includes the use of school-wide positive behavior supports to prevent behavior problems.

Tier I Assessment Processes

An essential feature of RTI lies in the utilization of curriculum based measures in early reading, written language, and math skills administered to students three times per year. These assessments are preferably spaced evenly throughout the school year, such as in September, January, and May. Aggregated data is collected by school staff, and primarily used as baseline data in order to determine the effectiveness of the core curriculum as a whole. Changes are generally made to the core curriculum when a larger than normal number (e.g., in excess of 20 percent) of students do not make appropriate academic progress. Therefore, rather than penalizing the student, or automatically assuming lack of progress is attributed to intrinsic characteristics such as lower cognitive skills, processing deficits, or some educationally disabling condition, the primary focus lies on establishing a more "student-friendly" yet evidence based core curriculum at large. Any changes in the overall curriculum are generally made for a period of six to eight weeks and then a re-assessment is conducted to monitor collective student response. The individual student data is analyzed to determine which students should be considered at-risk, and such students are provided with more intensive levels of intervention (Tier 2). Definitions of at-risk vary among RTI models, but a commonly suggested criteria is a student who scores at or below the 10th percentile during a screening assessment (McCook, 2006). District and class norms are generally preferable for these determinations, although such norms are often not available for many educators particularly when districts are just beginning to implement an RTI model. It should be noted that Tier 1 data is primarily compiled, recorded, and analyzed by school system personnel in *regular education*. The role and function of the school psychologist or special education team in this stage is essentially one of professional consultation. Certainly, all preliminary data should be verified by other sources of information, such as teacher input or ratings, suggesting at-risk status as well (McCook, 2006).

Table 2-3

Examples of Tier 1 Reading Interventions

1. *Rigby Literacy (Harcourt Rigby Education, 2000)*

2. *Trophies (Harcourt School Publishers, 2003)*

3. *The Nation's Choice (Houghton Mifflin, 2003)*

4. *Macmillan/McGraw-Hill Reading (2002)*

5. *Open Court (SRA/McGraw Hill, 2002)*

6. *Reading Mastery Plus (SRA/McGraw Hill, 2002)*

7. *Scott-Foresman Reading (2004)*

8. *Success For All (1998-2003)*

9. *Wright Group Literacy (2002)*

Tier 2 Processes

Once sufficient data is collected, students who are classified as at-risk begin to receive increased instructional supports and are monitored more frequently (every one to four weeks) with curriculum based measures. Once again, these students are not necessarily labeled as having an educational disability warranting special education services, but rather are deemed in need of additional instructional supports and assistance within the regular educational setting. Certainly, definitions of adequate progress may vary from school to school, though two criteria are suggested for most school systems. First, students must be making less weekly progress than the average grade level student who achieves at the 25th percentile relative to local and/or classroom norms. A second suggested criteria is simply the at-risk student is performing below the 10th percentile as compared to local and/or classroom norms. Consequently, progress monitoring is an extremely critical component of all RTI models because some low achieving students, particularly those who lack early skill exposure rather than an inherent learning disability, may eventually make appropriate progress without individualized or small-group interventions. In such cases, these students may simply require more time, as opposed to additional supports, to narrow the initial gap in skill development between their progress and that of students who are not considered at-risk.

Students who remain at-risk due to low academic skills acquisition, or poor progress after an initial six to eight-week period, are then recommended for Tier 2 interventions. Tier 2 instruction is designed for the approximately *20 to 30* percent of students who do not display sufficient skill development in an evidence based core (Tier 1) curriculum. Students who have not made sufficient progress in Tier 1 most likely require supplementary supports and services, in addition to the regular core curriculum. Screening measure data for such individuals can be analyzed in order to determine the intensity, setting, and nature of the Tier 2 interventions that are provided. Tier 2 interventions are generally implemented for a specified period of time, with progress monitoring occurring more frequently in order to measure how the student is responding. Progress monitoring is generally increased in frequency to every one to two weeks. It is important to note that frequent progress monitoring using curriculum based measures, as opposed to nationally norm-referenced tests, are critical components within the preliminary stages of RTI.

Tier 2 interventions typically involve an increase in the direct instructional time in the specific areas of weakness. Most RTI models recommend that Tier 2 interventions entail an additional 30 minutes of instruction and support in the academic domain or specific skill area that is hindering school achievement. Current research suggests that appropriate time frames of nine to twelve weeks are commonly recommended for Tier 2 interventions (Kovaleski, 2002; McCook, 2006). Tier 2 interventions tend to be delivered by individuals other than the regular classroom teacher, such as a reading specialist, and are generally provided in small groups of three to five students having similar delays in skill development. Students who respond well to Tier 2 interventions are often successful in closing the achievement gap and progress to grade level skill development. Students who do not display sufficient progress through Tier 2 interventions are provided with an array of even more intensive intervention procedures that is referred to as Tier 3.

Table 2-4

Possible Examples of Tier 2 Reading Interventions

1. *REWARDS (Sopris West)*

2. *Read Well (Sopris West)*

3. *Early (Soar to) Success (Houghton Mifflin)*

4. *Early Reading Intervention (Scott Foresman)*

5. *Ladders to Literacy*

6. *Reading Mastery Plus (SRA/McGraw Hill, 2002)*

7. *Road to the Code*

8. *Great Leaps (Diamuid, Inc.)*

9. *Earobics*

10. *Peer Assisted Learning Strategies (PALS)*

Tier 3 Processes

Tier 3 is regarded in some RTI models as the most intensive level of intervention, and cannot typically be sustained in the regular education setting without special educational services. The impetus behind a Tier 3 intervention is to establish a particular level of support capable of addressing significant academic skill deficits, without actually requiring a full commitment to special education services. The ideal scenario involves a student responding favorably to the increases in allotted instructional time and more intensive remedial instruction provision at Tier 3 and thereby avoiding the need for special education services.

Generally, students at Tier 3 receive even more direct and explicit instruction than students at Tiers 1 or 2. In some cases, scheduling changes are needed to allow for an additional hour of direct instruction beyond that provided in Tier 1, and this typically requires at least one-half hour more of daily direct instruction than in Tier 2. Furthermore, these scheduling changes may require the sacrifice of non-academic classes (e.g., art, music, gym, etc.) in order to allow ample time for instruction within one or more research-supported intervention programs. Typically, instruction at Tier 3 involves remediation of multiple aspects of the curriculum, and not just a single aspect of the curriculum. For instance, a student in Tier 3 may need assistance in improving decoding skills, reading fluency acquisition, and also passage comprehension skills. However, a student in Tier 2 often receives instructional assistance on just one specific curricular goal, such as reading fluency. Therefore, a student requiring more intensive instruction in both phonics and fluency might receive instruction through both the *Corrective Reading* and the *Read Naturally* series, and this may occur in more than one educational setting. Tiers 2 and 3 generally make use of similar evidence based intervention programs; however, the intensity and duration of instruction within these programs is much greater in Tier 3 (McCook, 2006). Progress monitoring requirements become even more intensive at Tier 3, with recommended measurement of progress occurring a minimum of one to two times per week.

Table 2-5

Suggested Examples of Tier 3 Reading Interventions

1. *Corrective Reading (SRA)*

2. *Language! (Sopris West)*

3. *Wilson Reading System*

4. *Reading Mastery*

5. *Alphabetic Phonics*

6. *Read Naturally*

7. *REWARDS*

8. *Horizons*

9. *PLATO Focus Reading Series*

It is important to note that students who do not respond to Tier 3 interventions are not automatically assumed to have a learning disability qualifying them for special education services, but it does suggest that a disability may exist. However, from solely a legal standpoint, students who do not respond to Tier 3 interventions can be considered disabled under the eyes of the law, and are therefore entitled to the rights and protections under IDEA. Additionally, students who *do* respond sufficiently to Tier 3 interventions, but remain dependent upon these high levels of support to be educationally successful, can also be considered legally entitled to the same rights as special education children. Herein lies the loophole between the legal justification for specialized instruction and the research based definition of an educational disability. The legal mandate postulates that successful educational progress that cannot be sustained in the regular curriculum without specially-designed instruction *may* be grounds for making an eligibility decision. Therefore, students who fail to respond sufficiently to Tier 3 interventions can be *considered* eligible for special education services due to a presumed learning disability. However, consideration for a disability is a far cry from actually possessing one, and it remains a slippery slope to diagnose any disability on the basis of an educational outcome without further examining neurocognitive processes. Still, there is no dispute that students who fail to make appropriate educational progress despite intensive exposure to evidence based intervention programs implemented with fidelity clearly are in need of more intensive supports and services.

KEY LEARNING POINT	Students who fail to respond sufficiently to Tier 3 interventions can be considered eligible for special education services due to a presumed learning disability. However, consideration for a disability is a far cry from actually possessing one, and it remains a slippery slope to diagnose any disability on the basis of an educational outcome without further examining neurocognitive processes.

Tier 4 Processes

Tier 4 is generally regarded as the stage where a comprehensive multidisciplinary evaluation (MDE) is conducted to determine a student's eligibility for special education services. As stated earlier, the evaluation should include a comprehensive review of all possible barriers to learning and intervention response. In RTI models that specify only 3 tiers, a MDE generally occurs after insufficient response to Tier 3. From a clinical standpoint, a student's lack of response to a specific intervention in and of itself is not a sufficient procedure or criterion for determination of a student's eligibility or need for special education services (Hale, Kaufman, Naglieri, & Kavale, 2006). School teams must still conduct relevant and thorough evaluations of students in all areas of a suspected disability before determining eligibility for special education services. However, this does not mean that school psychologists should simply revert back to administering individual IQ and achievement tests and then utilize the discrepancy model to confirm the presence of a learning disability.

In contrast, psycho-educational assessments spearheaded by school psychologists should continue in the spirit of RTI and emphasize thorough data gathering techniques to determine if a disability is indeed the primary cause of student under-achievement. Therefore, it is critical for all school psychologists to have necessary training in curriculum based data gathering techniques, as well as a comprehensive understanding of the fundamental learning tenets inherent in academic learning. For instance, the assessment of a reading disability should include cognitive ability testing, but with less emphasis on determining an overall IQ score. Instead, cognitive ability testing should be administered in order to gain insight regarding information-processing strengths and weakness (Hale & Fiorello, 2004). Additionally, knowledge of phonological processing, orthographic processing, subtypes of dyslexia, executive functioning, and working memory are just some of the examples covered in this book as being paramount to understanding the reading process. It is critical that all potential barriers precluding educational success be considered. Finally, merely diagnosing the neurocognitive strengths and weaknesses of individual learners is not enough. There must be important linkages made to connect a student's learning profile with a particular intervention strategy in order to ensure the best chance for educational success.

Figure 2-1 depicts an example of a two-hour block of reading and language arts instructional time within a school district that employs a 3-tier RTI approach. The district's specific choice of Tier1 core curricula and evidence based intervention programs for Tiers 2 and 3 are listed. As Figure 2-1 indicates, all students participate in one full hour of instructional time within the core curriculum, though some students at Tier 2 or 3 receive in-class small group instruction during this first hour of core curricular instruction. The second hour of this two-hour reading and language arts block finds students participating in homogenous (skill-level based) grouping with more individualized instruction methodologies in various environments that vary based upon individual student need and Tier membership.

Figure 2-2

Pleasantville School District's Two-Hour Reading/Language Arts Block

Tier I
Heterogeneous Grouping
All Students in grade level core - Instruction tied to anchors
(I hour daily)

Tier I	**Tier 2**	**Tier 3**
Homogeneous Skill Groups **(I hr. daily)**	Homogeneous Skill Groups **(I hr. daily)**	Homogeneous Skill Groups **(I hr. daily)**
• Workshop	• Workshop	• Flexible group I
• Trade-books	• Flexible group I	• Flexible group 2
• Literature Circles	• Comprehension	• Fluency
• Inquiry piece from core	• Open Court Intervention-Option I	• Read Naturally
	• Fluency	• Decoding
	• Great Leaps	• Reading Mastery
		• Comprehension
		• SOAR to Success

Potential Pitfalls of RTI

The RTI model has clearly shown excellent promise as an alternative means of providing earlier intervention services for all students, regardless of whether they possess a learning disability. Perhaps the greatest contribution of RTI is that it provides a systematic way of reducing the likelihood that academic problems will arise from poor or inconsistent instruction. Thus, RTI appears to be a very effective way of reducing or even eliminating the possibility for students to become *curriculum casualties*. Inevitably, however, problems will exist that cannot be fully addressed solely through the adoption of an RTI model. First, the RTI model presumes that at-risk learners will universally respond to standard protocol interventions. This is not necessarily the case for students whose learning problems result from unique profiles of cognitive functioning and unusually variable information-processing capacities. Clearly, some at-risk learners will display such complicated learning profiles that simply increasing the intensity or duration of direct instruction will not be terribly successful. In such cases, RTI can still impose a *wait-to-fail* scenario similar to that which it was intended to avoid. For instance, there may be some students who display highly unique cognitive characteristics and information-processing deficits, such that a strict application of the RTI model would require them to progress through each of the three or four tiers before being considered potentially eligible for special education services.

For some students, an inadequate response to standard protocol interventions can likely be predicted from early awareness of their highly unusual cognitive characteristics such as those seen in many low incidence disorders or neurological conditions. Some examples might include conditions such as Autism Spectrum Disorders (especially Asperger's Disorder), Tourette's Disorder, Attention-Deficit/Hyperactivity Disorder (ADHD), Obsessive-Compulsive Disorder, Seizure Disorder, exposure to toxins (lead, etc.), Traumatic Brain Injury, and a wide variety of low incidence metabolic, genetic, and neurodevelopmental conditions. For these students, it would likely be more helpful to engage in targeted individual assessment activities even as they progress through Tier 1, and especially as they enter Tier 2 (Della Toffalo, 2006; Hale et al., 2006).

KEY LEARNING POINT	RTI can still impose a *wait-to-fail* scenario similar to that which it was intended to avoid. For instance, there may be some students who display highly unique cognitive characteristics and information-processing deficits, such that a strict application of the RTI model would require them to progress through each of the three or four tiers before being considered potentially eligible for special education services.

Certainly, for some at-risk learners, a comprehensive assessment may be the only way to accurately determine the source or extent of their resistance to quality instruction and to develop appropriate individualized interventions that address those specific barriers and related needs (Della Toffalo, 2006). In other words, if there is reason to believe that a student will probably not respond to standard protocol interventions, why not engage in targeted assessment activities to try and find out what unique interventions or accommodations may be required to increase their chance of success in response to interventions? For example, some older students may have such pronounced phonological processing deficits that specific remediation of phonics by established programs such as *Orton-Gillingham* may not be as effective as utilizing a more balanced literacy program such as *Read 180* to better accommodate the learner. Therefore, in the spirit of data based decision making, an appropriate assessment of neurocognitive strengths and weaknesses should be sought before making this type of recommendation. This seems a decidedly better alternative to waiting until a student fails to display sufficient response to specific interventions at Tiers 2 or 3 and then wondering why their response was insufficient. In conclusion, an in-depth multidisciplinary assessment may occur at any tier of the RTI process depending on the individual learning needs and neurocognitive profile of the student in question. As will be discussed in Chapter 7, any such evaluation aimed at producing data to inform intervention should be conducted with assessment measures that ultimately sample the fundamental cognitive constructs deemed vital for the specific task at hand. In the case of reading, this may involve measures that tap phonological processing, rapid naming skills, working memory, and executive functioning skills. Not only would such a dynamic and comprehensive evaluation provide information regarding the likely source of a student's learning problems and assist in designing appropriate interventions, it would also assist in identifying any additional barriers to learning that may arise from comorbid conditions such as ADHD or behavioral disorders.

A second general concern with over-relying on RTI to determine eligibility for special education services is the RTI process is presently well defined only in the curricular domain of reading skill development, and this is typically limited to earlier elementary school-age levels. While reading problems do indeed represent the overwhelming majority of reasons for special educational referrals, there are students who display academic struggles in other curricular areas in addition to reading problems (Fiorello, Hale, & Snyder, 2006). Some examples include mathematics, writing skills, social skills, and emotional functioning. The RTI framework for tiered intervention is presently much less well defined for intervening in these other areas of academically-relevant functioning. While efforts are being made to extend the RTI process to other curricular areas as well as behavior, there are far fewer existing tiered intervention models available on which to base such efforts.

Future Considerations for RTI

At its core, RTI has provided educators with a fairly systematic and standardized methodology for the application of educational resources and interventions. Certainly, future research is needed to properly develop more evidence based interventions, especially in academic domains and curricular areas other than reading. Specifically, the potential benefits of RTI will not likely be fully realized until an array of standard protocol interventions are developed for learners who struggle in other curricular areas such as math skills and writing skills, and non-curricular skill areas such as study skills, social skills, and behavioral management. In addition, the RTI model is in need of an upward extension and adaptation for use as an intervention model at the upper elementary, middle school, and high school levels.

One way to increase the likelihood of success for all at-risk learners is to develop mechanisms of enhanced diagnostic assessment in the early phases of intervention. For example, rather than waiting until a student has failed to respond sufficiently to 3 tiers of interventions and then performing diagnostic evaluation, targeted assessment and screening should be conducted much earlier. Such targeted assessment should be conducted to explore potential information-processing barriers toward standard protocol interventions. For instance, deficits in memory functions, language skills, sensory or perceptual functions, motor skills, and executive functions have the potential to impose constraints of varying severity on the ability of students to respond to evidence based instructional methods (Della Toffalo, 2006; Hale et al., 2006). Such deficits can be identified through targeted assessment activities at any tier of the RTI model, but clearly hold the greatest potential for positive educational impact when identified as early as possible.

In summary, school psychologists are the most appropriately trained individuals in the educational arena to recognize constraints that can inhibit learning, and school psychologists are the most appropriately trained individuals to assess for such constraints. RTI has the potential to free school psychologists from being burdened with a stockpile of unnecessary assessments, and to engage in more focused assessment activities as part of an RTI and pre-referral problem-solving process. With the passage of IDEA 2004, school psychologists are no longer required to perform routine lock-step administrations of intelligence and achievement tests in order to determine eligibility for special education services. Given this new degree of freedom, it is incumbent upon school psychologists to acquire advanced skills in targeted assessment in order to facilitate the most effective application of the RTI framework. It also requires school psychologists to increase their understanding of the neuropsychological processes inherent to the reading process in order to both explain why a particular intervention failed, as well as why another may succeed. In the following chapters, a detailed discussion of the core cognitive constructs related to reading will be reviewed and highlighted by *Key Learning Point* text boxes. In addition, there will be a thorough review of 20 evidence based intervention techniques for educators to choose from based upon the unique learning profile of the child. After all, the goal of any assessment is to gather enough data to make a logical choice pertaining to the type of intervention strategy which best suits a particular child. To accomplish this mission, let's begin the discussion by reviewing the most important psychological process necessary for adequate reading to commence in younger students: namely, phonological processing skills.

CHAPTER 3

The Phonological Processor: How Reading Emerges at the Sub-Lexical Level

Cognitive neuropsychology has emerged as the leading discipline in forging the inevitable alliance between science and education. Whether guided by political forces such as the 2002 No Child Left Behind law, or inspired by neuroscientific consensus in the learning arena, public schools have made a renewed commitment toward using evidence based instructional techniques as the foundation for sound educational practice. Hence, strategies such as open classrooms, utilizing visual perceptual training or colored lenses to assist with reading, or incorporating pseudoscientific learning modules such as *Brain-Gym* are no longer endorsed. With public scrutiny of school performance intensifying, there has clearly been a dramatic shift in policy toward evidence based instruction, school accountability, and progress monitoring as the barometers for a successful learning experience. Why? According to Moats (2004) the National Assessment of Educational Progress estimated that 38 percent of all students will experience significant difficulty learning to read by 4th grade, and lack the necessary foundation skills to participate in the day-today rigors of grade-level instruction. Nevertheless, fewer than 6 percent of all students are identified for special education services due to a reading disability, leaving the vast majority of struggling learners subjected to "quick fix" programs that overwhelmingly fail. At a time when traditional services are being challenged and alternatives are being considered, the evidence based practice movement in schools has provided a conceptual framework to sculpt the learning, behavioral, and mental health needs of all children in three primary ways as outlined in Table 3-1 (Kratochwill, Albers, & Shernoff, 2004).

Table 3-1

Three Influences of Evidence Based Movement

1. Embrace the value of science as an appropriate methodology in educational practice.

2. Make a commitment toward selecting and implementing school-based prevention and intervention programs based upon evidence from scientific research.

3. The effectiveness of prevention and intervention programs that are implemented must be properly monitored and evaluated.

The trickle down effect of utilizing science and evidence based instruction as the foundation for educational practice quite naturally has opened the door for the study of brain-behavioral relationships as a dominant force in crafting educational policy and unifying education with science. As Moats (2004) succinctly noted, conceptions of reading instruction, reading development, and ultimately reading disabilities should take their lead from the neurosciences in order to provide a scientific rationale for the selection, implementation, and monitoring of reading programs designed to meet the needs of children who manifest early reading difficulty.

In 1998, the United States Congress stepped into the fold when a panel of 14 reading researchers and designated experts was commissioned to craft a reading policy based upon a meta-analysis on the existing literature. The National Reading Panel (2000) identified more than 100,000 research articles published on reading since 1966, though the overwhelming majority of these studies were discarded due to methodological failures. The rigorous standards set forth by the National Reading Panel included articles published only in English, articles that used an experimental or quasi-experimental design with a control group or multiple base line method, articles that clearly detailed characteristics of the normative sample, articles with specific interventions that allowed for replication, and finally articles containing a detailed analysis of how long treatment effects lasted. Cunningham (2001) criticized the scientific approach of the panel's research and questioned the use of reading intervention studies to discuss best practices for reading in general education. Furthermore, Burns (2003) questioned the panel's statistical interpretations regarding the use of qualitative approaches to determine effect sizes among the individual studies. Clearly, not every reading related issue or topic was addressed by the panel, nor was there a strategic emphasis placed upon studying second language learners, spelling, or the effects of integrating reading and writing.

Nevertheless, the conclusions reached by the National Reading Panel (2000) have served as the gold standard for evidence based instruction by identifying five linguistic skills children need to acquire in order to become functionally independent readers. As noted in Figure 3-1, the five pillars for reading success centered around *phonemic awareness* (manipulation of spoken syllables in words), *phonics* (letter-sound correspondences),

Figure 3-1

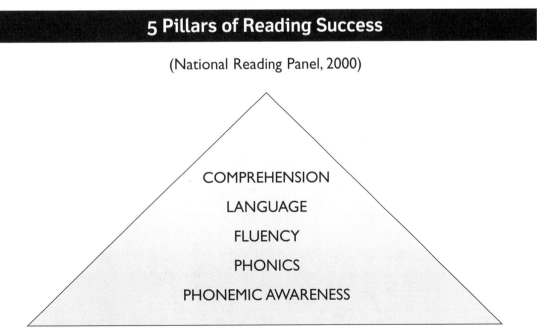

5 Pillars of Reading Success

(National Reading Panel, 2000)

COMPREHENSION

LANGUAGE

FLUENCY

PHONICS

PHONEMIC AWARENESS

fluency (reading speed and accuracy), *vocabulary* (lexicon of known words), and *comprehension skills* (ability to derive meaning from print). Furthermore, the panel concluded that all students, whether dyslexic or non-disabled, would benefit from instructional techniques involving explicit teaching of phonemic awareness and phonics. Hence, the genesis for a *balanced literacy* instructional approach was set in motion. The specific findings of the panel were largely based on a meta-analytic review of the literature, but in many respects did not differ from previous landmark research. For instance, Jeanne Chall (1983) also conducted a meta-analysis on the reading literature and determined that explicit phonological instruction in the early grades produced greater gains in reading by 3rd grade in comparison with most other approaches to reading instruction. Similarly, Marilyn Adams (1990) also carried out an extensive review of the literature and concluded that not only must letter-sound connections be taught in the early grades, they must also be linked to the actual reading process so students can have direct application of these connections to text. More recently, Snow, Burns, and Griffin (1998) concluded that direct systemic instruction in phonemic awareness and phonics was more effective in teaching reading than other forms of instruction. The National Reading Panel's (2000) findings were summarized by Alexander and Slinger-Constant (2004):

Table 3-2

National Reading Panel Conclusions

Kindergarten Through 1st Grade

1. The younger the child, the better the outcome.

2. The *"at-risk"* child responds best to small group instruction (3:1), with phonological awareness training being combined with explicit phonics instruction.

3. Highly trained teachers achieve the best results.

4. Frequent instruction (4-5 days per week) was more effective than sporadic instruction (2 days per week).

5. Gains were maintained in most children at long-term follow-up.

6. The following characteristics of the child were associated with poor outcome:
   a) attention or behavioral concerns   c) poor verbal skills
   b) low socioeconomic status   d) poor rapid naming skills

Table 3-3

National Reading Panel Conclusions

2nd Through 6th Grades

1. Readers at this age respond to explicit phonological instruction with improved word reading, but the gains were not as strong as with younger children.

2. These readers were less responsive to explicit phonics, though they did better in one-to-one or small group instruction.

3. More intensive work for a longer duration was required.

4. Spelling and fluency did not improve very well, though some improvement was noted with reading comprehension.

5. Gains were maintained in most children at long-term follow-up.

6. Computer instruction served as an effective aid, but was not effective by itself.

7. The following characteristics of the child were associated with poor outcome:
   a) attention or behavioral concerns
   b) low socioeconomic status
   c) poor verbal skills
   d) poor rapid naming skills

Table 3-4

National Reading Panel Conclusions

Text Comprehension

1. Fluency is better achieved by repeated guided oral reading than by silent reading practice.

2. Vocabulary instruction should be taught by both direct and indirect methods, with computer programs as merely adjuncts.

3. Comprehension is developed by fluent word reading and vocabulary strength. In addition, meta-cognitive strategies should be used to assist the child in connecting with the text.

The diligent work of the National Reading Panel (2000) to consolidate best practices in reading instruction is both invaluable and strikingly incomplete. An exhaustive review of the literature corroborated findings known by most savvy educators in the field: namely, that early intervention with an explicit phonics approach in a consistent small group atmosphere tends to produce the best results. The gist of these results was parlayed into federal legislation in December 2004 when President Bush signed the reauthorization of the Individuals with Disabilities Act (IDEA) bill into law. Among the many provisions in this bill, states were finally allowed to opt out of using a *discrepancy model* to identify reading disabilities, and replace it by using a Response-to-Intervention (RTI) model. In other words, rather than comparing a student's level of academic achievement with their purported intelligence, school districts were given the flexibility to craft a policy whereby students who do not respond to scientifically based early reading programs may be considered eligible for special education services. Furthermore, the law also required districts with significant over-identification of minority students to consider eliminating IQ testing and establish procedures to reduce disproportional representation of minorities in special education.

However, the National Reading Panel (2000) failed to explain why *older* children have greater difficulty remediating core phonological deficits than younger ones, why rapid naming skills tend to be a good predictor of reading success, why some children can read fluently despite significant phonological deficits, why attention deficits coupled with lower language skills tend to impair reading comprehension, and, most importantly, what exactly constitutes a reading disability? In other words, the National Reading Panel (2000) made few attempts to delve into the neurobiological basis of reading, though in all fairness that was never the intended mission.

Most prudent educators, psychologists, school administrators, and parents yearn for a greater insight into the neurobiological building blocks necessary for children to acquire literacy skills. There has traditionally been a clear and distinct disconnect between those who comprehend the functional organization of the human brain (genotype) and those who merely comprehend the observable portions of human behavior (phenotype) in the academic arena. Precisely how does the typical pre-literate kindergarten child with a vocabulary of some 3000 to 4000 words upon entering school develop a working vocabulary of better than 50,000 words upon graduating from high school (Pinker, 2000)? Furthermore, what are the neurobiological mechanisms that allow students to rapidly and automatically recognize a given word in a mere 200msec? The cognitive machinery necessary for the average child to acquire some 10 new words per day over the next 12 years of their academic career begins with an exploration of the neural pathways mediating the reading process. It is critical that educators become aware of the neural underpinnings of learning in order to create a more *brain-friendly* academic environment consistent with evidence based instruction. As Goldberg (2005) noted:

"I have always been dumbfounded by academic psychology being dominated by individuals not only ignorant about the brain, but were proud of being ignorant. An infatuation exists with the bogus notion that it is somehow possible to study cognition in its Platonic isolation."

The Phonological Processors: The term *phonological awareness* refers to an awareness of the spoken word form, as opposed to its actual meaning. Of critical importance is a working knowledge of the serial position of the sounds that comprise the acoustical properties of the word. In the English language, there are 44 phonemes that represent the sound properties of words. According to Uhry and Clark (2005), it is important to distinguish between *phonics knowledge*, which is more of a lower-level, paired associate type of skill linking letters with sounds, with *phonological awareness*, which is the metacognitive understanding of the spatial arrangements of sounds in words. Phonological awareness has been researched quite extensively, with most studies falling into one of three types of categories: namely, *post-mortem studies, structural anatomy studies, and functional neuroimaging studies.*

Post-Mortem Studies: The initial delve into the world of phonological processing from a brain-behavioral standpoint was conducted by Gallaburda (1989) and consisted of post-mortem analysis of adults with developmental dyslexia. There was clear evidence of cortical dysgenesis in the brains of individuals with dyslexia. The dyslexic brain evidenced anomalies from a cellular level, specifically in the left hemisphere around the *planum temporale*. The planum temporale is a triangular landmark region of the brain situated on the top (superior) portion of the temporal lobes just behind *Heschl's gyrus* along the *Sylvian fissure* (see Figure 3-2). It is a crucial region in the language processing center of the brain, specifically in terms of modulating the 44 phonemes that comprise the English language.

Figure 3-2

Superior Temporal Gyrus

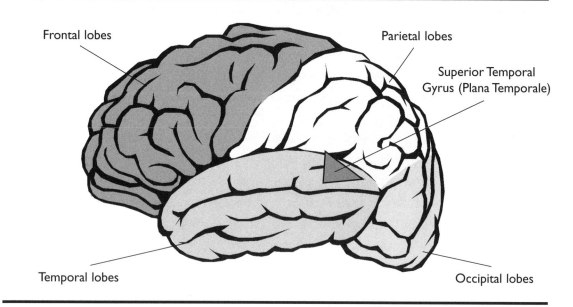

Typically, the left and right plana temporale are asymmetrical, with the left being somewhat larger than the right, due primarily to the left hemisphere being the repository of most linguistic related skills. As Goldberg (2005) noted, the left hemisphere tends to have more gray matter than the right hemisphere, as there are more neurons densely packed together that tend to interconnect in relatively short distances. Consequently, certain speech zones in the left hemisphere tend to be larger than those in the right hemisphere. In contrast, the right hemisphere is comprised of more white matter (glial cells) and is wired for more heteromodal or long-distanced associations between neurons, as evidenced by the abundance of spindle cells in this hemisphere. Gallaburda's (1993) findings suggested the presence of abnormally placed neurons, called *ectopias*, in the brains of dyslexics, along with an unusual symmetry in the plana temporale. In other words, from a cellular level, the dyslexic brains possessed a rather unusual architecture, characterized by numerous misplaced neurons. Similarly, from a structural level, the left hemisphere of the dyslexic brains did not exhibit the classic asymmetrical pattern between the left and right plana temporale. In some cases, there was perfect symmetry in the plana temporale between each hemisphere, or the right plana was actually larger than the left. Despite the robustness of these findings, Heim and Keil (2004) suggested brains of dyslexic subjects in post-mortem studies might reflect natural cell shrinkage if stored for a protracted period of time that could skew the results. Furthermore, these studies focused only on adult brains, and there was relatively little information regarding the specific type of reading disability each individual possessed. Still, the quest for a neurobiological explanation of dyslexia was underway, with specific landmarks on the journey pointing toward the relative contribution of the plana temporale in the left hemisphere as being a key region in the development of phonological awareness.

Structural Anatomy: The next body of research examined structural differences in the brains of dyslexics, with its initial focus on microscopic changes or differences in the dyslexic brain. It is important to note that a 2% change in the amount of genetic material (e.g. 46 vs. 47 chromosomes) can produce a 33% difference in brain structure as evidenced by conditions such as Down's Syndrome (Byrnes, 2001). Consequently, there was much interest in the individual neuron itself, specifically misplaced ones called ectopias, as possibly being the neurological signature in the dyslexic brain. Ectopias begin to emerge in the developing brain of the fetus before the sixth month prenatally, since most neurons find their adult positions by that time. This process of neural migration to form the various sulci and gyri of the brain is guided by radial glial cells (Burns, 2000). These guiding cells act like ropes that allow individual neurons to climb in order to reach their predestined location as biologically determined by each cell's DNA. At the end of the climb, a membrane acts like a ceiling so the cells remain where they belong. If there is any sort of breach or crack in the membrane, the cells migrate through the breach, and overshoot their predestined location. Hence, neurons that migrate incorrectly and overshoot their initial position; namely ectopias, never mature properly and become a functional part of the human cerebrum (Burns, 2000). Initially, researchers believed that a mother's immune system might play a part in the development of ectopias, though it is now generally agreed that ectopias are derived from faulty genetic scripts or possibly emerge due to toxins and outside agents during the prenatal period. For instance, teratogens such as prenatal alcohol consumption, nicotine consumption, and exposure to high levels of lead have the potential to interfere with cellular migration (Byrnes, 2001). These focal malformations have been found and confirmed in fMRI studies, specifically in the left perisylvian region of the dyslexic brain (Galaburda & Cestnick, 2003). It has been speculated that ectopias and focal malformations may prevent rapid auditory processing skills, as well as rapid visual-verbal processing skills, all of which lead to deficits with reading fluency and the automatic recognition of words in print (Galaburda & Cestnick, 2003).

One final structural hypothesis was developed by George Hynd, generally believed to be the pioneer of school neuropsychology, who championed the theory that structural differences exist not just in the relative sizes of the plana temporale, but also in the *corpus callosum*. The *corpus callosum* is a band of some 200 million axonal nerve fibers serving as an information highway of sort, mediating the cortical connections and relative communication between both cerebral hemispheres. The corpus callosum tends to be topographically organized, meaning that projections from specific cortical regions in the cortex are mapped to specific regions along the corpus callosum. Hynd et al. (1995) noted that dyslexics had a relatively smaller *genu* region in the corpus callosum, which is located at the extreme anterior or frontward end of the corpus callosum. Furthermore, there was a significant positive correlation between the size of the genu and reading achievement. Conversely, Duara et al. (1991) noted the most posterior region of the corpus callosum, termed the *splenium* and mapped directly to the plana temporale, was larger in dyslexic men than controls. Taken together, these conflicting results suggest a lack of consistency when attempting to link structural correlates of the brain with developmental dyslexia (Heim & Keil, 2004). Clearly, factors such as how to define specific regional boundaries in the brain, different measurement techniques used, the relative heterogeneity of dyslexia, and co-morbid subject conditions and/or characteristics may be leading to inconsistencies in these findings.

In summary, the aforementioned studies focused on structural regions of the brain, and attempted to correlate specific shapes and sizes of the cerebral cortex with reading skills. Certainly, critics of this methodology have argued that these types of scientific quests are tantamount to phrenology, the 19th century pseudoscience that examined the relationship between bumps on the head to intellectual and personality function. However, there is relatively little argument about the role of utilizing modern neuroimaging techniques to explore the relative function, not structure, of the brain's capacity to modulate a highly complex skill such as reading. Three specific neuroimaging techniques will be highlighted in order to demonstrate that phonological processing is a by-product of the functional integrity of the *temporal-parietal* junctures in the left hemisphere.

Positron Emission Tomography: Let's begin our discussion with Positron Emission Tomography (PET), which is used to provide a measure of brain functioning based upon blood flow and metabolism. In essence, the technology behind PET imaging techniques is based on radioactivity (Bremner, 2005). Glucose is the primary energy source of the brain, and increased brain activity when engaged in a specific cognitive task causes an increase in glucose uptake. Naturally, with an increased glucose demand comes an increase in blood flow. PET procedures are geared toward measuring the increased cortical blood flow in a rather invasive manner, as a radioactive substance is first injected into the person. A computer program constructs an image of the precise metabolism or blood flow patterns in the brain when engaged in the cognitive task. PET studies have consistently noted a decreased activation in the left temporal-parietal regions and the superior temporal gyrus (plana temporale) during phonological processing tasks such as rhyming or segmenting various sounds in words (Rumsey, 1996; Paulesu et al., 1996; Pugh et al., 2000, Sandak et al., 2005). Figure 3-3 provides a general schematic of the temporal-parietal junctures in the left hemisphere of the human brain.

KEY LEARNING POINT	The neuropsychological signature for phonological processing, a key factor involved in the acquisition of literacy skills as outlined by the National Reading Panel (2000), is the temporal-parietal regions of the left hemisphere.

Figure 3-3

Temporal-Parietal Juncture of the Cerebral Cortex

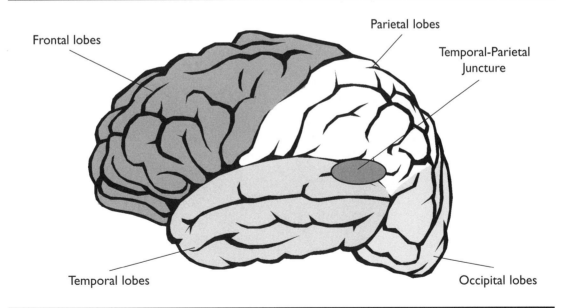

A brief review of cortical functioning may shed further light on the significance of the temporal parietal juncture being the true *"phonological processor"* in the human brain. According to Goldberg (1989), cortico-cortico connections *(e.g. temporal to parietal)* are mediated by continuous interactions within the grey matter, which tend to involve mostly shorter fibers which are non-myelinated. The left hemisphere is clearly differentiated from the right by its increased grey matter and relatively shorter cables or connections (Goldberg, 2005). Consequently, there is more of a continuous or *gradiental* division of labor between two cortices, as opposed to a fixed demarcation between the relative functions of two cortical structures. Therefore, the temporal lobes in the left hemisphere have long been associated with a multitude of functions involving linguistic skills. The posterior portions of the parietal lobes have long been linked with modulating spatial activity. Hence, the interface of the temporal and parietal lobes represents a natural symbiosis in the brain involving the spatial relationships of acoustical codes. As most good reading teachers are aware, *phonological awareness* represents a series of sounds that occupy a particular sequential order (e.g. temporal-parietal), as opposed to *phonological knowledge*, which represents an awareness of just an individual sound. As Adams (1990) observed, the following hierarchical structure in the teaching of phonemic awareness should be helpful in developing the *phonological processor*.

Table 3-5

Developmental Sequence of Phonological Processing

ACTIVITY	AGE	PURPOSE	BRAIN DEVELOPMENT
1. Response to Rhymes	3–4	Three and four year old children can memorize nursery rhymes, rhyming songs, and provide the final word in rhyming text.	The myelination of the auditory cortex in the temporal lobes allows children at approximately age three to more closely discriminate speech sounds. (Berninger & Richards, 2002)
2. Classifying Phonemes	4–5	Children at this age begin to match similar sounds together and can pick the sound that does not belong (e.g., book, look, took, cat).	Brain development tends to progress from the right hemisphere to the left. By age four, children can begin to take sound discriminations from the right hemisphere and classify them in the left, as the brain now allows for crosstalk between the hemispheres. (Berninger & Richards, 2002)
3. Segmenting Words	5–6	Five-year-olds can isolate sounds in the beginning and end of words and are capable of inventive spelling (e.g., KT for cat).	Cross-modal associations now become more automatic, allowing for visual or orthographic representation of words *(parietal lobes)* being stored in an auditory manner *(temporal lobes)*.
4. Phoneme Segmentation	6–7	By 1st grade, children can tap out the number of phonemes in a word, and can often represent all the sounds in a word by inventive spelling.	Brain development and myelination also proceeds from back to front, especially in language zones. Posterior regions code the sounds while anterior structures arrange them sequentially. (Berninger & Richards, 2002)
5. Phoneme Deletion	7–8	Depending on the complexity of the word, children can delete or can substitute the sound of one word to create another word (e.g., "say the "sting" without the "t").	The instructional environment is crucial in sculpting the tertiary regions of the brain for higher-level thinking and the manipulation of phonemes.

Functional Magnetic Resonance Imaging: For more than 100 years, neuroscientists have recognized that changes in blood flow and blood oxygenation in the brain (known as hemodynamics) are closely linked to specific neural activity. The second strand of neuroimaging studies linking the phonological processor to the temporal-parietal regions of the brain are from fMRI's. Functional Magnetic Resonance Imaging (fMRI) seeks to detect subtle magnetic changes in the brain brought on by cognitive activity. In other words, physiological changes in the brain occur with each passing thought, fleeting memory, or random cognitive endeavor. Similarly, nerve cells tend to consume oxygen at a relative pace and intensity commensurate with the cognitive task. Thus, listening to music or passively reading a cheap novel will demand less cognitive energy and thereby use less oxygen than a demanding cognitive activity such as performing mental math or studying for a test. The local response to this oxygen utilization is an increase in blood flow to regions of increased neural activity, occurring after a delay of approximately 1-5 seconds. The magnetic resonance (MR) signal of blood is therefore slightly different depending on the level of oxygenation. The main advantages of fMRI as a technique to image brain related activities are: 1) there are no invasive injections of radioactive isotopes, 2) the total scan time required can be very short, and 3) the in-plane resolution of the functional image is generally about 1.5 x 1.5 mm although resolutions less than 1 mm are possible (Bremner, 2005).

In the classic Connecticut Longitudinal Study, Sally & Bennett Shaywitz (2005) used fMRI technology to study 144 children as they read both real words and pseudowords (made-up words with no meaning). Once again, the primary sites activated during these reading tasks were areas in the left hemisphere around the temporal-occipital regions of the brain, along with the middle temporal and middle occipital gyri (Shaywitz et al., 2002). However, this research also allowed for the examination of compensatory systems on which dyslexic readers tended to over-rely. For instance, during some of the more challenging phonological awareness tasks, dyslexic readers actually engaged anterior brain regions in both the left and right inferior frontal gyrus (Shaywitz, 2004). Conversely, skilled readers relied on the more posterior regions, such as the temporal-parietal regions, to process phonological tasks such as nonword rhyming tasks. This was especially true for older students as compared to younger ones. Therefore, fMRI technology not only verified and reiterated the anatomical regions associated with phonological processing, but also illustrated the role of the frontal lobes in compensating for this process among dyslexic students (Figure 3-4).

Figure 3-4

Nonimpaired vs. Dyslexic

Nonimpaired readers activate primarily posterior portions of left hemisphere while impaired readers under-activate posterior regions and activate primarily frontal areas.

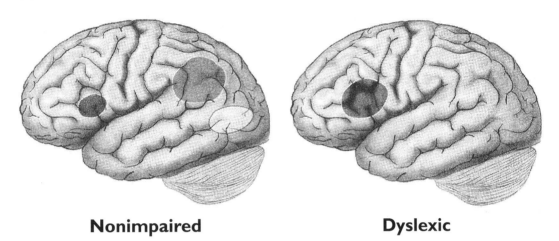

Nonimpaired　　　　**Dyslexic**

Adapted from: *Shaywitz, S. (2004). Overcoming dyslexia. New York: Random House. Printed with permission.*

According to Noble and McCandliss (2005), reading-impaired children actively recruit regions in the frontal cortices as well as the right hemisphere as a form of compensatory strategy in the reading process, as new pathways and alternative, though less effective, processing strategies emerge. As discussed in Chapter 6, there appears to be a large price to pay for the frontal lobes being involved in the phonological process; namely, comprehension and fluency tend to suffer. For instance, the frontal lobes mediate conscious problem solving endeavors. Therefore, in the process of sounding out words, the frontal lobes transform this task into an overly conscious endeavor, thereby precluding reading from becoming a reflexive or automatic process. Consequently, the reading process tends to become slower paced and rather arduous as each phoneme is overanalyzed in the attempt to recognize words in print. Furthermore, there tends to be too much cortical energy devoted to "crashing through" words, thereby sacrificing precious cognitive counterspace to begin the comprehension process. As a result, oral reading becomes much more effortful than it needs to be, and these children quickly lose interest and motivation to read outside of scholastic endeavors.

KEY LEARNING POINT	Students with dyslexia tend to activate other brain regions, most notably frontal lobe sites, to assist them with phonological processing skills. The consequence for recruiting these brain regions is a tendency to consciously focus on the phonetic properties of the word, thereby leading to reduced fluency and poor comprehension skills.

Diffuse Tensor Imaging (DTI): is the third imaging technique worthy of mention, and involves the functional organization of white matter tracts. DTI research has identified microstructural anomalies of perisylvian white matter in the left hemisphere of both children and adults with dyslexia (Noble & McCandliss, 2005). Because white matter is deeper in the brain than gray matter, it has often remained less visible to researchers and its structures are often missed by magnetic resonance imaging (MRI) and other techniques. Basically, conventional imaging techniques reveal major anatomical features of the brain (gray matter), which is made up of nerve cell bodies. However, neuroscientists believe that the gray matter is merely the tip of the iceberg, as cognition may be rooted in subtle "wiring" problems involving axons, the long, thin tails of neurons that carry electrical signals and constitute the brain's white matter. As Goldberg (2005) noted, there tends to be more white matter in the right hemisphere than the left, with nerve fibers capable of traversing great distances in the brain. With DTI, researchers can now begin to explore the complex network of nerve fibers connecting different regions of the brain. Essentially, radiologists use specific radio-frequency and magnetic field-gradient pulses to track the movement of water molecules in the brain. In most brain tissue, water molecules diffuse in all different directions. However, they tend to diffuse along the length of axons, whose coating of white, fatty myelin holds them in. DTI technology allows cognitive neuroscientists to actually create pictures and examine the functional integrity of axonal pictures by analyzing the direction of water diffusion According to McCandliss and Noble (2003), the diffusion of water tends to follow a more directional or anisotropic pattern in more healthy, and robustly dense white matter tracts. However, reading impairments tend to be associated with decreased anisotropy (lack of directional flow) in the white matter tracts of the temporal-parietal regions. In fact, the degree of anisotropy in the left temporal-parietal region was highly correlated with reading skill in both dyslexic and control subjects (McCandliss & Noble, 2003). As Temple (2002) observed, most dyslexics have difficulty with phonological processing which may indeed stem from disorganization of white matter tracts connecting the temporal-parietal regions with other cortical regions involved in the reading process. These additional cortical regions are the next topic for further exploration.

CHAPTER 4

The Orthographic Processor: Establishing the Neural Code for Automaticity and Fluency

The evolution of the brain is dominated by one grand theme, a gradual transition from a *hardwired* design to a more *open-ended* design (Goldberg, 2005). The human brain is not born a *tabula rasa*, the sixteenth century theory proposed by British philosopher John Locke stating that the mind is an empty shell waiting to be filled with the spirit of life through the richness of experiential learning. From an evolutionary standpoint, it seems necessary that the 40,000 generations of men and women who preceded our own must have had some means of passing along the accumulated knowledge and cognitive acquisitions discovered during their existence. Here lies the great dilemma. Throughout the brain's five million years of evolution, the ability to pass down knowledge through written transcription has only been available for the past 5000 years, and the ability to pass down knowledge through oral discourse a mere 50,000 years. Perhaps the survival instincts of our species can be attributed in part to the genetic scripts within the nucleus of individual neurons, and their ability to forge connections and communicate information without the luxury of environmental experience. In other words, a strong case can be made that the human brain comes pre-wired, with some synaptic connections making their first appearance within the cortical plate at approximately 23 weeks gestational age (Aylward, 1997).

According to Byrnes (2001), the functional adaptability of the brain begins with an initial overproduction of neurons. In fact, 90 percent of the neurons that are made during fetal development eventually die (apoptosis), leaving the brain with some 100 billion nerve cells to establish functional circuits comprised of some 100 trillion synapses (Stahl, 2000). At birth, the brain stem and the spinal cord are almost 100 percent myelinated, ensuring that the parts of the brain needed to support life are functional (Berninger & Richards, 2002). Consequently, subcortical regions such as the *thalamus, basal ganglia, midbrain regions,* and *cerebellum*, all of which modulate more sensory and motor functioning skills, are further along in their circuitry during the first two years of life, than higher level cortical functions responsible for more complex types of cognitions. Still, the cerebral cortex itself comes pre-wired for certain types of basic pattern recognition skills. Luria (1970) articulated this notion when noting that primary projection systems have a rather linear and simplistic type of neural organization system, resulting in more *"one-on-one"* types of neural mappings. Hence, basic sensory and motor skills, along with basic visual and auditory pathways, tend to be pre-wired at birth. However, the establishment of higher level cortical functioning involved in more complex machinations such as reading, require the development of secondary and tertiary brain regions. The more complex association *(heteromodal)* areas have little pre-wired knowledge, and are more modular or gradient in their make-ups leading to "one to many" types of brain mappings (Goldberg, 2005). In other words, the higher level or more sophisticated cognitive machinery of the brain receives neural input from multiple brain regions, and thus is more open-ended, meaning that environmental input plays an important role in sculpting neural connections. Since the human brain weighs just 25% of its adult weight at birth, yet reaches 90% of its adult weight by age five (Stahl, 2000), there is plenty of opportunity in the early years for neurons to establish important cortical connections necessary for the development of higher level complex tasks. Certainly, an enriched linguistic environment cultivating language acquisition skills remains paramount for the development of the reading brain. As Byrnes (2001) observed, there are two types of neural connections that forge the structural integrity of the brain's capacity to develop higher level learning:

Experience-expectant: This type of neural wiring is greatly influenced by consistencies in environmental stimulation. Experience-expectant circuits are predictable neural connections more likely to develop and strengthen in response to a repeated stimulus within the environment. According to Aylward (1997), *expectant* synapses are genetically programmed to receive experiences that are adaptive, species specific, and highly likely to occur. For instance, neuroscientists have found that if a monkey is trained to use a particular finger for a specific task, and the animal repeats the task a thousand times per day, there tends to be an over-representation of cells in the area of the post-central gyrus that corresponds to the specific finger used (Restak, 2001).

KEY LEARNING POINT	Basic sensory and motor skills, along with basic visual and auditory pathways, tend to be pre-wired at birth. However, the establishment of higher level cortical functioning involved in more complex machinations such as reading, requires the development of secondary and tertiary brain regions.

In human beings, studies have shown the post-central gyrus of the brain, which modulates tactile functioning, also becomes enlarged for blind readers of Braille as the fingertips become increasingly more attuned to subtle changes in tactile sensitivity (Restak, 2001). This same phenomena has even been observed in the brains of violin players who have enlarged cortical regions and pathways representing the thumb and fifth finger on the left hand, the so called fingering digits, in the right *post-central gyrus*, as a result of extensive practicing with the instrument (Ratey, 2001). It's as though neurons are in constant competition for cortical survival by establishing and strengthening neural connections for maximal cortical representation. As Berninger and Richards (2002) noted, genes may dictate the overall direction and growth of axonal development, but environmental experience shapes the strength of their functional connectivity. Hence, the development of reading pathways will no doubt follow along this basic neural axiom, in that sheer practice and repetition of the reading process will strengthen neural connections to facilitate this skill.

It is important to note that experience not only establishes and strengthens neuronal connectivity, but lack of experience tends to diminish or even eliminate cortical connectivity. As previously noted, fetal development can be characterized by a sheer overproduction of neurons due to a prolonged proliferation period lasting through the third trimester in the development of the human brain (Aylward, 1997).

Consequently, there is a natural pruning process beginning around 7 months of age and lasting throughout adolescence (Berninger & Richards, 2002). The purpose of the pruning process is to develop the most economical circuit possible for task efficiency by scaling back unwanted cortical connections. For instance, the notion of *auditory pruning* follows the same learning progression. Every child is born with the ability to distinguish all possible sound patterns and variations due to an overabundance of neurons in the auditory cortex produced during the proliferation stage. However, based on exposure to cultural specific dialects, a child becomes attuned only to sounds from their host language. As a result, neurons that respond to more subtle sounds not readily present in a child's host dialect are discarded, and only neurons stimulated by frequently heard sound patterns are retained. This pruning process of unused synapses in the auditory pathways explains why some adults such as Arnold Schwarzeneggar who are born in another country continue to have foreign language accents if brought to the United States after auditory pruning has occurred. Conversely, children exposed to a second language prior to the completion of the pruning process can learn to speak this language without the residue of their host tongue, due to the retention of neurons dedicated to processing these types of sounds. In essence, there does seem to be a critical window of time in which certain types of neurons must be activated or they simply die out. Simply put, if two neurons become activated at the same time, there is a greater chance they will not only form a synaptic connection, but also increase their chances for survival. The developing brain tends to be rather redundant in the formation of neural connections, almost to ensure some sort of innervation takes place, though by adolescence the human brain pares down these connections to just 60 percent of the maximum density seen at age two (Aylward, 1997). Therefore, the brain comes relatively "hardwired" for more basic self-regulatory processes at birth, though relatively "softwired" for more higher-level and complex cortical functions such as reading. This is good news for educators, who can alter and strengthen synaptic connectivity through repetition and practice in critical brain regions needed to modulate the complexities of reading.

Experience-dependent: This mechanism of change is not the natural elimination of neurons through a pruning process, but rather the ability to create new synapses and reorganize synaptic connectivity in order to modulate a unique task in the environment. These synaptic connections are in essence dependent upon environmental experience to sculpt the neural connectivity in a rather new, unique fashion. The modus operandum is not repetitive environmental stimulation to trigger a predictable firing pattern. Conversely, these synapses are less genetically programmed, and their subsequent wiring is determined more from novel, as opposed to redundant, environmental experiences (Holtmaat, Wilbrecht, Knott, Welker, & Syoboda, 2006).

KEY LEARNING POINT	The brain comes relatively "hardwired" for more basic self-regulatory processes at birth, though relatively "softwired" for more higher-level and complex cortical functions such as reading. This is good news for educators, who can alter and strengthen synaptic connectivity through repetition and practice in critical brain regions needed to modulate the complexities of reading.

Perhaps Hubel and Wiesel (1970) were the first to illustrate the differences between experience-dependent cells and experience-expectant cells in their landmark discovery that sensory experience is vital to teaching "higher level" neurons their specific job or duties. In their Nobel-winning experiments (Hubel & Wiesel, 1970), kittens were deprived of light during their first 8 weeks of life, and then responded to the environment as if they were blind despite relatively normal visual systems. Thus, without the sensory input of light, neurons in the visual cortices simply failed to establish critical cortical connections to develop sight. Hence, these neurons tended to die out, or they simply gravitated toward other regions of the brain in hopes of finding a specific role or function to establish some degree of usefulness. An experience-expectant cortical connection is pre-programmed to fire in a particular manner when triggered by a specific stimulus, whereas an experience-dependent cortical connection is the reorganization of synapses to fire in a unique manner when triggered by a multitude of stimuli.

Without a doubt, the process of reading begins as a novel learning experience, as there really is no ready-made word recognition center in the brain. In other words, the ability to rapidly and automatically recognize words in print is more a reflection of a progressive skill, shaped and cultivated by earlier mastery of phonetic decoding ability (McCandliss, Cohen, & Dehaene, 2003). For literate adults, the perceptual features of a word can be converted to having linguistic value and semantic understanding, despite wide variations in script, font, or size in just 250 ms. That translates into rapid and automatic word recognition skills at a pace of some 240 words per minute. According to McCandliss et al. (2003), there is significant evidence that specific neurons exist in the brain to comprise a *visual-word form area*, specifically in the extrastriate cortex of the occipital lobes around the *fusiform gyrus* in the left hemisphere (See Figure 4-1).

KEY LEARNING POINT	An *experience-expectant* cortical connection is pre-programmed to fire in a particular manner when triggered by a specific stimulus, whereas an *experience-dependent* cortical connection is the reorganization of synapses to fire in a unique manner when triggered by a multitude of stimuli.

Figure 4-1

Visual-Word Form Area (Fusiform Gyrus)

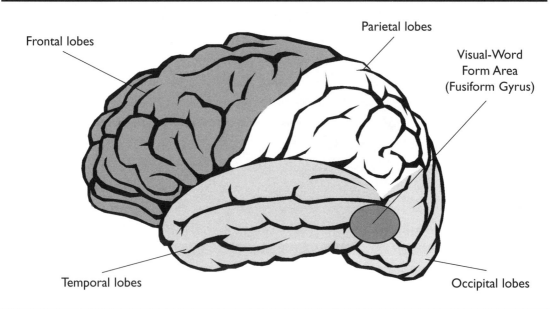

Just as Hubel and Wiesel (1970) noted that light is the environmental trigger for the visual system to emerge, Shaywitz et al. (2002) concluded that phonological skills were the trigger for the development of a brain region allowing for automatic word recognition skills, or what is referred to as a visual-word form area. In other words, the visual-word form area emerges from the experience-dependent synaptic pathways created through phonological decoding skills. Using fMRI technology, Shaywitz et al. (2002) demonstrated that activation of the visual-word form area was correlated with decoding skills, even when the effects of age were taken into account. In summary, there may be a certain symbiotic relationship between phonological decoding skills and the rapid ascension of automatic word recognition skills.

A brief review of Luria's (1970) exquisite knowledge of brain behavioral relationships may explain why. Luria (1970) conceived of a three-way organizational structure of the cortex, with the highest cortical levels of cognitive functioning being the tertiary levels, integrative brain regions as being secondary levels, and basic perceptual areas as being primary levels. In the visual system, the tertiary levels not only process higher level, unique visual perceptions, but also are comprised of experience-dependent synaptic connections. Conversely, the primary projection areas of the visual system (most basic levels) are comprised mainly of experience-expected synapses. These primary cortical zones are modality specific and receive direct input from the senses. Consequently, primary zones tend to be fully functional by the first year, which leads one to conclude that these cortical connections are primarily genetically controlled.

However, secondary zones integrate modality specific information from the primary zones, and therefore are not relatively functional until later in childhood. Now, let's take a look at the interplay of these zones in the reading process. The basic perception or recognition of the shape of a letter may be an example of a primary projection zone in the occipital lobes. However, the previous chapter discussed the cross modal association capabilities of the temporal-parietal regions that actually map letters to sound, and may be an example of a secondary zone in the reading process. However, most educators know the goal of reading is not solely the development of sound mapping, but also the ability to automatically recognize words in an effortless fashion for effective comprehension. Hence, automatic word recognition may be an example of a tertiary zone, as input from a variety of associative brain regions is assembled. These tertiary zones consist of more experience-dependent synaptical connections due in part to their relatively late emergence and reliance upon earlier, novel stimulation. The eventual formation of the visual-word form area may represent a reconfiguration of the synaptic connections in the visual system which were previously mapped out by earlier decoding skills, as children learn to match sounds with visual stimuli (McCandliss et al., 2003). Hence, phonological development is simply an intermediate step in the reading process, as decoding skills allow for the mapping of highly sophisticated neural synapses to be coded in the fusiform gyrus (visual-word form area) of the left hemisphere for the eventual automaticity of word reading. Herein lies the core of what truly may be dyslexia. The combination of either a structural or functional abnormality in the temporal-parietal regions that subserve phonological processing may have a cascading effect on the development of rapid word recognition processes during critical points in development, when the visual-word form area is becoming increasingly specialized to respond to words in print (McCandliss & Noble, 2003).

KEY LEARNING POINT	Phonological development is simply an intermediate step in the reading process, as decoding skills allow for the mapping of highly sophisticated neural synapses to be coded in the fusiform gyrus of the left hemisphere for the eventual automaticity of word reading.

Dyslexia in Other Languages: The assertion that phonological processing serves as a conduit for the development of rapid and automatic word recognition skills can be further explored by examining dyslexia in other languages, especially ones that are more phonologically consistent than English. The English language is a relatively hybrid tongue, consisting of a Germanic core, though influenced by Latin and Danish languages during three epochs (Old English, Middle English, and Modern English). Consequently, it is estimated that approximately 25% of the words in the English language are phonologically irregular, and do not follow a predictable sound to symbol relationship (Uhry & Clark, 2005). In comparing the visual-word form area of dyslexics in other languages, research has shown that despite the language, the posterior regions of the brain around the visual-word form area are under-activated (Paulesu et al., 2001). Hence, the posterior portions of the brain are critical, no matter what the language or culture, for the rapid and automatic recognition of words in print. The authors (Paulesu et al., 2001) concluded two important postulates regarding dyslexia. First, despite the language or culture, there are certain universal truths in how the human brain acquires linguistic codes pertaining to reading. As neuroimaging data revealed, the superior temporal regions of the left hemisphere (phonological decoding) and areas around the middle occipital lobe regions (automatic word recognition skills) were much more activated for non-impaired readers than dyslexics. Second, the differences in reading performance among cultures may be highly attributed to the complexities of the orthographical rules of the language itself. For instance, the English language has more than 1,100 ways of representing 44 sounds (phonemes) using different letter combinations (graphemes). Mapping letters to word sounds is a rather inexact science, as illustrated by pairs of words such as "pint" with "mint". By contrast, in Italian there is no such ambiguity and just 33 graphemes are sufficient to represent the 25 phonemes. This means that the same letter groups in Italian almost always represent the same unique sound, which makes the written language logical, easier to read, and more phonologically consistent. It seems plausible to assume that the more phonologically inconsistent languages, such as English, most likely have a higher incidence rate of dyslexia than more phonologically consistent languages such as Italian. Certainly, there are many cultural, environmental, and socioeconomic forces that also factor into this equation. However, as depicted in Table 4-1, the prevalence of dyslexia across several countries show a relationship between the degree of difficulty in the orthography of the language and incidences of dyslexia (Smyth, Everatt, & Salter, 2004).

Table 4-1

Dyslexia Prevalence Rates Across the Globe

Lowest Incidence		Highest Incidence	
Slovakia	1 - 2%	China	5 - 8%
Italy	1.3 - 5%	United States	5 - 10%
Czech Republic	2 - 3%	Russia	10%
Britain	4%	Israel	10%
Poland	4%	Finland	10%
Belgium	5%	Nigeria	11%
Greece	5%	Australia	16%
Japan	6%	India	20%

Clearly, there are numerous moderating variables that contribute to the incidence rates of developmental dyslexia. These include the definitional criteria used to assess a learning disability, the instructional methods used to teach reading, the skill level of practitioners to diagnose learning disorders, and differences acquiring a logographic versus alphabetic script. However, it is interesting to note that language systems do affect academic performance, even in mathematics. For instance, Campbell and Xue (2001) explored why Asian students tended to outperform North American students in mathematical performance. Among their conclusions was the actual script of the language system offered students an advantage when engaged in math calculation activities. Most European derived languages such as English or French do not correspond to the base-10 ordinal structure of the Arabic number system. In other words, what does the number *twelve* have to do with a base-10 counting system in mathematics? In contrast, most Asian languages have linguistic structures much more consistent with a numeric counting system, and thus counting past *ten* is a much more standard feature of the language. Therefore, the number twelve is represented as *"ten-two"* allowing for more efficient direct retrieval. Perhaps the relatively complexity of the orthographic structures of the English language system also provide students with a disadvantage in learning to master the reading process.

Toward an Integrative Model of Fluency: To date, there is converging evidence that successful oral reading involves three distinct brain systems. The first is more involved with dorsal (top) regions of the brain in the temporal-parietal cortices that modulate phonology, while the second is more involved with ventral (bottom) regions of the brain in the occipital-temporal regions (fusiform gyrus) involved with fluency (Pugh, Mencl, Jenner, Katz, Frost, Lee, Shaywitz, & Shaywitz, 2000). The temporal-parietal system is associated with rule-based analysis and learning, and tends to be critical in the initial mapping of graphemes with phonemes (Pugh, et al., 2000). This system is a relatively slower paced pathway, and tends to be used by beginning readers to learn how to sound out words (Shaywitz, 2004). Conversely, the occipital-temporal pathways are highly interconnected neural systems that respond in just 200ms to the visual features of a word to allow for automatic and rapid word recognition skills. Hence, during curriculum-based measurement and fluency types of tests, the integrity of the occipital-temporal stream, or what some refer to as the visual-form word area, is really being measured. A third system, located in the frontal regions of the brain around Broca's Area, also emerges as being the endpoint of the inner articulation system that fine-tunes the ability to orally sound out certain words. This system is also a relatively slower functioning reading pathway, as words are slowly stretched and sounded out. As Shaywitz (2004) noted, dyslexics fail to activate the quicker reading pathways in the posterior brain regions, and consequently, over-activate frontal regions of the brain, thus reading at a much slower and more methodical pace. Figure 4-2 illustrates the relative function of these three brain systems.

Figure 4-2

Major Neural Circuits Involved With Reading

Adapted from Pugh et al. (2000)

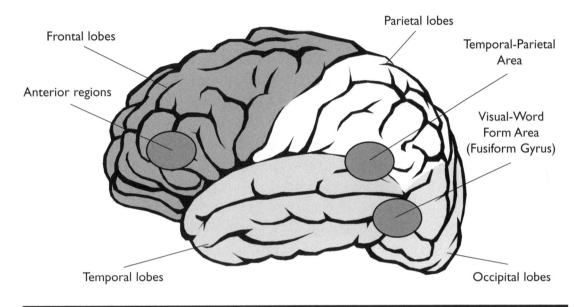

Table 4-2

Function of Each Brain Region

Temporal-Parietal (Dorsal) Region - Rule based analysis and the integration of orthographical and phonological information. A relatively slower paced pathway.

Occipital-Temporal (Ventral) Region - A linguistically structured memory based word form recognition area. A relatively fast system.

Anterior Regions - The endpoint of inner articulation system involved in fine grain articulatory recoding. A slower paced system.

Certainly, the goal of any good reading program is ultimately for the quicker paced pathways in the occipital-temporal regions of the brain to assume responsibility for the reading process, thereby freeing up other cortical regions to assist in comprehension. Should the slower paced neural circuitry in the temporal-parietal regions of the brain assume full responsibility for the reading process, fluency may then become compromised and reading becomes an effortful and mundane process. However, as previously mentioned, the English language is a relatively complex and irregular language to map consistently on to cortical structures. Since there are over 1100 different variants to map out the 44 phonemes of English, perhaps further cortical areas are needed to assist students in mapping out those difficult phonologically irregular words, such as *"one"*, which cannot be coded in a one-to-one correspondence. That is exactly what some of the newer, state of the art research in dyslexia is beginning to note. In particular, Owen, Borowsky, and Sarty (2004) have further explored a crucial brain region in the reading process, often hidden from fMRI technology, called the *insular cortex*.

KEY LEARNING POINT	There are three regions of the brain that modulate reading. The first is more involved with dorsal (top) regions of the brain in the temporal-parietal cortices that modulate phonology, while the second is more involved with ventral (bottom) regions of the brain in the occipital-temporal regions (fusiform gyrus) involved with fluency (Pugh, Mencl, Jenner, Katz, Frost, Lee, Shaywitz, & Shaywitz, 2000). A third system, located in the frontal regions of the brain around Broca's Area, also emerges to fine tune the ability to orally sound out certain words.

The role of the insular cortex: The insular cortex (also often referred to as just the insula) lies deep to the brain's lateral surface, within the lateral sulcus which separates the temporal lobe and inferior parietal lobe. This brain region is relatively complicated, and specializes in a variety of perceptive experiences. The insular cortex is well situated for the integration of information relating to the affective and reactive components of pain, and is part of the circuitry related to fear avoidance. Certainly, the question begs as to what does a brain region, which is primarily geared to modulate emotional and perceptive centers of the brain, have to do with reading?

The initial exploration of the insular cortex was conducted by Posner and Raichle (1994), who noted that insular cortical activity increased as a result of practice. These researchers used PET neuroimaging procedures to determine the effect of practice on the language system. When students were spontaneously given a list of nouns, and asked to pair a verb with each noun (e.g., hammer with pound) without any practice, areas of the left temporal cortex, Broca's area, and anterior cingulate were activated. However, when the students were allowed 15 minutes to practice intensely and therefore memorize in advance which verb would be selected to pair with each noun, an entirely new pathway was activated. In essence, this latter task was more associated with the automatic retrieval of archived information, and different brain structures; namely, the insular cortices of both hemispheres were activated (see Figure 4-3). Therefore, the insular cortex may be responsible for "word habits", which is the automatic retrieval of archived information without the need for further analysis or breakdown. Clearly, skilled reading involves the activation of "word habits" which is the automatic recognition of words consisting of familiar orthographic stimuli. The key word here is familiar, as students would need to have some familiarity with these words and have practiced them repeatedly. Most educators would refer to these words as "sight words" or in some classrooms, "word wall words", and expect students to automatically recognize them without the need to apply decoding skills. Hence, could the insular cortex actually be the anatomical structures involved in reading fluency? Furthermore, are curriculum based measurement techniques that overrely on the automaticity of rapid word recognition skills simply barometers for measuring the integrity of the insular cortices?

Figure 4-3

Insular Cortex Activity for Practiced Tasks

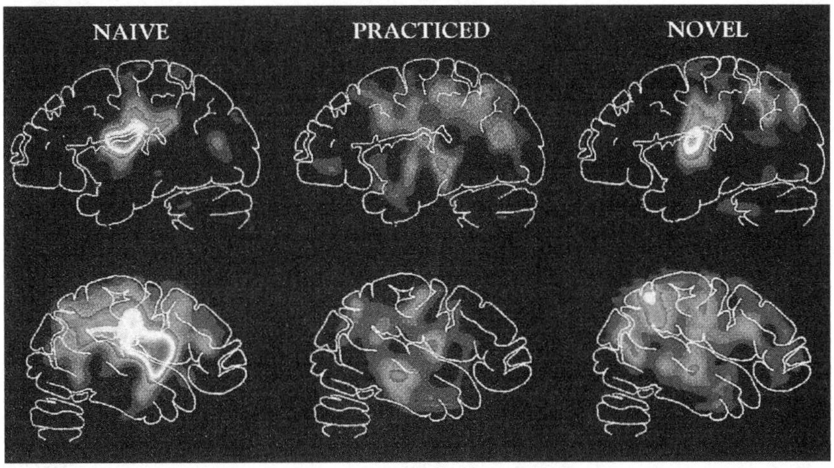

These images reverse the color coding normally used in PET scans, with decreases in activity represented by the darker colors. The insular cortex is activated when tasks are practiced and over-learned, though remain inactive during new trials. Adapted from Posner and Raichle (1994) with permission.

Owen et al. (2003) devised a series of neuroimaging experiments to further explore the anatomical nuances of reading fluency, and more accurately measure how these *"word habits"* are formed. The subjects were asked to determine whether a series of nonwords rhymed (e.g., "nirm and glirm"), and then were also asked to pronounce a pseudohomophone . A pseudohomophone is a made-up word that looked and sounded like an actual word (e.g., "brane"). It was hypothesized that determining whether two nonwords rhymed basically involved the acoustical regions of the brain; namely, the temporal-parietal circuit as well as phonological working memory skills. In essence, this was more of a bottom-up processing task. The pseudohomophone task was also a phonological processing task, but more on a whole-word or lexical (top-down) level. The results suggested that the insular cortex was *only* involved in the pseudohomophone or whole-word task, as was the inferior frontal gyrus. The rhyming task *did not* activate the insular cortex, though as predicted, it activated the temporal-parietal regions of the left hemisphere. This suggested that certain phonological processing tasks at the sublexical level that require bottom-up processing skills are modulated by the temporal-parietal lobes; however, other phonological processing tasks requiring more top-down processing (pseudohomophones) are modulated by the insular cortex. This is good news for educators, who may want to consider reading programs that utilize a top-down phonological method (e.g., LiPS, Wilson) for students who do not respond to traditional bottom-up phonological programs (e.g., *Road to the Code, Ladders to Literacy*). Still, the question remains as to how many brain circuits are truly involved in the automaticity of reading?

According to Borowsky, Owen and Masson (2002), reading fluency is primarily driven by two circuits, one which involves primarily the automatic word recognition centers around the fusiform gyrus, and the other that also involves the same circuit *in addition* to the insular cortex. Perhaps the added circuit involving the insular cortex serves as more of a "lexical checking system", which allows the reader to double check that phonologically irregular words are indeed a part one's lexical memory of the English language (e.g., "brane"). This circuit may be tantamount to an ad hoc mechanism designed to account for an unexpected pattern of results. Additionally, Borowsky et al. (2002) noted that subjects were slower to name pseudohomophones than just garden variety nonwords that were clearly unrelated to any familiar English word. These results suggested the more closely aligned a pseudohomophone was to an actual familiar word, the more time the brain needed to differentiate the unique characteristics of the pseudohomophone. Therefore, the insular cortex may be responsible for "double checking" and making sure that a word processed phonologically is indeed a real word that is part of the student's lexicon. Figure 4-4 presents a graphic illustration of the critical cortical components needed to read words in fluent manner.

Figure 4-4

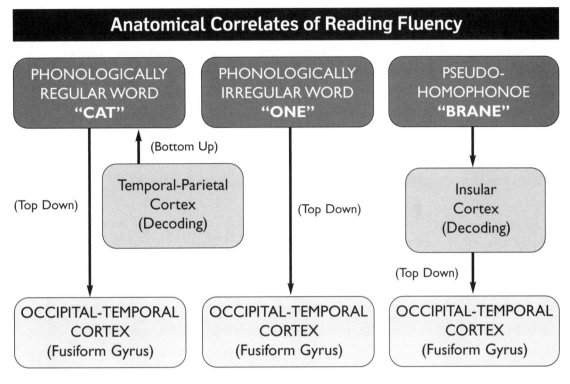

Anatomical Correlates of Reading Fluency

| PHONOLOGICALLY REGULAR WORD "CAT" | PHONOLOGICALLY IRREGULAR WORD "ONE" | PSEUDO-HOMOPHONOE "BRANE" |

(Bottom Up)

Temporal-Parietal Cortex (Decoding)

(Top Down)   (Top Down)

Insular Cortex (Decoding)

(Top Down)

| OCCIPITAL-TEMPORAL CORTEX (Fusiform Gyrus) | OCCIPITAL-TEMPORAL CORTEX (Fusiform Gyrus) | OCCIPITAL-TEMPORAL CORTEX (Fusiform Gyrus) |

KEY LEARNING POINT

The insular cortex may be responsible for "double checking" and making sure that a word processed phonologically is indeed a real word that is part of the student's lexicon. Having an additional system is good news for educators, who may want to consider reading programs that utilize a top-down phonological method (i.e., LiPS, Wilson) for students who do not respond to traditional bottom-up phonological programs (i.e., *Road to the Code, Ladders to Literacy*).

In conclusion, there appears to be compelling evidence that skilled readers activate the quicker, more rapid and automatic pathways to decipher words in print (Pugh et al., 2000; McCandliss & Noble, 2003; Shaywitz, 2004: Owen et al., 2004). This pathway is primarily situated in the posterior portions of the brain, along the interface of the occipital and temporal lobes, in a brain region called the fusiform gyrus. Conversely, dyslexics do not activate these pathways, but instead rely on different pathways, forged in part by compensatory mechanisms, which are slower and less efficient to assist with word recognition skills (Shaywitz & Shaywitz, 2005). These slower pathways, which over-rely on breaking down each word into its phonological core, are referred to as the *dorsal stream*. The quicker, automatic pathway which processes words at the lexical level, is sometimes referred to as the *ventral stream*. Lastly, yet another brain region, the insular cortex, may be of assistance when automatically processing unusual spellings of words, which tend to be common in the English language (Owen et al., 2004).

Implications for Teachers: As discussed in the previous chapter, the National Reading Panel (2000) identified reading fluency as one of the five pillars of reading. It is especially critical for educators to begin recording reading fluency and speed using curriculum based measurement techniques. This will help enable teachers to closely monitor reading proficiency, and from a neuropsychological standpoint, measure the extent with which the ventral stream has become acclimated to taking over the process of reading from the slower paced dorsal stream. Curriculum based measurement (CBM) has provided psychologists and educators with a quicker, more cost effective, and more ecologically valid means of measuring reading progress in children than nationally-normed tests. According to Shinn (2002), curriculum based measurement can be set apart from other curriculum based assessment models because it is explicitly linked to a direct problem solving model. As Fuchs (1998) noted, when teachers utilize CBM techniques to write specific data-based goals and objectives, as well as monitor academic progress, student achievement improves. The basic tenets of curriculum based measurement involve testing a student with brief fluency indicators. For instance, reading is assessed by randomly selecting a passage from a basal reading series, and recording the number of words read correctly in a minute. Usually, students are given three attempts at the passage, with the highest score and the lowest score being discarded. Instead of comparing fluency scores with an artificially contrived measured of intellectual potential, scores are compared to other students from the same class using localized norms. The data is further analyzed within the context of a problem solving model, which allows schools to identify the problem, and then explore solutions using a survey level assessment technique linking interventions with assessment. Table 4-3 provides current national norms for reading fluency for fall, winter, and spring, along with average weekly gains. Most school districts are gravitating toward these national benchmark measures instead of developing localized measures. It is critical that educators sample periodically reading fluency rates to determine student progress, as well as monitor the effectiveness of a particular reading intervention. In summary, reading fluency rates are not only an excellent predictor of reading comprehension in the early grades, but also reflect the brain's ability to synthesize a very complex process so vital for future learning success.

Table 4-3

					Avg. Weekly
Grade	**Percentile**	**Fall WCPM***	**Winter WCPM***	**Spring WCPM***	**Improvement****
1	90		81	111	1.9
	75		47	82	2.2
	50		23	53	1.9
	25		12	28	1.0
	10		6	15	0.6
2	90	106	125	142	1.1
	75	79	100	117	1.2
	50	51	72	89	1.2
	25	25	42	61	1.1
	10	11	18	31	0.6
3	90	128	146	162	1.1
	75	99	120	137	1.2
	50	71	92	107	1.1
	25	44	62	78	1.1
	10	21	36	48	0.8
4	90	145	166	180	1.1
	75	119	139	152	1.0
	50	94	112	123	0.9
	25	68	87	98	0.9
	10	45	61	72	0.8
5	90	166	182	194	0.9
	75	139	156	168	0.9
	50	110	127	139	0.9
	25	85	99	109	0.8
	10	61	74	83	0.7
6	90	177	195	204	0.8
	75	153	167	177	0.8
	50	127	140	150	0.7
	25	98	111	122	0.8
	10	68	82	93	0.8
7	90	180	192	202	0.7
	75	156	165	177	0.7
	50	128	136	150	0.7
	25	102	109	123	0.7
	10	79	88	98	0.6
8	90	185	199	199	0.4
	75	161	173	177	0.5
	50	133	146	151	0.6
	25	106	115	124	0.6
	10	77	84	97	0.6

*WCPM=Words Correct Per Minute   **Average words per week growth

Jan Hasbrouck and Gerald Tindal completed an extensive study of oral reading fluency in 2004. The results of their study are published in a technical report entitled, "Oral Reading Fluency: 90 Years of Measurement," which is available on the University of Oregon's website, brt.uoregon.edu/tech_reports.htm.

Students scoring in the 50th percentile using the average score of two unpracticed readings from grade-level materials need a fluency-building program. In addition, teachers can use the table to set the long-term fluency goals for their struggling readers.

CHAPTER 5

Subtypes of Dyslexia

There tends to be an inclination in our society to over-rely on linear, one-dimensional models to explain virtually all walks of modern life. For instance, in the political arena, the discourse continues to be somewhat tired, as the Republican proponents of the right denounce their Democratic counterparts on the left, and vice-versa. Herein lies an optimal example of how human intellectual prowess has been cheaply dichotomized in a binary, one dimensional fashion: namely, liberal versus conservative. Though many Americans tend to lean a bit toward being both socially liberal and fiscally conservative, political pundits and so-called media experts prefer to label beliefs, thoughts, opinions, and preferences using a singular and modular category. The categories are predictable, monolithic, and somewhat stereotypical as well. For instance, conservatives are supposedly religiously driven, favor big business, have rather black and white views on ethics and morality, and demonstrate devout nationalistic pride. On the other hand, liberals are supposedly more secularly driven, have ethical and moral views which are more relative than fixed, and denounce big business in favor of providing aid to the environment and less able individuals. The fact remains that most individuals have opinions on issues that vary not just along a singular left-right dimension, but also along an informed (deep) vs. uninformed (shallow) dimension, as well as a cerebral (top-down) versus emotional (bottom-up) dimension.

In a much more benign regard, the world of education also tends to view students from a rather binary perch, namely, regular education students versus learning-disabled students. This is especially evident in the field of learning disabilities. According to Spafford and Grosser (2005), nearly half of all students in special education are identified as being learning disabled, yet as many as 20 percent of the entire regular education population may be dyslexic. There are multiple reasons why students who may be dyslexic are often not identified for special education. First, certain subtypes of dyslexia do not always have a significant education impact (e.g., surface dyslexia), which is often defined as reading at least two grade levels below. Second, there have been numerous inconsistencies in the definitions of what constitutes a learning disability (LD) over the years. According to Kavale and Forness (2000), the evolution of LD definitions has resulted in the following ideas:

Table 5-1

Common Themes Among LD Definitions

1. LD is marked by heterogeneity

2. LD involves psychological processing disorders

3. LD is associated with underachievement in school

4. LD can be manifested in spoken language or in academic work

5. LD occurs across the lifespan

6. LD does not emerge from other conditions

Nevertheless, the fact remains that LD has not been quantified with much exactitude, leaving Kavale and Forness (2000) to conclude that an operational definition of LD still remains as elusive as ever, despite the neuropsychological literature providing a much more sophisticated and substantiated view of the cognitive processes involved in learning.

Lastly, there remains a seductive appeal in the educational arena to erroneously view a learning disability under the "disease model" of interpretation, meaning that a student either has "it", or does not have "it". As Goldberg (2001) noted, human cognition is a multidimensional phenomena distributed throughout the cortex in a continuous and graduated fashion, not in a linear and modular one. Hence, there are degrees of differences in learning and cognition that must be explored through a multidimensional survey of brain functions, as opposed to lumping all cognitive capacities into a meaningless numeric valued known as IQ. As Hale and Fiorello (2004) stated, ever since Binet created the first intelligence test, psychologists have never truly measured this intangible construct but instead have parceled out a confusing blend of cognition and information processing, coupled with achievement. Perhaps this is why 50% of students actually classified as having a learning disability do not demonstrate a significant discrepancy between aptitude and achievement (Kavale & Forness, 2004). Therefore, creating artificial cut-points through ability-achievement discrepancy models as the sole basis for identifying a learning disorder not only denies students (most notably, students with lower IQ's) from receiving services, but also continues to propagate an educational myth that views learning disabilities along a one-dimensional continuum between students with the disorder, and those without. At best, school systems that over-rely on aptitude-achievement discrepancy models to identify learning disorders are merely identifying school underachievement. Consider the current definition of dyslexia by the International Dyslexia Association (2003):

> *"Dyslexia is a specific learning disability that is neurological in origin. It is characterized by difficulties with accurate and/or fluent word recognition and by poor spelling and decoding abilities. These difficulties typically result from a deficit in the phonological component of language that is often unexpected in relation to other cognitive abilities and the provision of effective classroom instruction. Secondary, consequences may include problems in reading comprehension and reduced reading experience that can impede growth of vocabulary and background knowledge."*

Upon closer inspection, this definition has several noteworthy phrases, beginning with the notion that dyslexia is merely a subset of a learning disorder, and not a separate entity in and of itself. Second, the term dyslexia simply refers to a reading disorder that is presumed to have a neurological origin. Third, dyslexia involves multiple aspects of the reading process including phonological awareness and/or reading fluency and/or passage comprehension skills. Lastly, there is no indication of a minimum intelligence score needed to be identified with dyslexia, or a quantitative definitional boundary between aptitude and achievement. In fact, full scale intelligence test quotients are not even mentioned. Why? Simply because most research suggests that measures of intelligence account for little more than a meager 10% to 35% of the variance on measures of reading achievement (Vellutino, Scanlon, & Lyon, 2000). In fact, Shaywitz (2004) argues that measures of intelligence have virtually no relationship with the acquisition of phonological awareness skills.

As Carl Sagan noted (1997), "Science invites us to let the facts in, even when they don't conform to our preconceptions." Therefore, the marriage between education and neuropsychology will no doubt end in divorce unless educational leaders alter their preconceptions of what truly constitutes a reading disorder. The time has come for the educational community to shed any binary distinctions between reading and non-reading disabled students, as well as discard any notion about arbitrary cut-points between ability and achievement as the basis for a reading disorder. Instead, educators need to acknowledge that reading occurs along a continuum, with various brain regions contributing to the multidimensional process of executing such a complex linguistic skill. Therefore, nonspecific terms such as a "learning disability" are not terribly helpful in linking the assessment process to a particular intervention. It is incumbent upon each evaluator to go beyond simplistic classification schemes that hide behind IQ scores, and truly pinpoint the specific subtype of reading disorder a student may manifest, in order to create a blueprint for educational success. Good assessments should link specific test results with specific interventions. In the case of reading, this process begins with an understanding of the specific reading subtypes that can derail successful learning. These subtypes begin to emerge by an examination of reading through the multidimensional lenses of a brain-based learning perspective, where various circuits and neural networks modulate this all important skill. As will be discussed, the neural circuits underlying reading are extremely susceptible to environmental influences, meaning the quality and frequency of an educational intervention can assist the brain in re-wiring itself to allow the reading process to unfold in an unfettered fashion. However, the key to any intervention is to strike early and often, use a *balanced literacy model* as an ultimate goal, and to effectively utilize the combination of curriculum-based measurement techniques with cognitive neuropsychology to create optimum learning instruction for each student. Figure 5-1 illustrates the three-headed monster of reading, which educators need to tame in order for successful learning to take place. Next, a discussion of three major subtypes of reading disorders.

KEY LEARNING POINT	The time has come for the educational community to shed any binary distinctions between reading and non-reading disabled students, as well as discard any notion about arbitrary cut-points between ability and achievement as the basis for a reading disorder. Instead, educators need to acknowledge that reading occurs along a continuum, with various brain regions contributing to the multidimensional process of executing such a complex linguistic skill.

Figure 5-1

3-Headed Monster of Reading

SUBTYPE #1: DYSPHONETIC DYSLEXIA

The hallmark feature of dysphonetic dyslexia is an inability to utilize a phonological route to successfully bridge letters and sounds. Instead, there tends to be an over-reliance on visual and orthographic cues to identify words in print. Since there is little reliance on letter to sound conversions, these readers tend to frequently guess on words based upon the initial letter observed. For instance, the word "cat" may be read as "couch" or perhaps "corn". These students tend merely to look at the initial letter "c", search their lexicon for stored sight-words beginning with "c", and then randomly guess. Hence, students with dysphonetic dyslexia have tremendous difficulty incorporating strategies to allow them to crash through words in a sound-based manner, tend to be relatively inaccurate, and often approach reading by simply memorizing whole words. There is usually a steep price to pay for attempting to learn some 50,000 to 60,000 words over the course of an academic career through sheer memorization. For instance, these students often have difficulty reading words in different fonts, as well as in different contexts, as words tend to be memorized only in the font and context in which they were initially observed.

According to Noble and McCandliss (2005), poor phonological processing in the early years leads to inefficient neural mappings between letters and sounds. As noted by the National Reading Panel (2000), phonemic awareness and phonological processing are two of the five pillars for successful reading. Failure to develop these critical skills in the reading process may lead to a host of academic deficiencies including poor spelling skills, slower paced reading fluency skills, and ultimately difficulty with passage comprehension skills. In order to fully derive meaning from print, the process of reading needs to be as effortless and automatic as possible, thereby freeing up cognitive *counter-space* to assist with comprehension as opposed to word decoding skills. Moats (2004) examined the precursors to instant word recognition skills, and determined the building blocks for reading begin with speech-sound identification skills, letter recognition skills, alphabet recognition skills, and finally sound-symbol association skills.

Phonemic Awareness - As previously mentioned, the roots of literacy begin long before a child enters formal schooling. Phonemic awareness involves the abilities to hear and discriminate between sounds. Tallal, Miller, and Fitch (1993) attributed phonological awareness deficits to difficulty detecting rapidly changing acoustic elements of speech. Thus, subtle auditory perceptual deficits, such as differentiating between a "ba" sound and a "da" sound may be the underlying deficit in phonological dyslexia. Clearly, there are children with seasonal allergies or frequent occurrences of ear infections who may be prone to auditory perceptual deficits due to fluid in the middle ear hindering sound discrimination skills. However, it is important to note that phonemic awareness deficits are not due to a conductive hearing loss per se, but rather due to the auditory sensitivity of the temporal lobes, particularly in Heschl's gyrus and Wernicke's area. In fact, the very notion that auditory discrimination deficits ultimately lead to deficits in phonology remains one of the basic premises behind the *Fast Forward* technique, a reading intervention described in the final chapter.

Still, auditory discrimination alone is not sufficient for the development of phonological processing skills. According to Uhry and Clark (2005), phonemic awareness involves a multitude of auditory discrimination skills, as the beginning reader must learn to not only isolate sounds but also develop a spatial awareness of the temporal ordering of sounds in words. For instance, phonemic awareness involves being able to produce the final sound in "map," isolate the middle sound in "tap," or understand that by substituting a "m" sound for the "t" sound in the word "stock," a new word has been created ("smock"). Therefore, phonemic awareness involves the understanding of the sequential arrangement of sounds in words. As Uhry and Clark (2005) noted, phonemic awareness in verbal speech is rather straightforward, as most words break apart fairly naturally by syllables. However, individual phonemes within each syllable can be somewhat elusive to separate in the verbal speech stream. In fact, many consonants either close off the airflow rather quickly (d) or distort the vowel sounds preceding them (e.g., "r" in the word "car"), thereby causing confusion on the part of young readers (Uhry & Clark, 2005). Consequently, Moats (2004) advocates having the classroom teacher actually model the appropriate mouth positions of sounds and to provide corrective feedback as a means to utilize oral-motor formation as a learning cue. The *Lindamood-Bell* program, discussed in the final chapter, is based on this precept. In summary, the process of learning to read by differentiating acoustical properties in the spoken word, as well as being able to manipulate the ordering of sounds within words, lies at the heart of phonemic awareness. By definition, dysphonetic dyslexia constitutes a deficit with learning to read in a bottom-up fashion, as the sounds of language are inefficiently mapped to the printed word form.

Anatomical Correlates of Phonological Processing - According to Sandak et al. (2004), the chief brain architecture involved in mapping this neural network of sounds is called the dorsal stream. There are three main components of the dorsal stream, including the *angular gyrus* and the *supramarginal gyrus* of the left hemisphere, as well as the *inferior frontal gyrus* around Broca's area. These regions are primarily responsible for mapping visual percepts of print onto the phonological structures of language. It should be noted that the dorsal stream tends to respond to linguistic stimuli on a relatively slower time scale. In other words, learning to read in a bottom-up fashion by decoding each individual phoneme is rather time intensive. Figure 5-2 illustrates the flow of information along the dorsal stream.

Figure 5-2

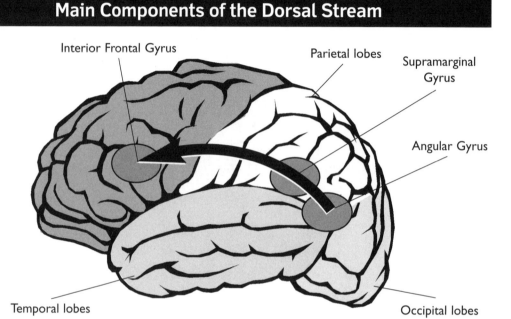

Main Components of the Dorsal Stream

Interior Frontal Gyrus

Parietal lobes

Supramarginal Gyrus

Angular Gyrus

Temporal lobes

Occipital lobes

Upon closer inspection of the dorsal stream, it becomes relatively apparent there is a separate brain region to tackle the rigors of phonemic awareness, and another brain region to handle the more complex chore of phonological processing. In particular, the top portion of the left temporal lobes, particularly in the areas around Heschl's gyrus, are responsible for basic sound discrimination skills as well as processing pitch changes in the auditory cortex (Ritter, Gunter, Specht, & Rupp, 2005). In a recent study by Golestani, Molko, Dehaene, Lebihan, and Pallier (2006), the actual anatomy of the white matter in the left auditory cortex was indeed associated with auditory processing efficiency, and partly predicted differences in rapid temporal processing among students. With respect to reading, the *superior temporal gyrus*, located on the uppermost crest of the temporal lobes, is critical for deciphering the 44 phonemes which comprise the English language.

Conversely, phonological processing refers to mapping out sounds to letters, and thus requires more cross modal associations between visual and verbal precepts. The *supramarginal gyrus*, located at the juncture of the temporal and parietal lobes, appears to be the key brain region responsible for phonological processing (McCandliss & Noble, 2003; Shaywitz, 2004; Sandak et al., 2004). According to Goldberg (1989), the left temporal lobe involves categorical representation of auditory stimulus patterns. This is critical for deciphering sound patterns that constitute words and language, as well as for the categorical perception of non-language sounds, such as a barking dog or a backfiring car. In many ways the concept of categorical processing of auditory perception can be viewed as a cultural precursor of language. The neuroanatomical location of the supramarginal gyrus lies at the intersection of the temporal and parietal lobes, and is anterior (in front) to the angular gyrus. Therefore, the supramarginal gyrus integrates the categorical representations of sounds (temporal lobe) with the spatial appreciation underlying sounds and symbols (inferior parietal lobe), thereby contributing to the temporal ordering of acoustical information.

KEY LEARNING POINT	The *superior temporal gyrus*, located on the uppermost crest of the temporal lobes, is critical for deciphering the 44 phonemes which comprise the English language. However, phonological processing refers to mapping out sounds to letters, and thus requires more cross modal associations between visual and verbal precepts. The *supramarginal gyrus*, located at the juncture of the temporal and parietal lobes, appears to be the key brain region responsible for phonological processing.

Lastly, the left *angular gyrus*, situated just behind the supramarginal gyrus, also represents a cross modal association area in the posterior portion of the brain. The angular gyrus lies in the posterior parietal lobe, near the superior edge of the temporal lobe and the extrastriatal cortex of the occipital lobes. This unique brain region is involved in a number of processes related to language and cognition due in part to receiving input from three cortices (parietal, temporal, and occipital lobes). Pugh et al. (2000) summarized converging evidence from the neuroscientific community suggesting that the left angular gyrus was pivotal for mapping a visual symbol in an acoustic manner. In the case of reading, this can be translated into looking at a letter or combination of letters, and assigning this visual precept a specific phonemic code. These researchers (Pugh et al., 2000) noted a disconnection between the angular gyrus and other regions of the dorsal stream when phonological assembly of a word was required for dyslexic readers. In fact, dyslexics tended to use compensatory mechanisms, particularly in the posterior regions of the right hemisphere, to assist with phonological processing. In summary, these findings support the overall conclusion that neurobiological anomalies in the phonological processing regions of the left hemisphere lead to the core deficits manifested in dysphonetic dyslexia. Table 5-2 summarizes the key brain regions contributing to this condition.

Table 5-2

Key Brain Regions in Dysphonetic Dyslexia

Heschl's Gyrus - auditory perception and discrimination.

Superior Temporal Gyrus - modulating the 44 phonemes of the English language.

Supramarginal Gyrus - cross modal association area underlying the spatial appreciation and positioning of sounds.

Angular Gyrus - cross modal association area underlying mapping symbols to sounds.

Inferior Frontal Gyrus - end point for inner articulation region.

Dorsal Stream - all of the aforementioned structures involved in the ability to phonologically assemble a word. A relatively slower paced learning network.

Interventions - The National Reading Panel (2000) found overwhelming evidence in the research literature that supports using an explicit phonics program as the primary remediation strategy for dysphonetic dyslexia at earlier ages. In other words, a bottom-up approach to reading should be emphasized when the primary deficit is dysphonetic dyslexia. For instance, Torgeson et al. (1999) conducted a study of severely at-risk kindergarten children who lacked appropriate reading readiness skills. The study compared three types of intensive interventions, all of which constituted a Tier III status in a Response-to-Intervention model. The first intervention was more of a whole language approach to reading, the second was an embedded phonics training where phonemic awareness was also learned in an implicit fashion, and the last was the *Lindamood Auditory Discrimination in Depth* program. The *Lindamood* program is predominantly a *bottom-up* approach to reading using sensory information to assist the development of more distinct phoneme representations (see Chapter Nine), whereas the other two programs were more top-down reading strategies. After intensive one-on-one interventions were administered to all students, 20 minutes per day, 4 days a week through 2nd grade, the bottom-up, explicit phonics program (*Lindamood*) was significantly superior to the others. Torgeson et al. (1999) concluded that younger learners, who have not developed the executive functioning capacities or abstract thinking abilities to sufficiently organize incoming information, respond best to a highly structured and explicit type of phonological training. The more *implicit* phonological approaches at this age were somewhat ineffective, despite the intensiveness of the training.

Similarly, Tunmer and Chapman (2003) examined the *Reading Recovery* program, which is also a Tier III type of reading intervention for 1st graders consisting of one-on-one instruction, 30 minutes per day, five days a week for 20 weeks. As Alexander and Slinger-Constant (2004) observed, *Reading Recovery* is more of a top-down program, emphasizing whole-word learning using semantic or syntactic clues for word reading. *Reading Recovery* does not contain the explicit phonological type of training found in more *Orton-Gillingham* or *Lindamood* types of remediation programs. The results suggested that 30% of students did not respond to *Reading Recovery*, indicating that intensive treatment alone is not sufficient for remediation dyslexia (Turner & Chapman, 2003). Instead, treatment must be used in conjunction with a specific type of reading intervention program which best meets the needs of the learner.

Pokorni, Worthington, and Jamison (2004) evaluated the effectiveness of *Earobics, Fast ForWord*, and the *Lindamood Phomeme Sequencing Program*. Each of these reading programs is described in further detail in the final chapter. After approximately 60 hours of training delivered in a small group setting, there were minimal gains observed in reading using each of these techniques. However, children exposed to the *Lindamood Phoneme Sequencing* program were significantly better at improving phonological awareness with noted gains in segmenting and blending, and the *Earobics* group also showed significant gains in phonemic segmentation. No significant gains were found in the *Fast ForWord* group. The researchers concluded that gains in auditory, phonological, and language processing can be immediately noted with some of these programs, though the most dramatic gains are often in programs that use systemic phonological awareness training. Once again, the specific type of reading intervention program, and not necessarily the intensity of the program, is paramount for developing reading success.

Lastly, Shaywitz and Shaywitz (2005) recruited a group of 2nd and 3rd grade children, all of whom had reading impairments, to receive two specific types of reading interventions. The community intervention group received a variety of school based interventions for 50 minutes per day for 8 months. The experimental intervention group received solely an explicit phonics program, very systematic in nature, and based primarily upon the alphabetic principle. Lastly, there was a control group consisting of non-impaired readers. All of the groups were scanned using fMRI technology on three occasions: pre-intervention, immediately post-intervention, and one year later. The results clearly indicated that children in the experimental group (explicit phonics instruction) made significantly greater gains in reading accuracy, reading fluency, and reading comprehension than did children in the community intervention group.

KEY LEARNING POINT	Torgeson et al. (1999) concluded that younger learners, who have not developed the executive functioning capacities or abstract thinking abilities to sufficiently organize incoming information, respond best to a highly structured and explicit type of phonological training. The more *implicit* phonological approaches at this age were somewhat ineffective, despite the intensiveness of the training.

Interestingly, these children also showed increases in activation in the temporal-parietal regions of the left hemisphere for at least one year after the end of the intervention. This study is one of the first to illustrate how brain chemistry and brain activation patterns can indeed be changed through educational remediation. Hence, the use of evidence based interventions involving explicit teaching of phonology can facilitate the development of specific neural systems that underlie reading (Shaywitz & Shaywitz, 2005).

However, there still remains the question as to why older children do not respond nearly as well to explicit, phonologically based instruction as younger children. Moats (2004) reported that students with reading disabilities require about 30 minutes per day in 1st grade, yet 3rd grade children require up to 2 hours per day to learn the alphabetic principle. The National Reading Panel (2000) also reported that students in 2nd through 6th grade were *less* responsive to explicit phonics instruction, and did not improve as significantly as younger children. Furthermore, more intensive remediation was required for older elementary aged children to demonstrate improved phonological processing and passage comprehension skills; nevertheless, spelling and fluency skills showed little improvement. Similarly, Torgeson et al. (2003) also examined the effectiveness of the *Lindamood Phoneme Sequencing Program* with 9 to 11 year olds. These older elementary aged children clearly showed improved accuracy and phonological processing skills, though little gains were noted in actual word reading fluency skills.

Perhaps the fundamental reason that older children are less responsive to explicit phonics instruction than younger children lies in what Ratey (2001) refers to as the *Neural Darwinism* of the brain. In other words, the old corollary "Use it or lose it" is very apropos when referring to the need for certain critical pathways to be explicitly stimulated, in this case with direct phonological instruction, for adequate reading to commence. Ratey (2001) used another adage, "neurons which fire together wire together" to explain that neural connections begin very early, and tend to stay intact and strengthen with continued and repeated exposure to a particular sensory stimulus. In fact, neurons tend to compete with other neurons for survival, and in the absence of proper stimulation, brain cells that do not form enduring cortical connections tend to die. According to Ratey (2001), the exact web of connections among neurons depends on a combination of genetic make-up, the environment, and the sum of experiences the brain has been exposed to. As noted by Kotulak (1996), as many as 500 trillion synapses may be present in the human brain, though this figure may go up or down by as much as 25 percent depending on environmental stimulation. Interestingly, Kotulak (1996) also reported autopsy studies revealing that brains of university graduate students had up to 40 percent more cortical connections than brains of high-school dropouts. Therefore, early environmental experience is critical in the development of literacy in children, so neural connections can be given the opportunity to form permanent synaptic connections. Consequently, students who are not offered explicit phonological instruction at early stages in the neural formation of literacy skills may have greater difficulty acquiring these skills at later ages due to inefficient pre-established neural connections. Therefore, phonological instruction at the later grades has the daunting task not only of forging new neural connections, but also disassembling previous ones. In order to facilitate this process, top-down types of phonological assembly approaches may be more beneficial than bottom-up methodologies, especially as executive functioning skills and abilities show continued maturation. Table 5-3 depicts specific interventions for dysphonetic dyslexia that have been hierarchically arranged from an emphasis on more bottom-up strategies in the early years, to more top-down or balanced literacy strategies for older students. Most programs are further described in Chapter Nine.

KEY LEARNING POINT	Students who are not offered explicit phonological instruction at early stages in the neural formation of literacy skills may have greater difficulty acquiring these skills at later ages due to inefficient pre-established neural connections. Therefore, phonological instruction at the later grades has the daunting task not only of forging new neural connections, but also disassembling previous ones.

Table 5-3

Remediation Strategies for Dysphonetic Dyslexia

TOP-DOWN

Over Age 12:
Wilson Reading System
SRA Corrective Reading
Read 180

Ages 7 - 12:
Alphabetic Phonics (Orton-Gillingham)
Recipe for Reading
SRA Corrective Reading
Earobics II
SIPPS
LIPS
LEXIA
Horizons
Read Well
DISTAR Reading Mastery

Under Age 7:
Fast Forword (Tallal)
Earobics I
Phono-Graphix
Lindamood Phoneme Sequencing Program (LIPS)
Success for All
Ladders to Literacy
Fundations
Road to the Code

BOTTOM-UP

SUBTYPE #2: SURFACE DYSLEXIA

Surface dyslexia, which is sometimes referred to as *visual word-form dyslexia* or *dyseidetic dyslexia*, is the exact opposite of dysphonetic dyslexia, as these students are readily able to sound out words but lack the ability to automatically and effortlessly recognize words in print. These readers tend to be letter-by-letter and sound-by sound readers, as there is an over-reliance on the phonological properties of the word, and an under-appreciation of the spatial properties of the visual word form. Most words are painstakingly broken down to individual phonemes and read very slowly and laboriously. Consequently, fluency, not necessarily phonological processing skills, tends to suffer the most with surface dyslexics. However, word accuracy may also be compromised especially when reading phonologically irregular words that lack a one-on-one correspondence between sounds and symbols. An error analysis of surface dyslexia might reveal the following:

Word	Read as:
island	izland
grind	grinned
listen	liston
begin	beggin
lace	lake

The Magnocellular Hypothesis and Reversals - Since phonologically irregular words by their vary nature do not follow a one-to-one correspondence between sounds and symbols, there must also be a more visually-based system to complement the phonological route in deciphering meaning from print. According to Stein (2000), the *magnocellular system* lies at the heart of processing the orthography of print in a rapid and automatic fashion. Since the initial stages of the reading process involve recognizing visual symbols, a brief explanation of the brain's two unique visual pathways will ensue. The visual system can be divided into two main types of cells. Approximately 90% are smaller types of cells called *parvo cells*, which basically respond to color and fine detail (Stein, 2000). However, the remaining 10% are magno (large) cells, as their dendrites cover a retinal area up to 500 times that of parvo cells. These cells are not only larger, but also are more heavily myelinated, meaning that these nerve signals have great conduction velocities, and can respond much faster than parvo cells. Hence, the magno cells tend to respond very quickly to visual motion, and the slower parvo cells respond more to color and detail. Both types of cells carry visual information from the retina, travel to the lateral geniculate nucleus of the thalamus, and finally relay the information to various visual cortices housed in the occipital lobes. The occipital lobes lie in the most posterior portion of the brain, so once the visual information is processed, it splits in two as the information is relayed back toward the anterior (front) portions of the cerebral cortex. The first pathway is known as the "what" pathway or *ventral stream*, and uses roughly equal portions of parvo cells and magno cells to assist in identifying what an object is (Stein, 2000). The ventral stream pathway essentially functions as the seat for visual-verbal learning. Often, students who are engaged in rapid and automatic naming tasks are basically activating the ventral stream or "what" pathway.

In contrast, the second pathway which visual information may take is called the "where" pathway or dorsal stream. This pathway travels upward from the occipital cortices and connects with the posterior portions of the parietal lobe. The "where" pathway is much quicker than the "what" pathway, and is vital for detecting the current position and motion of targets, and assists in the visual guidance of eye movements. It should be noted that this pathway is dominated by input from primarily magno cells, and not parvo cells. It is this pathway that is primarily responsible for visual tracking of letters and words while reading. Livingston et al. (1991) noted that dyslexics have up to 27 percent fewer neurons in the magno cellular layers of the dorsal stream or "where" pathway, thereby resulting in much slower visual processing. Therefore, the magnocelluar deficit hypothesis provides an anatomical explanation for slower reading speed and fluency. According to Stein (2000), about 75% of children and adults with dyslexia have poor motion sensitivity.

KEY LEARNING POINT	The magno cells tend to respond very quickly to visual motion, and the slower parvo cells respond more to color and detail. Livingston et al. (1991) noted that dyslexics have up to 27 percent fewer neurons in the magno cellular layers of the dorsal stream or "where" pathway, thereby resulting in much slower visual processing. Perhaps this explains why reading fluency and speed may be compromised in surface dyslexia.

There have been numerous studies which have linked the magnocellular pathway deficits to speed of visual processing (Demb, Boynton, & Heeger 1998). Furthermore, these magno cells also enervate the cerebellum, which is an ancient brain structure primarily responsible for fine tuning many skills, including motor skill functioning. Hence, the magno cellular system may also play a role in the relative motor clumsiness and awkward fine motor skills often seen in dyslexics (Stein, 2000). Lastly, the magnocellular system may also be related to the most common type of symptom seen in dyslexia; namely, reversals. Just what are the neural mechanisms seen in reversals?

Table 5-4

The Neurobiology of Letter Reversals

According to Stein (2000), most dyslexic children complain that letters seem to jump around when reading. During the reading process, the eyes remain fixated on an individual word for just 300msec before very subtle but rapid eye movements called saccades shift the eyes toward the next visual stimulus. Even during these brief fixations, the eye moves approximately 1 degree, or the equivalent of 4 or 5 letters. The magnocellular system allows children to stabilize this movement, but many dyslexics cannot, therefore transposing letters when reading. This unintended eye movement varies in each eye, thus resulting in a high level of binocular instability. Since this instability causes the line of sight for each eye to cross into an unintended visual field, the letters seem to change places.

It should be noted that the magnocellular hypothesis has not been fully endorsed by the neuroscientific community as a root cause for dyslexia, and remains a somewhat controversial topic. As Stein (2000) noted, many of the studies exploring the relationship between mango cells and reading disorders have involved small numbers of subjects, did not screen the subjects for specific types of reading difficulties, and tended to show only mild differences in vision contrast sensitivity. Furthermore, the findings from these studies have been difficult to replicate, and it has yet to be determined if the magnocellular deficits seen in children are the result and not the cause of dyslexia. For instance, perhaps these children were less skilled in taking in information in rapid eye successions because their reading difficulty precluded them from actively practicing this type of visual task. Consequently, over time there may be a gradual reduction in the number of visual cells assigned to saccadic eye movement simply because of a sheer lack of practice. As previously noted, visual neurons are particularly sensitive to environmental stimulation, and tend to adapt according to how they are stimulated.

Lastly, when a particular theory, especially a one dimensional causal type of theory such as the magnocellular hypothesis, claims as being the root cause for a particular disorder, then interventions tend to be skewed in a rather faulty direction. The educational community has probably seen enough of specialized visual training to cure reading problems. This includes treatments such as using rose colored paper or *dyslexic glasses*, both of which were intended to stimulate reading by altering contrast sensitivity between the print and paper. Furthermore, the days of visual perceptual training have long passed by as an appropriate intervention for dyslexia. However, Stein (2000) reported that binocular instability can be diminished by covering the left eye for reading, thus relieving any kind of perceptual confusion. After 3 months of occlusion, not only had some children's reading significantly improved, but some children could also fixate stably with their two eyes, and thus no longer needed to wear a patch (Stein, 2000).

Rapid Naming and Fluency - Surface dyslexia is basically a lack of reading fluency skills caused in part by difficulty rapidly and automatically recognizing the orthography of print. In other words, slower reading speed may be due to difficulty processing visual information in a rapid fashion. However, slower reading speed may also be due to difficulties in recognizing the linguistic value of the word itself, irrespective of the child's visual processing skills. Previous chapters have discussed two specific brain regions responsible for codifying visual information into a readily accessible linguistic format. First, the temporal-parietal circuit is vital for developing phonemic awareness and phonological processing skills. Second, the occipital-temporal regions of the brain constitute the essence of what Shaywitz (2004) referred to as the *visual word form area*. The visual word form area is primarily responsible for the rapid and automatic recognition of words, and to a certain extent, is very much dependent on the work of the temporal-parietal region. In other words, effective phonological mapping of sounds greatly enables the visual word form area to perform its job. Hence, there appears to be a certain symbiosis between phonological awareness and the automatic naming tasks. According to Schatschneider and Torgeson (2004), there are three ways in which phonemic awareness skills supports the growth of accurate word reading skills:

Table 5-5

3 Ways Phonemic Awareness Skills Support, Word Reading Skills

1. *It helps children understand the alphabetic principle.* Without some ability to identify sounds in words, it is difficult to see further relationships between letters in print and individual phonemes in spoken words.

2. *It facilitates the generation of possible words in context that are only partially sounded out.* For instance, if a child knows the sound that is represented by the first two letters in the word (e.g., "ch") they are more likely able to guess the correct word.

3. *It helps children notice the regular ways in which letters represent sounds in words.* If children can hear three sounds in the word "cat", it helps them notice the way letters correspond to sounds. This reinforces certain spelling patterns and serves as a mnemonic device so the child can automatically recognize words simply by glancing at them.

According to Sandak et al. (2004), there are many factors that contribute to the ability to rapidly and automatically recognize words in print, including the semantic properties of the word itself. In a series of cleverly designed experiments to assess the most efficient ways students learn words, students who used both phonological strategies and semantic strategies performed best. This was especially true for words that were highly imaginable such as nouns. Therefore, effective learning of new words essentially relies on both bottom-up strategies (phonological analysis) and top-down strategies (semantic analysis). The combination of these two strategies sets the foundation for *balanced literacy*, and will be discussed further in Chapter Nine.

Wolf and Bowers (1999) have shown that rapid automatic naming tasks are consistently predictive of word-level reading difficulties as well as passage comprehension. These researchers have highlighted the importance of early rapid naming skills with the subsequent development of reading fluency. Rapid naming involves the ability to look at a visual stimulus and assign a verbal tag to that stimulus. It is important to note that effective rapid naming requires numerous cognitive operations including attention skills, executive functioning skills, accurate retrieval skills, and processing speed (Wolf & Bowers, 1999). Most learning disabled students have difficulty with automatic and rapid naming tasks, as the ability to rapidly recall archived information such as letters, numbers, or words tends to be compromised. It is interesting to note that naming speed, and not phonological awareness skills, tends to be a better predictor of reading difficulty in languages which are more phonologically consistent such as German, Dutch, Finnish, and Spanish (Wolf, 1999).

Lastly, recent studies conducted by Mirsa, Katzir, Wolf, and Poldrack (2004) have suggested that not all rapid naming tasks were created equal. For instance, rapid letter naming tasks were more predictive of word level reading skills than tasks involving the rapid and automatic naming of familiar objects. Mirsa et al. (2004) noted that letter naming tasks resulted in greater activation of the angular gyrus, medial extrastriate regions, and other areas associated with phonological processing. Conversely, rapidly naming objects activated only the ventral stream, which connects the visual centers of the occipital lobe with the verbal centers of the temporal lobe, and not the phonological processing areas. Therefore, school psychologists who generally use tests of rapid naming such as the *Comprehensive Test of Phonological Processing (CTOPP)* or the *Process Assessment of the Learner (PAL)* should differentiate between the ability to rapidly name letters and phonemes versus rapidly naming objects. The prudent examiner may want to explore the DIBELS as a more viable measure of rapid naming skills pertaining to reading.

<table>
<tr><td>

**KEY
LEARNING
POINT**

</td><td>

Poor reading fluency may be due to difficulty processing visual information in a rapid fashion (Magnocellular Hypothesis). However, slower reading speed may also be due to difficulties in recognizing the linguistic value of the word itself, irrespective of the child's visual processing skills. Most learning disabled students have difficulty rapidly recalling archived information such as letters, numbers, or words. Tests that measure the rapid naming of letters and phonemes (i.e. DIBELS) tend to be better predictors of reading fluency than rapid naming of familiar objects.

</td></tr>
</table>

A crucial point when deciding upon an effective intervention strategy is that repetitive practicing of phonological processing skills does not necessarily result in better reading fluency skills for older students. Sandak et al. (2004) suggested that a closer inspection of the subcomponents of the ventral stream may help explain why. Within the ventral system, there are various sub-regions dedicated to processing certain elements of the printed word form. These regions tend to operate in a back to front fashion. The posterior, or very back portion of the ventral stream, is located in the extrastriate cortex of the occipital lobes (see Figure 5-3). This area is dedicated to processing individual letters. One of the first reading readiness goals in most kindergarten curriculums is for students to master all 26 upper case and all 26 lower case letters. Furthermore, Shaywitz (2004) indicated that mastery of alphabet letter naming is a better predictor of future reading abilities at this age than actual word reading skills. Therefore, the more posterior portions of the ventral stream, primarily in the extrastriatal cortex, are vital for developing automaticity with respect to letter naming.

Figure 5-3

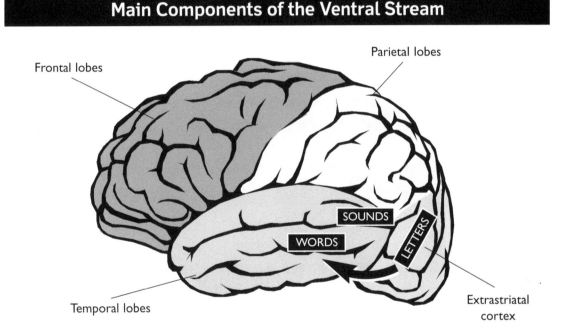

Main Components of the Ventral Stream

The temporal lobe region, which is more of a cross modal association area adept at processing letter sound combinations and pseudowords, can be found forward in the ventral stream. Similarly, Shaywitz (2004) noted that by 1st grade, knowledge of letter sounds, not letter names, becomes the best predictor of reading abilities. Finally, the front portions of the system located near the medial temporal lobes are dedicated more toward responding to actual printed words, as opposed to just random strings of letters (Sandak et al., 2004). This portion of the ventral stream may be where the breakdown or disconnection in surface dyslexia seems to be, as words are not automatically recognized but individual sounds are identified. Therefore, there is a logical progression within the ventral stream from back to front as certain brain regions are dedicated to recognizing letters, other brain regions for letter-sound combinations, and, lastly, an area of the brain specializing in whole word recognition. The following interventions for surface dyslexia are geared toward establishing the integrity of brain regions responsible for whole-word recognition skills, and consequently involve more top-down types of strategies. According to Sandak et al. (2004), the posterior or back regions of the brain are arranged toward phonological processing (bottom-up) strategies, but the more anterior aspects of the temporal lobes and frontal regions of the brain tend to process information in a more whole word (top-down) type of fashion. Table 5-5 depicts specific interventions for surface dyslexia that focus primarily on enhancing automatic and rapid whole-word recognition skills. Most of these programs are further described in Chapter Nine.

KEY LEARNING POINT	The posterior or back regions of the brain are arranged toward phonological processing (bottom-up) strategies, but the more anterior aspects of the temporal lobes and frontal regions of the brain tend to process information in a more whole word (top-down) type of fashion. The anterior portion (front) of the ventral stream may be where the breakdown or disconnection in surface dyslexia seems to be, as words are not automatically recognized, but individual sounds are identified.

Table 5-6

Remediation Strategies for Surface Dyslexia

Over Age 7:   Analytic or Embedded Phonics Approach ("top down" methodology)
Reading Recovery
Early Steps

Ages 7 - 12:   Great Leaps program
Read Naturally
Quick Read
RAV-O

Under Age 12:   Neurological Impress method
Wilson Reading System
Laubach Reading Series
Read 180

SUBTYPE #3: MIXED DYSLEXIA

With any disorder, there are varying degrees of severity, ranging from mild to moderate to severe. Mixed dyslexia generally represents the most severe type of reading disability for students as there is no usable key to unlock the functional code of literacy. Generally, these readers have difficulty across the language spectrum, and are characterized by a combination of poor phonological processing skills, slower rapid and automatic word recognition skills, inconsistent language comprehension skills, and bizarre error patterns in their reading. The term *double deficit* hypothesis often applies here, as there are numerous deficits which disrupt the natural flow of rapidly and automatically recognizing words in print. As Pugh et al. (2000) noted, more than one of the following processes depicted in Figure 5-4 tends to be disrupted:

Figure 5-4

Fundamental Processes in Reading

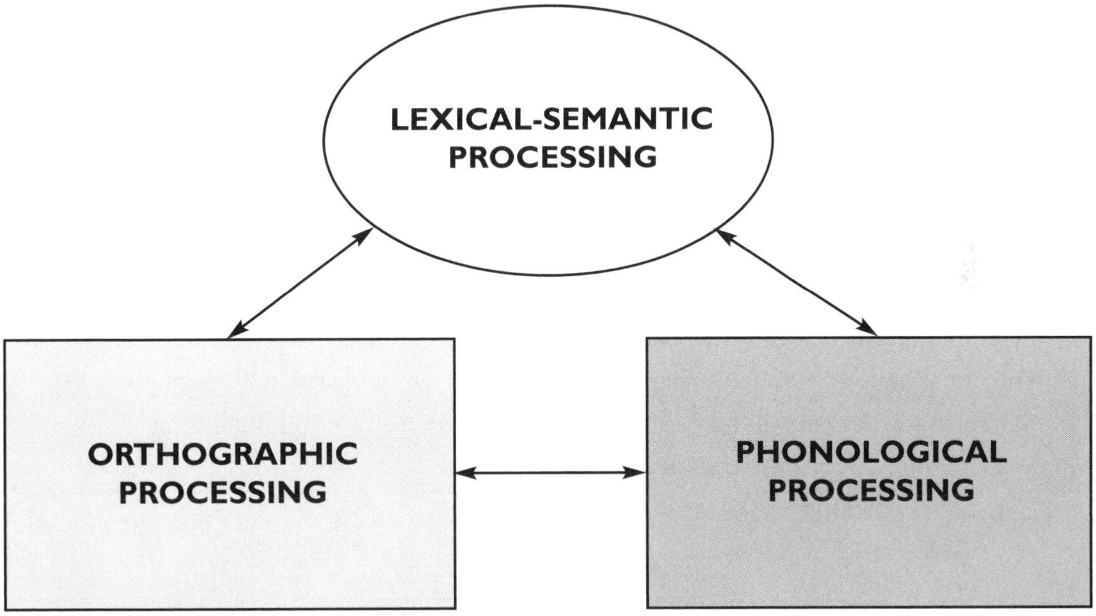

LEXICAL-SEMANTIC PROCESSING

ORTHOGRAPHIC PROCESSING

PHONOLOGICAL PROCESSING

The cerebral orchestra of reading has many key musicians that must play in perfect harmony to establish a seamless cacophony of neural processing. A disruption in any one of these critical brain regions may significantly impact the reading process. The neural symphony of oral word reading may include the following:

Table 5-7

Neural Symphony of Oral Word Reading

1. **Reticular Activating System** - basic level of arousal and orientation.
2. **Magnocells in Retina** - carry visual information of print to thalamus for processing.
3. **Lateral Geniculate Nucleus of Thalamus** - processes visual input and redirects to extrastriatal cortex in occipital lobes.
4. **Fusiform Gyrus** - occipital-temporal region of the brain that processes the visual word form automatically.
5. **Temporal-Parietal Circuit** - the central sound-symbol association area that processes unfamiliar words by phonological analysis.
6. **Arcuate Fasciculus** - main association fiber connecting anterior and posterior speech zones.
7. **Insular Cortex** - top-down modulation of phonological processing tasks as a sort of lexical checking system.
8. **Inferior Frontal Lobes** - Broca's area represents end point for inner articulation circuit and activated during oral word reading.
9. **Limbic System** - allows the reader to make some emotional connectivity with words in print.
10. **Hippocampus** - retrieval of memories stored throughout the cortex in sense of space and time.
11. **Inferior Parietal Lobes** - seat of higher level thinking and tertiary problem solving zones.
12. **Frontal Lobes** - syntactical arrangement of thoughts and ideas in a linguistic manner.
13. **Dorsolateral Prefrontal Cortex** - organization and planning of thoughts.
    - working memory to hold ideas in mind.
    - sustain attention to task at hand.
    - inhibit distracting thoughts.
    - initiate task and maintain motivational persistence.
    - self-monitor reading accuracy
14. **Orbitofrontal Cortex** - modulates emotional comprehension of material

The Shifting Hypothesis - According to Goldberg (2005), there is a very important evolutionary and universal rule evident among most cognitive tasks, whether verbal or visual-spatial in nature: namely, that information processing travels from right to left. In other words, the true distinction between the hemispheres of the brain lies in the right hemisphere's dominance for initial task acquisition, and with ever increasing skill mastery, the left hemisphere eventually takes over. This postulate holds true for virtually any learning endeavor. As Goldberg (2005) mentioned, music is an excellent example. When musically untrained individuals recognize melodies, the right hemisphere tends to be particularly active. However, in trained musicians, the left hemisphere tends to be particularly active and is the more dominant hemisphere in recognizing melodies. This type of cognitive shift further illustrates the subtle complexities involved with how the brain processes information through various stages of the learning process. Task efficiency is determined in part by the ability to automatically recognize patterns without the need for re-processing the same information in a naïve fashion. Therefore, not only are there multiple brain structures involved in the reading process as described in Table 5-6, and not only are the functional utility of some structures (e.g., visual word form area) dependent upon other structures (e.g., phonological processing zones), but the timing in which there is an information shift from the right to the left hemisphere remains critical as well.

Certainly, in mixed dyslexia there is an overwhelming concern about why reading continues to be such a difficult and effortful process, despite years of academic remediation attempts. Bakker (2006) suggested that severe forms of dyslexia may stem in part from issues surrounding this all important shift from right hemispheric modulation of reading, to left hemispheric modulation of the reading process. For instance, some children may get stuck using neural circuitry in the right hemisphere to assist with reading, and are unable to shift hemispheres. Bakker (2006) labeled these children as *P-type* dyslexics. Hence, reading is always a novel task and these readers tend to be relatively slower paced, less fluent, and somewhat fragmented in their skills. The task of reading even familiar words is always new, and tends to be somewhat cumbersome and effortful. Conversely, some students make this hemispheric switch too early, and force the left hemisphere to modulate the process of reading too prematurely. Bakker (2006) labeled these children as *L-type* dyslexics, as these readers move rapidly through the text but have no eye for the perceptual features of words, read through punctuation, lack the proper intonation when reading aloud, and tend to make numerous careless errors. Hence, more severe deficits with reading such as mixed dyslexia may stem from the timing of task acquisition, as the right hemisphere gives way to the left in order for more automatic and efficient processing.

However, it is vital to examine the brain along multiple dimensions, and not just linear ones. Certainly mixed dyslexia can stem from timing issues as information shifts from right to left, but also may derive from miscommunication from front to back. For instance, Temple (2002) referred to children with more posterior speech zones failing to communicate with more anterior speech centers as having a *disconnection syndrome*. Using diffusion tensor imaging, a relatively new technique that provides information about the microstructure of white matter, Temple (2002) reported atypical white matter distribution surrounding the temporal-parietal (phonological processing) centers of the brain. This region is primarily responsible for connecting the left hemispheric language areas to more frontal brain regions. Furthermore, the degree to which the left temporal-parietal white matter was disorganized was correlated with the severity of reading skills. Hence, mixed dyslexia may be a disconnection syndrome precluding multiple brain regions from communicating appropriately in order to identify words in print. This begs the question: what exactly is white matter, and what is its role in neural functioning?

White matter represents axons that carry nerve impulses between various cell bodies (grey matter). Generally, white matter can be understood as the parts of the brain and spinal cord responsible for information transmission, whereas grey matter is mainly responsible for information processing. In other words, white matter carries the signals generated by the grey matter. Another significant distinction between white matter and grey matter is the length of the cables. Grey matter is more densely packed within the left hemisphere, and therefore communicates through shorter connections. Perhaps this is why the left hemisphere is best at performing more automatic types of tasks. Conversely, the right hemisphere has more white matter, and, from a cellular level, is the repository of spindle cells. As Goldberg (2005) noted, spindle cells are rather prolific in the right hemisphere of human beings, are modestly represented in some apes, and virtually nonexistent in any other species on the planet. Spindle cells have a very unique ability to carry messages and relay information across great distances in the cerebral cortex, and may actually unite disparate brain regions that contribute to highly advanced attributes of the mind (Goldberg, 2005). Therefore, spindle cells may play a role in the white matter transmission of connecting speech areas across great distances in the human brain. Since spindle cells emerge postnatally to connect speech centers throughout the cortex, the integrity of these neural connections most likely depends upon highly stimulating environmental conditions (Allman, Hakeem, Erwin, Nimchinsy, & Hof, 2001).

KEY LEARNING POINT	There is evidence to suggest that mixed dyslexia may be a disconnection syndrome precluding multiple brain regions from communicating appropriately in order to identify words in print. Certainly, the timing in which there is an information shift from initially learning a task (right hemisphere) to developing mastery of the task in an automatic or over-learned fashion (left hemisphere) remains critical as well.

Herein lies the final, and perhaps most important point about developmental dyslexia, the quality and enrichment of the environment is critically important to shaping the neural mechanisms necessary for reading skills to emerge. According to Noble and McCandliss (2005), socioeconomic status (SES) is a very strong predictor of reading skills due primarily to the home literacy environment. Children without access and opportunity to books, computers, print exposure, early preschool experiences, and good linguistic role models are at risk for significant reading impairments in school. However, Noble and McCandliss (2005) caution that children from lower SES backgrounds with significant reading delays do not necessarily meet the neurobiological criteria for mixed dyslexia, but instead just seem just delayed in their reading skills. For instance, using fMRI technology, Shaywitz et al. (2003) examined children who were persistently poor readers with limited phonological awareness skills. These readers tended to come from more disadvantaged schools with lower IQ scores. Interestingly, these persistently poor readers tended to have similar brain-behavioral functioning to non-impaired readers. In other words, the left fusiform gyrus was indeed activated during more simplistic reading tasks, thus indicating functional integrity of the visual-word form association area in the brain. Conversely, children from more advantageous schools, though possessing similar deficits in phonological processing, demonstrated atypical cortical activation in the visual-word form association regions when exposed to a simple word reading task. Instead, these readers activated the right temporal and frontal regions of the brain as if to compensate for their phonological difficulties. Noble and McCandliss (2005) suggested that brain-behavioral differences may indeed exist between significantly reading impaired students from lower SES backgrounds versus higher SES backgrounds. In fact, the brain regions typically involved in reading may be quite malleable for the lower SES students, though these students may remain persistently poor readers due to lack of print exposure and practice in their environment. Conversely, students who demonstrate significant reading difficulties from a higher SES background are more apt to have atypical neural mechanisms contributing to their reading difficulties, and thus need to rely on more compensatory strategies to assist with reading skills.

KEY LEARNING POINT	Children without access and opportunity to books, computers, print exposure, early preschool experiences, and good linguistic role models are at risk for significant reading impairments in school. However, Noble and McCandliss (2005) caution that children from lower SES backgrounds with significant reading delays do not necessarily meet the neurobiological criteria for mixed dyslexia, but instead just seem delayed in their reading skills.

Interventions - Students with *mixed dyslexia* generally have the most severe forms of reading disorders found in school systems, and often need the most intensive (Tier IV) types of intervention. There are four general rules of thumb to keep in mind when working with students with significant reading deficits.

1. ***Balanced Literacy*** - The key to developing reading success with any student is to incorporate a balanced literacy approach. This is especially critical with students possessing mixed dyslexia, as there are often combinations of deficits including poor phonological processing skills, poor fluency skills, poor comprehension skills, poor verbal short-term memory skills, and poor language processing skills. Therefore, relying solely upon a phonological methodology (e.g., *Alphabetic Phonics*) may yield an unbalanced or negligible result. A balanced literacy approach using programs such as Read 180 or RAV-O that target multiple aspects of the reading process may yield the best opportunity for success.

2. ***Top Down Strategies*** - Most students with severe forms of dyslexia do not respond to conventional remediation programs due to atypical development in various regions of the brain responsible for modulating the phonological aspect of reading, and mapping these sounds to the visual word form association areas (Temple, 2002; Shaywitz et al., 2003; Noble & McCandliss, 2005). Rather than increasing the intensity and level of phonological instruction, educators should change the type of instruction from a bottom-up approach, to more of a top-down methodology. Utilizing a visual-phonics type of program (e.g., *Wilson*), or balanced literacy programs emphasizing morphological and vocabulary rules (e.g., *Read 180*) may prove more beneficial than sticking with bottom-up programs that consistently fail.

3. ***Socioeconomic Status*** - Students who come from poor environmental backgrounds are certainly "at-risk" for developing more significant reading problems. According to Noble and McCandliss (2005), socioeconomic status (SES) is a very strong predictor of reading skills due primarily to the home literacy environment. Therefore, every opportunity should be made to provide these children with more opportunities to read. Using behavior strategies such as rewarding books read per week, providing before and after school reading clubs, and working with parents to carve out 15 to 20 minutes per day of reading can be extremely beneficial. As noted by the National Reading Panel (2000), developing language skills are an essential component toward developing literacy skills.

4. ***Motivation and Confidence*** - Every effort should be made to keep the reading process as enjoyable and entertaining as possible. Today's youth are bombarded with an array of electronic activities competing for the attention of a child including GameBoys, Game Cubes, PlayStation portables, XBoxes, and iPods. It remains extremely difficult in this day and age for books to compete with that kind of entertainment value. Nevertheless, practicing reading and literacy exposure are the only way to develop skill mastery. Therefore, it is paramount to keep reading fun, and maintain a student's motivational interest. Have students practice reading materials such as *Sports Illustrated for Kids* or magazines such as *Popular Mechanics* to keep the reading process relevant and self-motivating. Also, having children read to younger students, or volunteering them to read to the building administrator may be motivational as well and help develop confidence in their skills. Lastly, reading programs such as *Great Leaps, Read Naturally,* and *Neurological Impress* tend to give immediate positive feedback to students, and can be used as a confidence builder as well.

CHAPTER 6

The Comprehension Connection

The field of school psychology is undergoing a paradigm shift. There is no longer an over-reliance on nationally norm-referenced tests, such as intelligence tests, in the assessment of learning disorders in children. Driven by new regulations contained in IDEA 2004, a greater number of practitioners are favoring a more pragmatic assessment approach, based upon how a student responds to a particular intervention, as the means of diagnosing a learning disorder. Proponents of a *Response to Intervention (RTI)* model discount the use of nationally norm-referenced tests, and favor a curriculum-based-measurement approach directly linking assessments with interventions. Such an approach forces practitioners to concentrate on targeting and monitoring interventions aimed at improving academic performance. According to Hale (2006), all schools should be using some of the major tenets espoused by RTI including research-based instruction, regular student progress monitoring, single-subject experimental designs, and empirical decision making within a problem-solving model. It stands to reason that repeated measurement of a child's performance in a particular curricular domain, which is the essence of curriculum-based measurement, should allow for greater treatment validity as test results can be applied directly to actual learning experiences (Shinn, 2002). The use of curriculum-based-measurement as a more appropriate and ecologically valid form of assessment has drawn the endorsement of the National Association of School Psychologists.

On the other hand, proponents of a cognitive assessment model attempt to pinpoint specific processing deficits, using nationally norm-referenced tests, in order to explain *why* a student may have difficulty acquiring a particular academic skill. Consider, for example, reading comprehension in children. Certainly, curriculum-based measurement approaches can be extremely beneficial in measuring reading fluency and speed by assessing the number of words a student can read accurately in one minute. However, reading is more than just the rapid and automatic recognition of print, and galvanizes the learning process by allowing students to broaden their knowledge base by extracting meaning from print. A cognitive processing model can be extremely beneficial in dissecting the critical components necessary for effective reading comprehension. These components include *executive functioning*, which involves the strategies students use to organize incoming information with previously read material; *working memory*, which is the amount of memory needed to perform a given cognitive task; and *language foundation skills*, which represent the fund of words with which a student is familiar.

Clearly, proponents of a curriculum-based measurement model would argue that fluency speed is still the best barometer for reading comprehension skills, and should be used as a critical measure of this skill. However, studies have consistently shown that the correlation between reading comprehension and word recognition is only meaningful at early grades and then rapidly declines until reaching an asymptote in middle school and high school (Francis, Fletcher, Catts, & Tomblin, 2005; Gough, Hoover, & Peterson, 1996). Most skilled practitioners and astute researchers recognize that the science side of psychology is not solely limited to a lock-and-step behavioral paradigm that examines linear cause and effect relationships such as the one between fluency and comprehension. Nevertheless, proponents of RTI would further endorse their behaviorally oriented perspective by claiming there are other curriculum-based techniques often utilized at later grades to decipher the relative understanding and mastery a student possesses from printed text. Most of these techniques simply involve counting the number of questions answered correctly after reading a passage. Therefore, arbitrary goals such as responding to *"eight of ten"* questions correctly *"75 percent of the time"* often find their way into a student's Individual Education Plan (IEP). Unfortunately, there are few specific instructional techniques offered on most IEPs, as learning objectives are ambitiously outlined, and like a rudderless ship, there is little guidance about how to reach these desired paths along the learning journey. Simply put, cognitive neuropsychology seeks to ask the fundamental question of *why?* Was the faulty comprehension due to an underlying condition hindering attention or memory, or a poor language base, or were there global cognitive pitfalls, or was the material simply taught improperly?

KEY LEARNING POINT	The correlation between reading comprehension and word recognition is only meaningful at early grades and then rapidly declines until reaching an asymptote in middle school and high school (Francis, Fletcher, Catts, & Tomblin, 2005; Gough, Hoover, & Peterson, 1996).

Reading comprehension is a remarkably complex skill derived from multiple cognitive factors, involving the interaction of approximately 30,000 human genes, of which half are expressed in the human brain. These genetic constellations form an infinite myriad of neural connections to modulate symbolic representations of print through various cognitive machinations. The underlying premise is that a deeper appreciation of the *multiple* factors that contribute to poor reading comprehension skills should put educators in a much better position to pinpoint specific interventions aimed at improving academic performance.

It has been estimated that some 10% of all school aged children have good decoding skills but possess specific difficulties with reading comprehension skills (Nation & Snowling, 1997). Certainly, students with conditions such as *hyperlexia* (the uncanny ability to decode words despite significant cognitive limitations) and *attention-deficit-hyperactivity disorder* (which often results in a lack of awareness to the content being read) are among those who suffer from significant reading comprehension difficulties. However, most students with reading comprehension deficits do not possess a co-morbid condition or any difficulties with reading fluency or decoding skills. In essence, these readers simply struggle to derive meaning from print despite good reading mechanics. Therefore, simply using curriculum-based measurement techniques as a barometer for making a predictive statement regarding comprehension skills may be rather misleading. Furthermore, erroneously believing that reading comprehension is merely an isolated reflection of word reading fluency can easily mislead educators into choosing an intervention aimed at improving phonology and word recognition skills as opposed to a direct intervention aimed at facilitating actual comprehension skills. Though most of the discourse in reading research is centered around teaching skills and strategies to foster the phonological processing of sounds in words, it is important to note that the ultimate goal of reading is to teach students how to derive meaning from print. Hence, phonological processing is merely a facilitator toward the universal learning platitude of knowledge acquisition through written text. In order to explore the phenomena of reading comprehension, a further discussion of single word comprehension at the morphological level must now ensue.

The Role of Morphology at the Text Level

Morphology refers to a given word structure, as well as the rules used to form new words including changes that affect word meaning. *Morphemes* are the basic units of morphology, and consist of the smallest units of meaning in language. A morpheme can be as small as an individual letter, such as an "s" added to a noun to create plural, or can be a complete word that can stand on its own. These types of morphemes are often referred to as *free morphemes*, whereas affixes, prefixes, and suffixes are often referred to as *bound morphemes*. There are two different kinds of bound morphemes. An *inflectional morpheme* is basically a group of suffixes used to express information without changing a word's part of speech. For instance, *waits* versus *waited* changes the tense of the word by adding an "s" or an "ed" to the root word wait, but does not alter its semantic meaning. On the other hand, *derivational morphemes* are affixes attached to a root word that actually create a new word, thus changing the word's semantic meaning as well as its part of speech. For instance, the word *attach* is a verb, though adding the suffix *"ment"* creates a new word, *"attachment"*, which is a noun. It is interesting to note that some languages, such as Hebrew, use morphological units that go in the middle of the word, rather than prefixes or suffixes.

The beginning reader is often caught in a tangled web of simultaneously having to recognize phonemes, while also searching for some underlying semantic comprehension of these sounds. Therefore, reading comprehension begins at the word level, as early readers need to understand both the relationship between letters and sounds (phonology) and the relationship between sounds and meaning (morphology). Certainly, there is a question as to whether or not there are distinct brain regions for a morphological crossover, or the ability to link sounds with meaning. In a fascinating series of experiments by Richards, et al. (2006), there is converging evidence indicating distinct brain signatures for the phonological, morphological, and orthographical properties of words. Two fMRI scans were performed on a group of children in grades 4 through 6 with dyslexia, as well as an aged-matched control group. One of the tasks scanned brain regions activated during *phoneme mapping*, and required the students to judge whether one or two-letter units stood for the same sound. The other task assessed brain activation during *morpheme mapping*, and required the students to make correct associations between word parts that signaled grammatical information, such as suffixes, and their meaning when affixed to a root word. For instance, the children were presented two words in both a visual and auditory format, such as *"corner"* and *"corn,"* and asked to determine whether the words were semantically related. Following an initial brain scan, the children with dyslexia then participated in a formal treatment program that involved 2 hours of instruction for 14 consecutive days. The treatment consisted of specific training emphasizing either phonological awareness or morphological awareness, but not both. Table 6-1 briefly outlines the methods used with both the phonological based intervention group and the morphologically based intervention group.

Table 6-1

Reading Treatments Used for Children with Dyslexia

(Richards, et al., 2006)

Phonological Treatment Group	*Description*
Word Building	Counting syllables and phonemes in pseudowords.
Word Generating	Giving examples of pseudowords containing target phonemes.
Unit Finding	Underlining spelling units and sounding out pseudowords unit by unit.
Transferring	Reading a different set of pseudowords than taught in unit finding lesson orally.
Relating Units	Deciding if letters in red in pseudowords are twins (i.e. stand for the same sound)
Sorts	Categorizing on basis of alternations (putting words that share a common spelling unit into the category that shares a common phoneme.
Does It Fit?	Sorting spelling units into word contexts to spell a real word.

Morphological Treatment Group	*Description*
Word Building	Creating new words from provided bases and affixes.
Word Generating	Giving new words containing same affixes.
Unit Finding	Underlining bases and circling affixes
Transferring	Reading of a different set of words with the same affixes orally.
Relating Units	Deciding if a second word comes from the first word.
Sorts	Categorizing on basis of spelling units with shared morphemes.
Does It Fit?	Sorting words with suffixes into sentences.

The results of this study indicated that *both* types of interventions significantly improved each student's performance on measures of accuracy and rate of phonological decoding, morphological awareness, accuracy of decoding words, and reading comprehension skills. However, the most salient aspect of this study was the appreciation of the cross-over effect between morphology and phonology with students in grades 4 through 6. Richards et al. (2006) reported that students in the morphological treatment group improved *significantly more* than students in the phonological treatment group on direct measures of phonological decoding. What could explain such a juxtaposition? The answer most likely lies in the brain's ability to engage in a crossover effect of mapping phonemes to morphemes, as children actually create mental maps based upon a complex webbing of phonology (sound units), orthography (letter shapes), and morphology (meaning). According to the National Reading Panel's (2000) report summarizing best practices in reading research, specific training in phonological awareness is most effective in 1ˢᵗ grade, then loses its effectiveness as children matriculate through school. The dyslexic students in this study were in grades 4 through 6. Hence, the students in early elementary school may learn phonology best through an actual mapping of phonology to orthographical units, or direct teaching of explicit phonics. However, students in later elementary school do not necessarily learn phonology best through a direct and explicit phonological program, but rather through teaching morphological rules. Table 6-2 details the specific brain regions responsible for phonological mapping and morphological mapping.

KEY LEARNING POINT	Students in early elementary school learn phonology best through an actual mapping of phonology to orthographical units. However, students in later elementary school do not necessarily learn phonology best through a direct and explicit phonological program, but rather through teaching morphological rules. (Richards et al., 2006)

Table 6-2

Brain Activation Patterns for Different Educational Treatment Conditions

(Richards, et al., 2006)

Educational Intervention	*Increased fMRI Activation*
Morphological Treatment	Left fusiform gyrus Left posterior insular cortex
Phonological Treatment	Left anterior insular cortex Left superior temporal gyrus Right superior frontal gyrus

In summary, there are three implications to be derived from this important piece of research (Richards et al., 2006). First, morphological treatment was associated with increases in phoneme mapping, whereas phonological treatment was associated with increases in brain activation during morphological mapping for older elementary students. This cross-over effect suggests that children learn to read by creating mental maps of the interrelationships among word forms. For reasons not completely understood, once these mental maps are established, it becomes increasingly problematic to influence a singular aspect of the reading process directly *(i.e. phonology)*. Instead, a certain symbiosis emerges between phonology, orthography, and morphology, forcing the educator to enhance the effectiveness of one by stimulating the other. Consequently, the second learning axiom derived from this research is that *bottom-up* educational processes such as teaching explicit phonics are most effective in 1st grade (National Reading Panel, 2000), but *top-down* methods such as using morphology and word meaning cues are most effective for older elementary school children to learn phoneme segmentation. Simply put, words live in families just like children do; therefore, to learn to read and spell children need to learn families of sounds, families of word parts for meaning, and families of letter units (Nagy, et al., 1994). Explicit instruction in word forms and their interrelationships can be balanced with instruction that also teaches vocabulary and comprehension (Stahl & Nagy, 2006). Thirdly, a *balanced literacy* approach, as opposed to a monolithic approach that only emphasizes phonology, may be best not only to teach reading for older elementary school students, but also to establish the foundational skills necessary for reading comprehension to emerge. In conclusion, the fundamental aspects of reading comprehension may truly begin with an understanding of the morphological principles of the English language at the individual word level.

KEY LEARNING POINT	Words live in families just like children do; therefore, to learn to read and spell children need to learn families of sounds, families of word parts for meaning, and families of letter units (Nagy et al., 1994). Thus, comprehension may truly begin with an understanding of the morphological principles of the English language at the individual word level.

The Role of Language and Comprehension:

There is a certain duality that occurs when analyzing the essential components of reading comprehension. As previously discussed, there is a word recognition component that assists in translating the printed word into language; however, the comprehension component also assists in making sense of this linguistic information. The comprehension component weaves a tapestry of seamless thoughts, ideas, and cognitions generated from these chains of linguistic islands, thereby creating a fabric of mind scripts that facilitate the process of learning. There is overwhelming support in the literature that children with poor reading comprehension skills also have deficits in receptive vocabulary development as well as semantic processing (Catts, Adloff, & Weismer, 2006; Nation et al., 2004; Nation & Snowling, 1998). Most of the aforementioned studies noted that students with poor reading comprehension skills also had difficulty responding to specific questions in a story when the passage was read to them, and especially struggled to draw inferences from passages (Cain, Oakhill, & Elbro, 2003). Furthermore, these children tended to have relatively normal phonological processing abilities, thus illustrating the dissociation, not association, between phonology and comprehension at the later elementary grades.

Nevertheless, according to Catts et al. (2006), most of the language problems of students with poor reading comprehension skills, such as poor vocabulary development and limited grammatical development, are sub-clinical in nature and do not meet the standard diagnostic criterion for language impairment in kindergarten. Since the vast majority of these children do not receive speech and language therapy services at the early elementary level, there is an increased burden among educators in the regular class setting to balance phonological decoding with text comprehension. However, this is rarely the case in most reading programs within a Tier I or Tier II intervention system under the RTI model. Why? Simply put, reading programs in the early grades tend to emphasize phonological processing and word recognition skills, as opposed to language comprehension skills. According to Catts et al. (2006), children with poor decoding skills often score very poorly on measures of reading comprehension skills in the early grades, thus establishing a linear pattern between these two reading attributes. Students with poor language comprehension skills in the earlier grades tend to score more like normal readers on measures of passage comprehension skills, and therefore are not perceived as having any learning deficits. However, these same students experience significant difficulty with reading comprehension by eighth grade due in part to the depth and linguistic demands of the curriculum (Catts et al., 2006). Herein lies a fundamental difference in the curriculum between an overemphasis on word recognition skills at the elementary level and a shift toward language comprehension at the secondary level. As Nation et al. (2004) noted, there is no support for the view that poor comprehenders at the secondary level have residual phonological processing deficits. Instead, students with poor reading comprehension skills are less successful due to language based deficits including semantic processing, morphosyntax, and higher level aspects of linguistic reasoning skills. Therefore, the intervention focus should be at the *language* level and not at the *phonological* level for students with poor reading comprehension skills. In summary, reading comprehension is a multi-faceted phenomenon, with deficits in part attributed to poor language comprehension skills that often do not manifest until the secondary grades.

KEY LEARNING POINT	Reading comprehension is a multi-faceted phenomenon, with deficits in part attributed to poor language comprehension skills that often do not manifest until the secondary grades.

The Role of Intelligence and Comprehension:

An important question to consider involves the relationship between intelligence and reading comprehension skills. For years, psychologists have been using intelligence test scores as a predictor variable to determine educational outcomes for children. There are many psychologists who continue to over-emphasize full scale intelligence test scores as the primary explanatory factor for student underachievement. As discussed in Chapter 1, the over-emphasis and misinterpretation of full scale intelligence test scores has led to a host of faulty educational decisions, and in some cases has basically rendered school psychologists impotent in making individual intervention decisions (Hale & Fiorello, 2004). However, the most degrading aspect of utilizing one numeric value to represent the wide spectrum of human cognitive abilities has been the notion that intelligence is merely a synonym for a student's *potential*. To assume that intelligence is tantamount to potential is to assume that intelligence is a fixed, immutable, and innate cognitive trait captured in its entirety by an IQ test (Sattler, 1988).

Still, an investigation into the cognitive profiles of students with reading comprehension deficits is certainly important. Nation, Clarke, and Snowling (2002) examined children in middle school in order to determine the relative cognitive profiles of students with reading comprehension deficits. Their results indicated that students with reading comprehension deficits scored in the *average* range on measures of general cognitive ability, though their scores were significantly lower than those of normal readers. Students with poor reading comprehension skills had an average general composite ability score of *94.1* compared to *107.6* in the control group (F=32.4, p<.01). In terms of cluster scores, students with poor reading comprehension skills differed most from normal readers in verbal ability scores, particularly in the areas of *word definitions* (defining words) and *similarities* (determining how two words were alike). It should be noted that both groups were matched on variables including chronological age and phonological ability. These researchers (Nation et al., 2002) concluded that children with poor reading comprehension skills were a fairly heterogeneous group. Most of these children had relatively normal intelligence, with comprehension deficits due primarily to specific aspects of verbal processing such as drawing inferences from the text, as opposed to more global deficits with speech and language processing. Certainly, there are some children who have difficulty with reading comprehension skills due to marked deficits with intelligence, as well as a small percentage of children who show relatively advanced phonological processing skills in lieu of reading comprehension deficits *(i.e. hyperlexic children)*. However, the vast majority of children with reading comprehension deficits do not have substandard intellectual skills or deficits with phonological processing (Nation et al., 2002; Nation & Snowling, 1998). The implications of these findings are twofold. First, what are the cognitive mechanisms in place leading to subtle language deficits hindering a student's ability to draw inferences from the passage? Second, what are the best educational methods and practices available to target students with poor reading comprehension difficulties? The answers to both questions lie in the cognitive construct known as executive *functioning skills*.

KEY LEARNING POINT	Most students with poor reading comprehension skills have relatively normal intelligence. Their comprehension deficits are primarily due to very specific aspects of verbal processing such as drawing inferences from the text, as opposed to deficits with more global aspects of speech and language skills or with phonological processing (Nation et al., 2002).

Executive Functioning and Reading Comprehension Skills:

Children who lack strategies to organize print and reflect upon new information being read, or have difficulty sustaining their attention to verbal information over protracted periods of time, are often unable to stitch together printed information into a river of cohesive thoughts. In other words, they tend to struggle with reading comprehension skills. The cognitive culprits responsible for a host of reading comprehension difficulties are a constellation of higher-level problem solving skills known collectively as executive functioning skills. Barkley (2001) defined executive functioning skills as a set of mind tools that facilitate adaptive behavior functioning during real world encounters. Hence, executive functions can be thought of as a set of multiple cognitive processes that act in a coordinated way to direct cognition, emotion, and motor functions. As discussed in Chapter 1, a litany of research has demonstrated that most executive functioning skills have a generalized neuroanatomical base housed within the prefrontal cortex (Moffitt & Henry, 1989; Malloy & Richardson, 1994; Mega & Cummings, 1994; Giancola, 1995). Hence, the prefrontal cortex plays a vital role in forming goals and objectives, devising plans of action to obtain these goals, selecting the cognitive skills necessary to execute the plan, as well as to evaluate the success or failure of a given plan (Goldberg, 2001). Therefore, executive functions are involved with, but not limited to, the direction of multiple cognitive processes toward the pursuit of a goal directed academic task for a successful learning outcome. A litany of executive functioning characteristics is highlighted in Table 6-3.

In essence, executive functioning skills are tantamount to a cerebral orchestra directing the constant flow and manipulation of cognition. However, like that of a fine philharmonic, the ensemble of players comprising the core components of executive processing takes time to fully develop. Barkley (2001) acknowledged that executive functioning skills develop in children through a gradual maturation process. In fact, the developmental trajectory of executive functioning skills begins with certain lower level skills being firmly established, such as expressive and receptive language development. However, more higher-order cognitive problem solving skills such as working memory skills, processing speed, and attentional control capabilities tend to occur in later adolescence (Anderson, Anderson, Northam, Jacobs, & Catroppa, 2001). Similarly, the educational curriculum often mirrors this pattern as drawing inferences from longer text, a fundamental component in the reading comprehension process, becomes more critical in the later grades.

Table 6-3

Executive Functioning Characteristics

- Inhibiting reflexive, impulsive responding
- Interrupting, and returning to, an ongoing activity
- Directing and focusing attentional processes, screening out interference and distractions, and sustaining attention
- Cueing the initiation of effort and judgments about the amount of effort required to complete a task, and the sustaining of a sufficient amount of effort to effectively complete the task
- Demonstrating flexibility in the shifting of cognitive resources to focus on new demands or to respond to new conditions or new information
- Directing the efficient use of, and alternation between, pattern and detail processing (knowing when to focus on the "big picture" and when to concentrate on the details, and when to switch between the two)
- Monitoring and regulating speed of information processing; finding the right combination of speed and accuracy for optimal performance of an activity
- Monitoring task performance for accuracy and efficiency
- Overseeing the selection of verbal-nonverbal and abstract-concrete processing mechanisms
- Directing motor output, altering performance based on feedback
- Directing the efficient use of fluid reasoning resources
- Directing the use of working memory resources - that is, directing the ability to mentally manipulate information
- Directing the efficient and fluent production of language when highly specific production demands are made
- Directing the integration of multiple abilities to produce oral or written responses or products that reflect the level of capacity of the component abilities involved
- Directing the efficient placement of information in long-term storage
- Directing the retrieval of information from long-term storage
- Regulating social behavior
- Regulating emotional control
- Enabling self-observation and self-analysis
- Making use of hindsight and foresight in the direction of current processing
- Enabling the capacity to "take the perspective of the other" in order to infer how someone is thinking or feeling at a given point in time

<table>
<tr><td>

**KEY
LEARNING
POINT**

</td><td>

Executive functioning skills do not represent intelligence, but rather cue and direct cognitive, emotion, and motor functions. Executive functions are thought to be housed in the frontal lobes, and involve a constellation of cognitive attributes that develop slowly over time. Processing speed, working memory, and sustained attention emerge somewhat later in development.

</td></tr>
</table>

Now, let us turn our attention to the executive functioning processes involved with reading comprehension skills. The aforementioned discussion has argued for an examination of reading comprehension essentially to begin at the word level (morphology), across words (semantics), and finally across different tiers or levels of cognition (executive functions). Hence, in this **trilogy** of comprehension components, executive functions basically represent a cascade of numerous cognitive constructs responsible for a variety of academic ventures necessary for learning, including initiating tasks, maintaining a persistent pattern of effort, resisting distractions, and plotting a general strategy or course of action when actively engaged in a problem solving task. The primary executive functioning characteristics associated with reading comprehension skills are highlighted in Table 6-4.

Children with dyslexia display marked deficits on selected aspects of executive functioning skills (Reiter, Tucha, & Lange, 2004). Without a doubt, the most crucial aspect of executive functioning impaired in children with developmental dyslexia is working memory skills (Vargo et al., 1995; Wilcutt et al., 2004; Reiter et al., 2004). Working memory involves the ability to hold representational knowledge of the world around us in mind, coupled with the mental flexibility to manipulate this knowledge in whatever manner we choose (Levine & Reed, 1999). Hence, working memory subserves the reading process by temporarily suspending previously read information while simultaneously allowing the reader to acquire new information. Deficits in working memory can certainly disrupt a student's ability to make appropriate linkages among information in the text. The concept of working memory skills and its critical importance to learning is perhaps best described by Baddeley's (2000) three-component system.

Table 6-4

Executive Functioning Characteristics in Reading Comprehension

Executive Functioning Trait	_Reading Attribute_
Planning Skills	Read with a specific question or purpose in mind when seeking specific information. Also involves strategic manner the reader uses to process new information.
Organization Skills	Stitch together text in a cohesive manner. Also, when distracted, the ability to return back to the text and resume the story flow.
Working Memory	Temporarily suspending previously read information in mind while simultaneously linking to new information being read.
Cognitive Flexibility	Shifting patterns of thought processes to the organizational parameters of the text being read, and not perseverating on material.
Verbal Fluency	Speed of processing linguistic information at the word level to facilitate passage comprehension at the text level.
Concept Formation	Depth of understanding of the text.
Response Inhibition	Refraining from jumping ahead when reading text and missing salient aspects of the passage.
Sustained Attention	The ability to stay focused on the text for prolonged periods of time and resist distractions.

According to Baddeley (2000), the first component of working memory is the *phonological loop*, which holds and manipulates acoustic and speech-based information The functional significance of the phonological loop in the reading process is twofold. First, working memory allows auditory and acoustically based information to linger longer for further processing to occur. Second, working memory can also assist at the word level, providing novel readers with an opportunity to consecutively stitch together a series of phonemes and graphemes in multisyllabic words.

The second component of working memory is called the *visual-spatial sketchpad*, and holds visual, spatial, and kinesthetic information in temporary storage in the form of visual imagery (Baddeley, 1998). The visual-spatial sketchpad of working memory seems to be more effective at storing a single complex pattern, but is not well suited for serial recall like the phonological loop. Still, the ability to *"think in pictures"* and rely on visual imagery for the memorization of specific letter formations, spelling patterns, and orthography of words plays a vital role in the efficacy of reading and spelling skills (Feifer & DeFina, 2002). According to Reiter et al. (2004), children with dyslexia demonstrate impairments in tasks that measuring both verbal working memory systems, as well as visual or figural working memory systems.

Lastly, the *central executive system* is the third cornerstone of Baddeley's (1998) working memory model, and serves as the command post for controlling both the phonological rehearsal loop and the visual-spatial sketchpad. One of the primary purposes of the central executive system is to allocate attentional resources in a manner whereby two or more cognitive tasks can be performed in a simultaneous manner (Baddeley, 1998). As Hopko, Ashcraft, and Gute (1998) noted, it is the central executive system that serves primarily to suppress or inhibit any negative distracters having an adverse effect upon learning. In fact, Brosnan et al. (2002) suggested that dyslexic adults and children consistently had difficulty both with response inhibition when distracters were present and recollection of the temporal order of items presented in a sequential fashion. Both sets of tasks have profound effects upon the reading process. First, recalling the sequential order of events in a story is paramount to organizing the information in a cohesive manner. In fact, most classroom teachers often lament the organizational difficulties of children with reading disabilities. Second, the inability to inhibit a response in context suggests that dyslexics may often be fooled or *"tricked"* by the phonological inconsistencies in the English language, and erroneously jump to a conclusion regarding the identification of a word irrespective of the context being read. Clearly, errors in this regard run the potential of altering passage comprehension skills.

KEY LEARNING POINT	The primary executive functioning skills diminished among dyslexics with reading comprehension deficits are working memory skills. Working memory subserves the reading process by temporarily suspending previously read information while simultaneously allowing the reader to acquire new information. Visual working memory deficits can impair the ability to recall the orthography of words, and consistently recall spelling rules and boundaries.

In terms of the relationship between other executive functioning skills and reading comprehension, the results have been somewhat mixed. For instance, some research studies have indicated children with dyslexia were markedly impaired on verbal fluency tasks (Brosnan et al., 2002: Reiter et al., 2004), though executive functioning skills such as the ability to plan and organize have not consistently been found to be impaired in children with dyslexia (Klorman, Hazel-Fernandez, Shaywitz, Fletcher, Marchione, Holahan, Stuebing, & Shaywitz, 1999). Nevertheless, it remains problematic to draw specific conclusions regarding the precise relationship between a particular aspect of executive functioning and reading comprehension since different measures of reading comprehension tap different types of skills. In other words, the successful comprehension of printed text relies in part on the specific type of question being asked. For instance, Cain and Oakhill (1999) reported that students with poor comprehension skills performed at a comparable level to same age peers on questions tapping more basic or literal types of information, as opposed to drawing inferences from the text. However, as students progress through their academic careers, the types of questions being asked tend to be more inferential in nature, and less literal with each successive grade. With respect to the term *"inferential,"* Table 6-5 depicts five types of inferential questions typically required of students (Bowyer-Crane & Snowling, 2005).

Table 6-5

Subtypes of Inferences

(Boyer-Crane & Snowling, 2005)

1. **_Elaborate inferences_** - These types of inferences are not necessary for comprehension, but allow the text to be further elaborated upon based on real-world knowledge. For instance, making a prediction about a possible outcome from a description of events would elaborate on the information given in the text.

2. **_Cohesive inferences_** - These inferences rely on linguistic cues present in the text. For instance, to comprehend the phrase _"Tim hit Jill with his tennis racket"_ the reader would need to infer that the tennis racket belonged to Tim, since Tim is the only male mentioned in the phrase.

3. **_Knowledge-based inferences_** - These inferences rely on the application of real-world knowledge to the text. They differ from elaborative inferences in that they are necessary for actual text coherence. For instance, in the following two sentences _"The campfire started to burn. Tim grabbed a bucket of water,"_ the reader must activate the idea that water puts out the fire; otherwise the two sentences remain disjointed.

4. **_Evaluative inferences_** - These inferences relate to the emotional outcome of an event, and like knowledge-based inferences, rely upon the reader's background knowledge to interpret the text.

5. **_Literal inferences_** - These questions require no inferences to be made as the information is literally written directly in the text.

In fact, Bowyer-Crane and Snowling (2005) also determined that students who had difficulty with reading comprehension but demonstrated adequate reading accuracy skills were likely to have difficulty drawing inferences from text. However, the performance of these same children improved on text-connecting inferences when the children were allowed to _refer back to the text_. Therefore, there may be two very important factors influencing text comprehension. First, certain reading comprehension measures such as the _WORD (Wechsler Objective Reading Dimensions Test of Reading Comprehension)_ were less likely to discriminate among students with poor reading comprehension skills due to the literal nature of the questions. (Bowyer-Crane & Snowling, 2005). Second, some measures of reading comprehension skills such as the

Woodcock-Johnson III may also be less likely to discriminate among students with poor reading comprehension skills because students are allowed to go back and re-read the passage, thus reducing the working memory demands of the task. Conversely, other tests of reading comprehension that place more emphasis on knowledge-based inferences, such as the *NARA II (Neale Analysis of Reading Ability)* or *Gray-Oral Reading Test-Fourth Edition (GORT-IV)*, and do not allow students to re-read the passage may better discriminate among poor comprehenders (Bowyer-Crane & Snowling, 2005). Taken together, these studies suggest that children with comprehension difficulties would benefit from direct instruction on utilizing background knowledge and cues to elaborate upon and draw inferences from the text, as opposed to further practice on reading fluency to assist with comprehension skills.

In summary, specifying the underlying linguistic and cognitive factors associated with poor reading comprehension skills may be helpful toward developing more effective intervention strategies to assist children throughout their learning journey. As discussed in Chapter 3, the National Reading Panel (2000) classified reading comprehension skills and vocabulary development as being two critically important learning pillars in the reading process. The ability to utilize background knowledge and draw inferences from the text also facilitates the comprehension process and allows for a deeper and more enriched engagement of the passage. Clearly, executive functioning skills represent a student's ability to stitch together relevant aspects of the text in order to derive meaning from print. The most salient aspect of executive functioning vital for effective passage comprehension skills is working memory. Working memory subserves the reading process by temporarily suspending previously read information while simultaneously allowing the reader to acquire new information. Deficits in working memory can certainly disrupt a student's ability to make appropriate linkages among information in the text. Finally, vocabulary development remains a crucial aspect to support the comprehension of text acquisition, and can be enhanced by an understanding of the morphological underpinnings of words, and relationships between root words and derivational prefixes and suffixes.

Lastly, a discussion of reading comprehension cannot be complete without touching on *content affinity*. Certainly, there are emotional factors as well that facilitate the interest level each reader brings to the text. In other words, reading about baseball, Yu-Gi-Oh, or the secrets to mastering a PlayStation game is probably more intrinsically appealing to a 3rd grader than a thorough review of the geopolitical strategies that brought an end to the Cold War. In the human brain, the *amygdala*, a central component of the limbic system, tends to register the emotional valence of incoming information by triggering important regions for memory functioning including the *hippocampus*. Therefore, information that is more emotionally relevant and important to a child's life automatically registers a greater charge within this learning circuit to allow for greater interest and more scrutinized reading by the child. With respect to specific learning strategies that educators can use to assist students in their passage comprehension skills and consequently greater content affinity, the following recommendations in Table 6-6 are offered.

Table 6-6

Reading Comprehension Interventions

a. **Stop and Start Technique** - The student reads a passage out loud, and every 30 seconds the teacher says "stop" and asks questions about the story. Eventually the time interval is lengthened.

b. **Directional Questions** - Ask questions at the beginning of the text instead of the end so students can become more directional readers.

c. **Story Maps** - A pre-reading activity where graphic organizers are used to outline and organize information prior to reading the text.

d. **Narrative Retelling** - Have the child retell the story after reading it aloud.

e. **Read Aloud** - Reading out loud allows students to hear their own voices and can facilitate working memory.

f. **Multiple Exposure** - Encourage students to skim the material upon reading for the first time, with emphasis on chapter and text headings. Read for detail on the second exposure of the text.

g. **Active Participation** - Encourage active reading by getting children in the habit of note-taking or putting asterisks next to important material in the text.

h. **Create Questions** - Have students write their own test questions about the material.

i. **Reduce Anxiety** - Anxiety inhibits working memory, and leads to ineffective recall. Children who are anxious about reading out loud in front of their classmates should be provided an opportunity to read in a *"safety zone"* in class. This may also help to eliminate distractions as well.

Table 6-6

Reading Comprehension Interventions

j. **Medication Management** - Often students with attention-deficit-disorder struggle with passage comprehension skills. Proper medication management of the disorder can help foster better comprehension.

k. **Practice Terminology** - Practice defining new terms and concepts prior to reading material with dense language. Vocabulary enrichment is often the key to improving comprehension.

l. **Classroom Discussions** - Introduce new topic areas with general classroom discussions to capture a student's attention and interest prior to reading the material.

m. **Sequencing Tasks** - Present random words out of sequence and have children arrange them to make a sentence. Next, present sentences out of sequence and have children arrange them to make a paragraph. Lastly, present paragraphs out of sequence, and have children arrange them to make a story. This type of organization drill will facilitate sequencing linguistic material.

n. **Increase Fluency** - For younger students, greater fluency allows for reading to become a more automatic process, thereby freeing up cognitive resources to concentrate on the passage itself, as opposed to mechanically decoding each word in the passage.

CHAPTER 7

Integrating RTI With Cognitive Neuropsychology

Whether students participating in special education programs actually benefit continues to be a challenging issue to document unequivocally. What remains clear is that data based decision making based upon effective progress monitoring remains an often overlooked attribute driving educational policy decisions. The goal of RTI is, first and foremost, to instill a scientific process back into the public educational arena when making programming decisions regarding student achievement. Therefore, RTI is a *process*, not a panacea or a flawless diagnostic tool, that educators can use in a systematic fashion to ensure that educational resources are applied in the most judicious and prudent manner possible. It is both a creation, as well as a reallocation, of resources to allow schools to screen for educational problems at an earlier age, assess learning rates and levels of performance, provide tiered levels of intervention, monitor the effectiveness of interventions, and to prevent learning and behavioral issues from developing into more severe deficits. Through collaborative data based decision making, RTI seeks to prevent the inherent problems that have emerged from the traditional "test and place" philosophy that currently dominates the landscape of special education. Some of the more salient issues plaguing the current special education instructional model are highlighted in Table 7-1.

Table 7-1

Traditional Problems With the Special Education Service Delivery Model

- A deliberate separation of regular education from special education.

- Undocumented benefits of special education effectiveness for children with both high and low incidence disabilities.

- A disconnect between testing for eligibility decision purposes versus testing for what interventions best assist a child.

- A reduced emphasis on pooling resources toward early intervention and establishing prevention types of programs.

- Individual Education Plans (IEPs) that rarely emphasize the "I" but rather are Generic Education Plans (GEPs) that do not consistently implement evidence based instructional supports.

- An overrepresentation of minority students in special education programs.

- Poor ability to identify students at earlier ages for effective intervention strategies.

- Inconsistent qualification decisions because there is no universal agreement as to what constitutes a 'significant discrepancy' between intelligence test scores and scores from nationally-normed achievement tests.

Chapter 8 provides two case studies to illustrate the relative strengths that both RTI and cognitive neuropsychological assessment can play in the identification and remediation of reading disorders in children. Unfortunately, most educators are facing an artificial dilemma with regard to implementing both approaches. Rightfully so, the "ability-achievement" discrepancy model has increasingly come under fire as both unnecessary and insufficient for identifying learning disabilities. However, in denouncing the "discrepancy model," many educators have mistakenly interpreted the "ability-achievement" discrepancy model and all of its inherent flaws as synonymous with a cognitive processing model of assessment for learning disabilities. Therefore, proponents of RTI tend to dismiss cognitive neuropsychological assessment as being nothing more than an extension of, or a thinly-disguised version of, the discrepancy model and therefore believe it has no place in the process of identifying learning disabilities. What critics often say is that cognitive neuropsychological assessment promotes the false notion that "fuzzy" psychological processes and artificial discrepancies are related to reading disorders.

This incorrect notion that cognitive neuropsychological assessment and the discrepancy model are one in the same has led many to conclude that all nationally-normed tests are irrelevant in the identification and remediation of learning disorders (Reschly, 2003; Fuchs et al., 2003). Nevertheless, the true culprits are not the tests themselves, but rather the psychologists, administrators, special educators, and other educational personnel who have historically interpreted these measures in a pseudoscientific manner while fervently searching for the previously all-important 'significant discrepancy.' In reality, both proponents of RTI and proponents of cognitive neuropsychology firmly agree that the discrepancy model is neither a reliable nor a valid method to identify learning disorders in school. In addition, both proponents of RTI and proponents of cognitive neuropsychology agree that earlier intervention and the use of evidence based intervention techniques are essential in efforts to remediate struggling learners and must permeate the thinking behind any educational reform. Lastly, proponents of both RTI and cognitive neuropsychology acknowledge that the core factors illustrated by the National Reading Panel (2000) including phonemic awareness, phonics, fluency, vocabulary, and comprehension are vital components of the reading process.

It should be noted that RTI has also faced scrutiny from the cognitive neuropsychology community, and has subsequently been criticized for a variety of factors as well. For instance, Hale (2006) argued that, with the exception of word reading and fluency, RTI has largely ignored most academic domains and does not address optimal instructional techniques across grade levels and curricula. Hale has also pointed out that RTI seems to have turned a blind eye to the multifaceted nature of learning disabilities (LD) and has failed to determine objective criteria for what constitutes a response failure to a particular intervention. Certainly, there are limitations to RTI, but there are also pragmatic limitations to cognitive neuropsychology as well. While the debate rages and the battle lines have been drawn, educational researchers and practitioners need to avoid the pitfalls of arguing for the competitive sake of winning a philosophical point, and instead should work together to develop a comprehensive method of identifying and assisting struggling learners. Unfortunately, this argument has polarized the profession of school psychology. Most professionals who view learning from a behavioral paradigm favor RTI, while others who use a more cognitive processing perspective tend to favor neuropsychological assessment. The time has come to acknowledge that both a cognitive neuropsychological approach and an RTI approach will work best when combined to form an integrated model where one does not exclude the other. Research in the cognitive neuropsychology of reading has shown us that the time has also come to stop questioning whether neuropsychological processes (including phonological processing, language development, working memory, and rapid naming skills) are related to reading skill acquisition. Lastly, the time has come to stop viewing a cognitive neuropsychological assessment model in the same vein as the flawed discrepancy model.   Table 7-2 lists the relative strengths and weaknesses of both RTI and cognitive neuropsychology.

Certainly, there are inherent weaknesses in utilizing any singular methodology when determining an educational disability in a child. From a statistical point of view, in order to minimize the chances of committing a Type I error (mistakenly classifying a child as being disabled) or a Type II error (failing to classify a child as being disabled when indeed they are), one should adhere to the relative merits of combining multiple methods of data collection within a multi-layered framework (Hale et al., 2006). In other words, RTI needs to be integrated within a cognitive neuropsychological assessment framework to maximize the effectiveness of both models. What remains clear is that neither RTI nor the discrepancy model addresses the current definition of a learning disability as outlined by IDEA 2004 (Hale, 2006). A specific learning disability has consistently been defined as a disorder of a basic psychological process that interferes with academic achievement. According to the U.S. Department of Education Learning Disabilities Roundtable (2002), *"The identification of a core cognitive deficit, or a disorder in one or more psychological processes that is predictive of an imperfect ability to learn, is a marker for a specific learning disability."*

Table 7-2

Relative Strengths and Weaknesses of RTI and Cognitive Neuropsychology

RTI STRENGTHS

- Enhanced ecological validity
- Quicker and cheape
- Specifically measures an area of academics
- Measures curricular learning
- Linked to a problem solving model
- Allows for more efficient progress monitoring
- Data can easily be linked to curricular decisions
- Encourages scientific interventions be used
- Allows students to receive help at earlier grades
- De-emphasizes labeling kids
- More collaborative decisions made
- Reduces "curriculum casualties"
- A proactive and not reactive model
- Eliminates the over-emphasis on IQ scores which can lead to a is proportionate number of minorities in special education

RTI WEAKNESSES

- Assesses limited aspects of academics
- Not a diagnostic approach
- Does not answer the WHY question
- Difficult to implement across grades
- Poor differential diagnosis
- Does not delineate a firm time line for a student to respond
- Difficult to apply to other academic endeavors besides reading
- Limited guidelines on how long to stay within each tier
- Discounts proven neurocognitive factors
- Does not address lack of evidence-based instructional techniques in math and written language.

NEUROPSYCHOLOGY STENGTHS

- A thorough and complete assessment of learning
- Provides diagnostic information
- Allows for differential diagnosis
- Answers the WHY question pertaining to student underachievement
- Can provide a HOW (for intervention)
- Constructs are scientifically-based
- Measures the National Reading Panel's five core constructs pertaining to reading (and not just fluency measures)
- Can explain what functions can be remediated versus what functions need accommodations
- Most likely assessment to hold up in due process hearing

NEUROPSYCHOLOGY WEAKNESSES

- Can be costly and time consuming
- Most psychologists trained in IQ testing and not cognitive neuropsychology
- Reports can be too long and technical
- Difficult for school systems to interpret
- Not useful for progress monitoring
- Recommendations often not practical
- Often completed by outside psychologists with little insight into school culture and climate or issues specific to learning
- Most effective only when students have not responded to earlier interventions; not a proactive method

Certainly, RTI can identify children with low achievement, but RTI alone cannot diagnose a core neurocognitive learning deficit, which clearly is the center piece in the definition of an educational learning disability. At best, RTI can lead to the assumption that a child did not respond to an evidence based intervention due to an inherent disability, though RTI cannot prove that one exists. Similarly, an ability-achievement comparison or discrepancy model can make the assumption that a student who is not achieving at a level commensurate with their cognitive abilities might possess a learning disability, though they cannot prove that one exists. The fact remains that neither the discrepancy model nor RTI alone can detail the intrinsic factors inherent in the neuropsychological make-up of an individual that impact reading. According to Semrud-Clikeman (2005), only direct school based neuropsychological evaluations examining core neuropsychological processes can directly assess for the presence of specific cognitive markers such as working memory deficits, executive dysfunction, poor retrieval fluency, and phonological processing deficits that may be the root cause for a reading disability. Therefore, the first step in fusing together the tenets of RTI within a cognitive neuropsychological framework is a comprehensive definition of a reading disability that takes into account both extrinsic and intrinsic factors that may hinder the learning process. While IDEA 2004 has crafted a rather generic definition of an educational disability at the federal level, each state and for that matter each school district will ultimately fill in the details with a more detailed set of procedures and standards defining an educational disability. The following 4-factor criteria outlined in Table 7-3 may be helpful to capture the essence of both RTI and cognitive neuropsychology.

Table 7-3

Proposed 4 - Factor Model of Defining a Reading Disability

1. There should be data to document that a student's RATE of learning in one or more aspects of reading skill development is substantially slower than grade level peers over a specified period of time.

2. There should be data to document that the student has not responded to evidence based interventions when compared to grade level peers over a specified period of time.

3. There should be data from cognitive neuropsychological assessment indicating the presence or absence of specific processing deficits that are directly related to the reading process. This should include measures of phonemic awareness, phonological processing, language skills, working memory skills, executive functioning skills, and rapid and automatic retrieval skills.

4. There should be data ruling out other major sources of constraints upon school success such as emotional, cultural, medical, or environmental factors.

The criteria proposed in the aforementioned 4-factor model virtually demands that a combination of both RTI procedures and cognitive neuropsychological assessment be used to determine the presence of a learning disability. Furthermore, the definition remains consistent with IDEA 2004, the U.S. Department of Education Learning Disabilities Roundtable (2002), and the International Dyslexia Association (2005). In essence, Tier I would consist of the standard RTI approach implemented by classroom teachers using evidence based instructional materials within a standardized core curriculum for all children. Tier I should be highlighted by differentiated instruction, meaning that children would participate in a variety of smaller reading groups within the regular classroom in order to best meet their instructional needs. Furthermore, there should be plenty of opportunities for re-teaching, as well as sufficient academic engaged time allotted to address each particular curricular goal. Lastly, a fundamental component of Tier I should be utilizing periodic curriculum based measurement probes to frequently monitor the progress of all students. The role of a school psychologist at Tier I should be primarily consultative in nature.

Tier 2 is designed for those students who fail to respond or maintain appropriate educational progress within the regular class setting. The primary advantage of Tier 2 is to immediately provide specific interventions for a child at early grade levels without necessarily labeling the child as having a disability. However, before a Tier 2 type of intervention is implemented, an individualized problem-solving approach should be undertaken by the school's intervention team. This may include the regular classroom teacher, a special education teacher, a reading specialist, the school psychologist, a speech and language therapist, and building administrator. There should be an emphasis not only on identifying the problem, but also attempting to form hypotheses about the potential source of the problem and determining its magnitude by using a variety of data gathering techniques. This may include curriculum based measurement reading probes, informal reading inventories, and reading readiness measures such as DIBELS. The goal of the intervention team is to brainstorm and explore possible solutions to the problem, and develop both short-term and long-term intervention objectives. For instance, suppose that, at the end of their 2nd grade year, a student was reading just 18 words per minute accurately in grade-level text and was developing increasing frustration within the classroom. The team might suggest movement to Tier 2 for a short-term intervention such as Targeted Reading Instruction, which involves a professional such as the reading specialist intervening for a specified period of time to provide extra support and assistance in developing reading fluency. The team should also develop a method for monitoring the effectiveness of the intervention, and set a specific date to reconvene and continue, modify, or discontinue the intervention as necessary based upon the student's response. The measured degree of response to this intervention should determine which course of action is most appropriate. Should the student fail to respond to the intervention, then a more intensive intervention or further assessment may be warranted.

The fundamental tenet within any RTI model is data collection. This can be done through a variety of processes already discussed, including the use of cognitive neuropsychological assessment. It is important to note that <u>cognitive neuropsychological assessment can occur at any point in the process</u>, and does not always need to be (nor should it be) deferred until the final Tier. If such assessment were restricted to the final Tier, then RTI would run the risk of imposing yet another 'wait to fail' process not unlike the one that has plagued the discrepancy model paradigm (Della Toffalo, 2006). Therefore, if the student reading at just 18 words per minute was resistant to a Tier 2 intervention, and was also manifesting attention problems in the classroom, struggling with written language skills, displaying difficulty with the rapid and automatic retrieval of math facts, and demonstrating both expressive and receptive language difficulties, then targeted assessment may be warranted prior to advancing to the next tier. The goal of this targeted assessment would be to use a variety of tools, including cognitive neuropsychological measures as needed, to determine the potential source for this student's variety of difficulties in order to determine the full scope and nature of interventions needed in order to address the variety of difficulties that they are displaying.

KEY LEARNING POINT	It is important to note that cognitive neuropsychological assessment can occur at any point in the RTI process, and does not always need to be deferred until the final Tier. If it were restricted to the final Tier, then RTI would run the risk of imposing yet another 'wait to fail' process not unlike the one that has plagued the discrepancy model paradigm.

Perhaps the core learning deficit in this type of example might be an inability to retrieve archived information from memory, whether in verbal or numeric form. Hence, interventions may need to be multifaceted and include a combination of language interventions, a behavior plan to address attention and impulsivity in the classroom, and specific methods to address reading, writing, and math deficits. In contrast, if a student simply possessed difficulties only with reading accuracy and fluency, then perhaps early targeted assessment would not be necessary; rather a more intensive intervention within a Tier 3 context should be sought before seeking assessment or a multi-disciplinary evaluation to determine the student's eligibility for special education services. Once again, this decision would need to be made by the school based intervention team through an analysis of the data collected. In this case, perhaps a systematic, daily, reading program such as *Alphabetic Phonics* (see Chapter 9) or *Horizons* (see Chapter 9) might be warranted rather than simply recycling the same intervention from Tier 2. In summary, the RTI process strives to incorporate a scientific process in school based decision making, as data from a single subject design is analyzed through effective progress monitoring and used as the justification for subsequent intervention decisions.

Clearly, by following an RTI model, the first two criteria depicted in Table 7-3 for the proper identification of a learning disability are quite easily assessed. In other words, RTI allows school systems to appropriately measure the rate of learning over a specific period of time, as well as to effectively measure a student's response to an evidence based intervention. Furthermore, by conceptualizing RTI within a framework that includes cognitive neuropsychological assessment as needed, the relative strengths of the model including early intervention, data based decision making, progress monitoring, and collaborative problem solving are clearly emphasized. Table 7-4 illustrates common myths that have been associated with an RTI framework.

Table 7-4

5 Common Myths About Response to Intervention

MYTH #1: **The outcome and intent of RTI is identification.**
There are two goals of RTI. The first is to deliver evidence based interventions and instructions for all students. The second is to use a student's response to an intervention as a basis for determining further instructional needs.

MYTH #2: **Tier IV is only special education.**
The last tier in any RTI model represents the most intense level of intervention, which may or may not include special education services.

MYTH #3: **RTI is only for pre-referral decision making.**
RTI is a comprehensive service delivery system that requires significant changes in how a school serves all students. When thought of solely as a pre-referral process, it tends to remain the province of special education only.

MYTH #4: **The main benefit of RTI is to identify those students who are not really LD, but simply are not achieving due to poor instruction.**
The main benefit of RTI is prevention. IDEA 2004 is clear that no single criterion can be used for special education eligibility.   Data collection during RTI implementation can be used as one source of information, but identification is an end-product of RTI, not the primary purpose.

MYTH # 5: **The research on RTI is solely based on beginning reading skills.**
Most of the research to date on RTI focuses on beginning reading skills. However, just as much research (if not more) has been produced on the use of a problem-solving model in treating behavioral problems in all ages. Future research is needed with respect to RTI and its effectiveness at the secondary level and with other academic domains.

Adapted from National Association of State Directors of Special Education. (2006)

In order to address the final two criteria in Table 7-3, cognitive neuropsychological assessment techniques will be needed. It is important to note that certain types of disabilities will be rather challenging for a pure RTI model to address, and therefore, may represent another 'wait to fail' set of procedures unless incorporated within a framework that includes cognitive neuropsychological assessment as part of the problem-solving process. In essence, many disabilities seen today produce highly unique sets of cognitive and learning characteristics, and many of the 'standard protocol' interventions that are successful for most struggling learners may be insufficient to address the needs of these more unique learners. When a Response to Intervention (RTI) methodology is implemented for identifying and intervening with struggling learners, it is imperative that schools use all available tools to ensure what the right interventions are for all struggling learners. Ultimately, it makes little sense to engage a student in a lock-step process of standard protocol interventions when there is reason to believe that such interventions are not likely to meet their needs. Instead, an RTI model integrated with school neuropsychological assessment would offer targeted assessment early in the RTI process in order to help determine the types of interventions that are most likely to assist unique learners. Perhaps, then, the true emphasis of this integrated model is RT**R**I (Response To the RIGHT Intervention).

KEY LEARNING POINT	An RTI model integrated with school neuropsychological assessment would offer targeted assessment early in the RTI process in order to help determine the types of interventions that are most likely to assist unique learners. Perhaps, then, the true emphasis of this integrated model is RT**R**I (Response To the RIGHT Intervention).

Table 7-5 depicts certain types of disabilities that may need further assessment immediately, rather than progressing through a tiered system of interventions in a lock-step fashion. Students with these types of disabilities typically display cognitive profiles notable for significant variability, and generally include unique profiles of strengths and weaknesses in processing different types of information. For instance, many students with disorders on the Autism spectrum such as Asperger's Syndrome tend to be hyperlexic. That is, they possess an almost uncanny ability to read words with correct pronunciation at a very high rate of speed despite significant cognitive limitations. For these students, curriculum based measures of reading skills commonly yield little information regarding their learning difficulties, since these students more typically struggle with comprehension rather than decoding or fluency. In fact, their comprehension deficits are often due to difficulties with the semantic and pragmatic qualities of language that are often an integral part of disorders on the Autism spectrum. These difficulties certainly have educational implications far more pervasive than simply reading problems. In fact, many students with Asperger's Syndrome also display a rather unique profile of cognitive strengths and weaknesses associated with right hemispheric dysfunction, and this type of learning profile has been thoroughly described in the literature as being a Nonverbal Learning Disability Syndrome (Rourke et al., 2002). This syndrome generally consists of cognitive features such as markedly stronger verbal skills than nonverbal reasoning skills, poor gross and fine motor coordination, difficulties learning new information and recognizing its applicability to previously-learned information, social skill deficits, difficulties understanding the perspective of others, difficulties understanding nonverbal social cues such as facial expressions and body postures, and impaired ability to engage in novel reasoning (Rourke et al., 2002). Of further interest, the syndrome of Nonverbal Learning Disability (NLD) has been described by Rourke (1995) as a 'final common pathway' for many other disorders—meaning that the unique cognitive profile characterized by this label often results from a wide variety of genetic, metabolic, acquired, and neurodevelopmental disorders. Examples include but are not limited to: Sotos Syndrome, Williams Syndrome, Callosal Agenesis, Early Hydrocephalus, Noonan's Syndrome, Fetal Alcohol Syndrome, Multiple Sclerosis, Turner Syndrome, Congenital Hypothyroidism, and Traumatic Brain Injury (Rourke, 1995).

Table 7-5

Examples of Students for Whom RTI Alone May Not Be Successful

- Autism Spectrum Disorders (especially Asperger's Syndrome)
- Tourette's Syndrome
- OCD and other anxiety related conditions
- Seizure disorders
- Medical disorders (diabetes, arthritis, cancer, etc.)
- Fetal Alcohol Syndrome
- Lead poisoning
- Traumatic Brain Injuries
- Low incidence disorders (metabolic, genetic, and neurodevelopmental syndromes such as hydrocephalus, callosal agenesis, tuberous sclerosis, etc.)
- Emotional disturbance
- Significant cognitive impairment

Furthermore, disorders involving seizures, exposure to ingested or environmental toxins, and traumatic brain injuries also result in highly individualized profiles of cognitive deficits that are inherently unpredictable in nature and often dynamic in their course. Individuals with these types of disorders often require unique approaches to instruction in order to learn new information or skills, frequently need assistance relating information to previously acquired skills, and often require support to retrieve or demonstrate previously-acquired knowledge (Della Toffalo, 2006). Fortunately, students who manifest these types of disorders constitute a relatively small percentage of children; however, these students may have their educational needs neglected if not provided with an appropriate psychological assessment detailing their unique educational needs. Clearly, an inflexible implementation of RTI in which students progressed through each of the tiers in lock-step fashion before being comprehensively assessed would certainly result in a 'wait to fail' scenario. Furthermore, it would be equally undesirable if the child's unique educational needs were undetected because they were not identified by the measures used for Tier 1 school-wide screenings. Table 7-6 illustrates a few key tips in order to address potential gaps in an RTI model.

Table 7-6

Key Tips in Addressing Gaps Within an RTI Model

1. Employ targeted assessment in Tiers 2 and 3 to assist in determining the applicability of standard interventions for individual students.

2. Use of assessment data to design interventions and/or test individualized specific accommodations (pre-referral intervention format such as Instructional Support Teams, Child Study Teams, etc.).

3. Integrating more specialized and targeted assessments to provide earlier identification of the *at-risk* learners who are not likely to be, or who have not thus far been, helped sufficiently by standard protocol interventions.

In an integrated model involving both RTI and cognitive neuropsychological assessment, it is vital that students immediately begin receiving academic interventions in their areas of need while further assessment (if needed) is being conducted. The goal of the assessment should be to gather further information leading directly to more appropriate interventions based on individual strengths and weaknesses, and to provide accommodations from which to judge a student's response to intervention. Clearly, the vast array of learning difficulties that may occur extends far beyond the scope of reading skills and can permeate any academic endeavor include socialization skills. Table 7-7 details the variety of learning pitfalls stemming from these types of disabilities.

Table 7-7

Sources of Academic Constraint That Suggest a Need for a Cognitive Neuropsychological Assessment

- **Reading difficulties** often involve a combination of factors that can include poor instruction, misguided or contradictory interventions, language deficits, executive function deficits involving the use of working memory, and impaired speed of access to lexical and/or verbal data. Sorting out which factors cause the apparent disability can be extremely difficult without systematic process-oriented assessment.

- **Math difficulties** can include a combination of factors such as sensory problems (visual and/or motor), language problems, executive function deficits, impaired speed/efficiency of access to information, and memory problems impacting recall of procedural knowledge when problem solving.

- **Written language** difficulties can be due to a wide variety of factors including motor skills deficits, perceptual difficulties, language deficits (receptive and/or expressive), poor abstract reasoning skills, and executive functions deficits in planning, organization, and working memory.

- **Attention deficits** might hinder any academic endeavor in addition to impacting listening comprehension skills and causing inconsistencies in learning. In addition, deficits in attention often result in impulsive classroom behavior that can lead to missed instructional time while related discipline issues are addressed. As well, attention problems may be the root cause of numerous social skills issues, or they may be a secondary deficit associated with primary emotional disorders.

- **Language skills** are fundamental to academic success as they provide the cornerstone for reading comprehension skills, written language skills, and allow for successful completion of word problems in mathematics. Furthermore, verbal reasoning measures and cognitive process measures reliably differentiate the faster and slower responders to remedial instruction (Berninger & Richards, 2002)

- **Behavioral deficits** can be due to a variety of intrinsic and extrinsic factors and therefore are just as subject to learning pitfalls as other more cognitively-oriented skills. Deficits in sensory functioning, language skills, executive functioning skills, attention skills, or sometimes just sheer frustration from being over-matched by the rigors of academic learning can lead to behavioral noncompliance and/or academic disengagement in the classroom. Targeted assessment can help pinpoint specific areas in which to intervene from an intrinsic end (counseling) extrinsic end (manipulating the environment for school success, and learning end (teaching desired pro-social skills).

The Process of School-Neuropsychological Assessment

A very thoughtful and pragmatic approach to school neuropsychological assessment has been proposed by Hale and Fiorello (2004) in their discussion of the Cognitive Hypothesis Testing (CHT) model. In this model, all available sources of information regarding a child's functioning are brought together to form specific hypotheses about the potential sources of constraints upon academic performance. Each hypothesis is then tested through a rigorous combination of assessment techniques designed to specifically tease out cognitive factors potentially hindering the learning process. For example, if a student displayed difficulty following verbal directions in the classroom, then a list of hypotheses is generated that includes all conceivable skill deficits contributing to difficulty following directions. These may include neurocognitive constructs such as auditory perception and discrimination, receptive language, sustained auditory attention, and executive functioning skills including working memory. There may be additional skill areas implicated if following verbal instructions also impacted note-taking skills, thus requiring further assessment of fine-motor skill development and visual perception as well.

Each hypothesis can be explored through a combination of four primary data collection techniques. The first includes a formal assessment of the particular construct in question. For instance, a test such as *Auditory Attention and Response Set* from the *NEPSY* may be administered to assess sustained attention to auditory stimuli. Second, qualitative information would need to be gathered not only from a classroom observation, but also by observing <u>how</u> a student performed on a given set of tasks. For instance, perhaps the student had many errors of commission, especially during part B of the *NEPSY Auditory Response Set*, thus implying that impulsive decisions tended to occur when following multiple, as opposed to single, sets of directions or task rules. Third, data collected through checklists completed by teachers and parents, rating scales, and observations can be helpful in determining the frequency and types of classroom situations where behaviors of concern occur most often (and sometimes, more importantly, where those behaviors *do not* occur). Lastly, non-normative data including teacher observations, work samples, grades, and actual classroom performance on various assignments need to be examined.

Typically, a thorough evaluation of a child's specific neurocognitive skill set requires the use of specialized assessment techniques and tools. These techniques are not available through lock-step administration of common intelligence tests or achievement measures because they are typically too "factorially-impure." In other words, the typical subtests on standardized assessment instruments often require a wide variety of neurocognitive skills in order to successfully complete the task. Consequently, when trying to determine the factors that influenced an child's performance on a particular task, there may be too many factors (skills) to consider. For example, if a student performed poorly on the *Digit Span* subtest from the *WISC-IV*, there may be a host of factors hindering test performance, including auditory sensory deficits, poor attention, poor working memory, limited understanding of the test directions due to language deficits, or even test anxiety. The goal of school based cognitive neuropsychological assessment is to determine what underlying factors are responsible for hindering learning, test performance, and classroom performance. Therefore, if a child performed poorly on a subtest measuring their ability to follow verbal directions, then the prudent examiner must explore an array of underlying factors to explain this poor test performance. As a result, further testing of multiple cognitive constructs needs to be explored in order to begin ruling-in and ruling out the potential sources of neurocognitive difficulty. In this example, if the child performed well on an individually administered test of verbal directions, then hypotheses about the reason for their difficulty in displaying this skill in the larger class setting would begin to focus less on auditory perception and receptive language deficits, and more on factors with attention. If the child also performed well on measures of attention, then analysis and hypothesis testing would begin to focus more on extrinsic factors such as motivation and emotional functioning.

The task analysis required for CHT can be performed on nearly any formal or informal assessment administered to a student. However, the ability to measure the individual skill areas identified by task analysis generally requires more specialized instruments designed specifically for a process-oriented assessment (Hale & Fiorello, 2004). One example familiar to most school psychologists is the structural format of the *Beery-Buktenica Developmental Test of Visual-Motor Integration*, 5th Edition (DTVMI-5). This measure is designed to assess the child's integration of visual perceptual skills and fine motor skills associated with drawing various geometric shapes. The main task of the DTVMI-5 requires the child to copy drawings of increasing complexity ranging from a basic horizontal line through line drawings of a 3-dimensional representation of a cube. Clearly, this test requires both visual-perceptual skills and fine motor coordination. If a student performs poorly on the overall task, the examiner can assume the child has skill deficits in either visual perception, fine motor coordination, or the integration of these two skill areas. Fortunately, this instrument provides more 'factorially-pure' supplemental measures for determining which specific skill area is most problematic for the child.

The first supplemental condition of the DTVMI-5 is called *Visual Perception*, and requires the child to look at a target shape contained in a dark box, then to select its exact match from among a number of similar choices below. The child is permitted either to make a pencil mark to indicate their choice, or to simply point. In this way, nearly all demands for motor skills are eliminated, and the results of this supplemental condition provide a more 'pure' assessment of visual perceptual skills. The second supplemental condition of the DTVMI-5 is called the *Motor Coordination* subtest, and attempts to eliminate the demand for visual perceptual skills in order to assess fine motor skills. This subtest requires the child to connect dots placed between two dark lines that form an outline of the same geometric forms contained in other portions of the test. This task still requires some rudimentary skills of visual perception, though the demand for such skills is greatly minimized by the presence of guiding lines and dots that must be connected in order to produce the required drawing. Therefore, it is possible to determine the relative integrity of each component skill on this test, namely, visual perception and fine motor coordination. The DTVMI-5 is not a neuropsychological instrument per se, though its structure clearly provides a very good example of how practitioners can employ a neuropsychological approach to engage in assessment as part of a Cognitive Hypothesis Testing (CHT).

The overarching philosophy of incorporating a school based cognitive neuropsychological assessment with respect to reading is to determine the underlying causes of a child's reading difficulties. As described in Chapter 3, there may be significant deficits with phoneme awareness or phonological processing—both vital in the early acquisition of literacy skills. As described in Chapter 4, there may be significant deficits surrounding the orthography of words, which can often lead to poor fluency skills as the visual aspects of reading never become fully automatic. As described in Chapter 6, there may be significant language-related deficits, working memory issues, or executive dysfunction hindering the comprehension process. As described in Chapter 5, there may be multiple cognitive constructs impairing the reading process resulting in a very severe form of dyslexia called Mixed Dyslexia. The fact remains that the underlying neurocognitive processes responsible for modulating the reading process need to be isolated, measured, and analyzed in order to determine why a student has not responded to evidence based interventions and, more importantly, to help determine what intervention a student may have more success with. As outlined in Table 7-8, the role of the school psychologist is vital during the data collection and decision making process within an integrated RTI model.

Table 7-8

Role of the School Psychologist in an Integrated RTI Service Delivery Model

- Participate in Data Analysis Teaming decisions at curriculum level for Tier 1 (using collective DIBELS, 4-Sight, statewide assessment, or other group achievement test data). These decisions should involve selection of core curricula based on review of evidence supporting curricula and review of school-specific data regarding the needs of each student as indicated by reviewing group achievement/progress data.

- Participate in pre-referral intervention at Tiers 2 and 3 by attending team meetings for individual students and helping to analyze individual progress data to determine whether the student needs a more intense intervention, a different type of intervention, or targeted assessment in order to determine the appropriate next step in intervention. At times, group data may still need to be analyzed at Tiers 2 and 3 in order to help assess whether evidence based interventions were implemented in the manner in which they are intended (with fidelity).

- Conduct a targeted or comprehensive assessment once parent permission is obtained, utilizing specialized individual measures targeting specific constructs involved in the reading process.

- Assist team in determining need for inter-tier movement of students based on individual needs, progress, or data from targeted assessment.

- Participate in all review meetings after unsatisfactory progress in Tier 2 or Tier 3.

- Conduct any additional assessment required after unsatisfactory progress in Tier 3. NOTE: This additional assessment should not only establish eligibility for special education, but also assist in providing guidance for the design of an appropriate IEP. By this point nearly all data necessary to determine eligibility should already have been gathered as part of the problem-solving pre-referral intervention process.

Key Components of School-Neuropsychological Assessment

Background History:

Effective school-neuropsychological assessment should begin with a careful review of background information and developmental history. This may uncover any potential neurocognitive risk factors such as peri-natal or post-natal exposure to toxins or infectious diseases, birth trauma such as oxygen deprivation (anoxia) during delivery, recurrent infections such as those associated with known neurocognitive impact such as HIV or strep infections, traumatic brain injury, birthing complications, and extended high fevers (Lezak, Howieson & Loring, 2004). It is helpful to use specific and comprehensive questioning to ascertain the full extent of relevant neurocognitive risk factors. Oftentimes, parents are unaware of the relevance of specific information and may fail to share potentially important details such as an injury, infection, or birth complication that may have seemed insignificant because it failed to yield any persisting physical symptoms. Such events may nevertheless have profound implications for the clinical presentation of their child (Rourke, van der Vlugt, & Rourke, 2002). One of the most important questions for the examiner to ask is whether or not there is a history of reading difficulties in the family. However, whether or not these difficulties led to a diagnosed reading disability is irrelevant due to historically extreme variability and dubious accuracy in prior identification of learning disabilities. According to Shastry (2007), most reading difficulties have an underlying neuroanatomical basis within the temporal-parietal or language centers of the brain. Furthermore, reading disorders are highly familial and heritable, with current research focusing on chromosomes 1, 2, 3, 6, 11, 13, 15, and 18. The most recent evidence suggests that dyslexia may have its roots in abnormal migration and maturation of neurons during early fetal development dictated by four candidate genes (KIAA 0319, DYX1C1, DCDC2, and ROBO1) (Shastry, 2007). Specific written questionnaires, developmental history forms, and parent interviews reviewing all available medical, educational, and prior evaluation activities and records are essential.

Observations:

Observations of the student are also important to provide a full picture of the child's functioning and also to assist in forming hypotheses regarding constraints on learning that can be tested through formal assessment procedures (Spreen, Risser, & Edgell, 1995). General observations should include information about the child's apparent attention capacity, ability to remain on-task, overall affect and mood, fine and gross motor coordination, interactions with peers and adults, and overall temperament style. Specific observations germane to the reading process should include reading rate and fluency, qualitative analysis of reading errors on phonologically-regular versus phonologically-irregular words, intonation when reading aloud, fatigue factors when reading, general language skills, decoding strategies for unfamiliar words, and comprehension skills.

Intelligence Test Measures:

Since the passing of IDEA 2004, the fundamental goal of intelligence testing should no longer be to determine a student's full scale intelligence score. Instead, intelligence testing should entail the use of process-oriented measures that enable the examiner to tease out specific patterns of strengths and weaknesses that, either beneficially or adversely, contribute to the learning process. Clearly, intelligence is a concept underscored by multiple cognitive and social constructs that contribute to the expression of intelligent behavior. However, the examiner must avoid asking the question of "How smart are you?" which was a necessary evil under the discrepancy paradigm, and begin asking a new question: namely, "How are you smart?" School psychologists are now beginning to understand that human intellectual functioning is comprised of multiple aspects of cognition, as reflected by the structural complexities and multiple scoring and interpretive options inherent in newer tests such as the Wechsler Intelligence Scale for Children - 4th Edition (WISC-IV) and the WISC-IV Integrated, the Woodcock Johnson - Third Edition, Tests of Cognitive Abilities (WJ-III), and Stanford-Binet 5th Edition. Table 7-9 highlights some very general patterns of performance sometimes observed on two of these instruments in individuals with reading disabilities.

Table 7-9

Intelligence Test Patterns Often Observed for Dyslexia Subtypes

WISC-IV DOMAIN PATTERNS:

Lower Verbal Comprehension Index = Dysphonetic Dyslexia

Lower Perceptual Resoning Index = Surface Dyslexia

Lower Working Memory Index = Comprehension Issues

Lower Processing Speed Index = Related to all of the above

WJ-III SUBTEST & INDEX SCORE PATTERNS:

Dysphonetic Dyslexia:

- Lower Verbal Comprehension
- Lower Auditory Processing (Sound Blending, Incomplete Words, etc)

Surface Dyslexia:

- Slower processing speed (lower scores on Visual Matching, Decision Speed, and Rapid Picture Naming subtests)
- Lower visual processing scores (Spatial Relations, Picture Recognition)

Poor Reading Comprehension:

- Lower Crystallized & Fluid Intelligence (Analysis-Synthesis, Concept Formation)
- Diminished working memory (Numbers Reversed, Auditory Working Memory)

Phonological Processing:

According to the National Reading Panel (2000), two of the five core linguistic skills that children need to acquire in order to become functionally independent readers are *phonemic awareness* (the manipulation of spoken syllables in words), and *phonics* (letter-sound correspondences. The term *phonological awareness* refers to an awareness of the spoken word form, as opposed to its actual meaning. Of critical importance is a working knowledge of the serial position of the sounds which comprise the acoustical properties of the word. In the English language, there are 44 phonemes that represent the sound properties of words. According to Uhry and Clark (2005), it is important to distinguish between phonics knowledge (which is more of a lower-level, paired associate type of skill linking letters with sounds) and *phonological awareness* (which is the metacognitive understanding of the spatial arrangements of sounds in words). As Temple (2002) observed, most students with reading deficits have difficulty with phonological processing that may stem from a neural disorganization of the temporal-parietal regions in the left hemisphere with other cortical regions involved in the reading process. In fact, functional MRIs have shown that individuals with dyslexia tend to activate other brain regions, most notably frontal lobe sites, to assist them with phonological processing skills (Shaywitz et al., 2003). The consequence for recruiting these brain regions is a tendency to consciously focus on the phonemic properties of the word, thereby leading to reduced fluency and poor comprehension skills. As Noble & McCandliss (2005) observed, there tends to be too much cortical energy devoted to "crashing through" words, thereby sacrificing the comprehension process. As a result, oral reading becomes much more effortful than it needs to be, and these children quickly lose interest and motivation to read outside of school as well.

Rapid Naming Tests:

Wolf and Bowers (1999) have shown that rapid automatic naming tasks are consistently predictive of word-level reading difficulties as well as passage comprehension. These researchers have highlighted the importance of early rapid naming skills with the subsequent development of reading fluency. Rapid naming involves the ability to look at a visual stimulus and assign a verbal tag to that stimulus. It is important to note that effective rapid naming requires numerous cognitive operations including attention skills, executive functioning skills, accurate retrieval skills, and processing speed (Wolf & Bowers, 1999). Most learning-disabled students have difficulty with automatic and rapid naming tasks because their ability to rapidly recall archived information, albeit letters, numbers, or words, tends to be compromised. It is interesting to note that naming speed, and not phonological awareness skills, tends to be a better predictor of reading difficulty in languages which are more phonologically consistent such as German, Dutch, Finnish, and Spanish (Wolf, 1999). Lastly, recent studies conducted by Mirsa, Katzir, Wolf, and Poldrack (2004) have suggested that not all rapid naming tasks were created equal. In other words, rapid and automatic letter naming tasks were more predictive of word level reading skills than tasks involving the rapid and automatic naming of familiar objects. Therefore, school psychologists who generally use tests of rapid naming such as the *Comprehensive Test of Phonological Processing (CTOPP)* or the *Process Assessment of the Learner (PAL)* should differentiate between the ability to rapidly name letters and phonemes versus rapidly naming objects. The wise examiner may want to explore the *DIBELS* as a more viable measure of rapid naming skills as they pertain specifically to reading.

Memory Tests:

Working memory subserves the reading process by temporarily suspending previously-read information while simultaneously allowing the reader to acquire new information. Deficits in working memory can certainly disrupt a student's ability to make appropriate linkages among information in the text and therefore hinder reading comprehension skills. The ability to utilize background knowledge and draw inferences from the text can facilitate the comprehension process by allowing for a deeper and more enriched engagement with the passage. Brosnan et al. (2002) suggested that deficits in working memory can also hinder a child's ability to recall the sequential order of events in a story and prevent the child from organizing contextual information in a cohesive manner. It is not surprising, then, that most classroom teachers often lament the organizational difficulties of children with reading disabilities.

According to Reiter et al. (2004), children with dyslexia demonstrate impairments in tasks that measure both verbal working memory systems and visual (or 'figural') working memory systems. Therefore, working memory deficits can also impair the ability to recognize words in print in addition to the aforementioned comprehension deficits. For instance, the inability to recall the orthography of words can lead to inconsistencies in recalling spelling rules and boundaries. Since phonological awareness involves an awareness of sounds that occupy a particular sequential order, deficits in working memory can also hinder the ability to stitch together sounds from a multi-syllabic word as the fledgling reader may forget the sequential arrangement of sounds.

Fluency Skills:

Research in the cognitive neuropsychology of reading has provided compelling evidence that skilled readers activate the quicker, more rapid, and automatic pathways to decipher words in print (Pugh et al., 2000; McCandliss & Noble, 2003; Shaywitz, 2004: Owen et al., 2004). This pathway is primarily situated in the posterior portions of the brain, along the interface of the occipital and temporal lobes, in a brain region called the fusiform gyrus. The occipital-temporal pathways form a highly interconnected neural system that responds in just 200 milliseconds to the visual features of a word to allow for automatic and rapid word recognition skills. However, dyslexics do not activate these pathways. Instead, they rely on different pathways, forged in part by compensatory mechanisms, which are slower and less efficient to assist with word recognition skills (Shaywitz & Shaywitz, 2005). These slower pathways over-rely on breaking down each word into its phonological core, and therefore the reading process never becomes automatic. This is often observed in children who default to diligently sounding-out all words that they see, even high frequency words such as /the/, /with/, /and/, etc. that tend to be more automatic for skilled readers.

The National Reading Panel (2000) identified reading fluency as one of the five pillars of reading. The goal of any good reading program is to ultimately have the quicker-paced pathways in the occipital-temporal regions of the brain assume responsibility for the reading process, thereby freeing up other cortical regions to assist in comprehension. When the slower-paced neural circuitry in the brain *(temporal-parietal regions)* assumes full responsibility for the reading process, then fluency may become compromised. In addition, reading becomes an overly effortful and mundane process thereby robbing the child of the most rewarding aspect of reading, comprehending the message from the words. It is important for educators to begin recording reading fluency and speed using curriculum based measurement techniques. This will help enable teachers to closely monitor reading proficiency, and from a neuropsychological standpoint, measure the extent with which these quicker pathways become acclimated to taking over the process of reading from the slower pathways. Curriculum based measurement (CBM) has provided psychologists and educators with a quicker, more cost effective, and more ecologically-valid means of measuring reading progress in children than nationally-normed tests. As Fuchs (1998) noted, when teachers utilize CBM techniques to write specific data based goals and objectives, as well as to monitor academic progress, student achievement improves.

Executive Functioning:

As discussed in Chapter 3, the National Reading Panel (2000) classified reading comprehension skills and vocabulary development as being two critically important learning pillars in the reading process. Executive functions basically represent a cascade of numerous cognitive constructs responsible for a variety of academic ventures necessary for learning including task initiation, maintaining a persistent pattern of effort, resistance to distractions, and selecting and/or revising a general strategy or course of action when actively engaged in a problem solving task. In the reading process, executive functioning skills represent a student's ability to stitch together relevant aspects of the text in order to derive meaning from print. It has been estimated that some 10% of all school aged children have good decoding skills but possess specific difficulties with reading comprehension skills (Nation & Snowling, 1997). Table 6-4 (see Chapter 6) represents the core facets of executive functioning and their relative contribution to the comprehension process.

Table 7-10 highlights specific resources for engaging in cognitive neuropsychological assessment of reading disorders by reviewing nine core constructs that should be measured and analyzed. Table 7-11 gives examples of instruments used in school neuropsychological assessment. The specific tests under each construct are not meant to represent an exhaustive list, but rather to provide the educational professional with a sample of instruments from which to choose. Each school based assessment team is encouraged to select an instrument under each construct in order to craft their own unique assessment battery to better identify reading disorders in children. Based upon the relative integrity of each construct, school teams can now begin to match an appropriate intervention strategy (See Chapter 9) with the unique neurocognitive profile of the child in order to provide the best chance for educational success.

Table 7-10

9 Core Areas to Assess and Examples of Instruments for Each

1. COGNITIVE FUNCTIONING:

Wechsler Intelligence Scale for Children - 4th Edition - Integrated (WISC- IV-Int)

Woodcock-Johnson - 3rd Edition, Tests of Cognitive Abilities (WJ-III: Cog)

Cognitive Assessment System (CAS)

Stanford-Binet Intelligence Scale - 5th Edition (SB-5)

Reynolds Intellectual Assessment Scales (RIAS)

---

2. PHONEMIC/PHONOLOGICAL AWARENESS:

WJ-III Cognitive:	Sound Blending Auditory Attention	Incomplete Words
WJ-III Achievement:	Spelling of Sounds Word Attack	Sound Awareness Spelling
WIAT-II:	Pseudoword Decoding	
NEPSY-2:	Phonological Processing	
KTEA II:	Nonsense Word Decoding	

Comprehensive Test of Phonological Processing (C-TOPP)

Process Assessment of the Learner (PAL):	Receptive Coding Pseudoword Decoding Phonemes	Rhyming Syllables Rimes

Table 7-10 (continued)

9 Core Areas to Assess and Examples of Instruments for Each

Test of Phonological Awareness Skills (TOPAS):	Incomplete Words Sound Sequencing	Rhyming Sound Deletion
DIBELS:	Phoneme Segmentation Fluency	NonsenseWord Fluency

---

3. RAPID NAMING TESTS:

WJ-III Cognitive:	Rapid Picture Naming	Retrieval Fluency
NEPSY-2:	Speeded Naming	Verbal Fluency
PAL:	Rapid Automatic Naming	
DIBELS:	Letter Naming Fluency	
D-KEFS:	Verbal Fluency	
KTEA II:	Naming Facility	

Rapid Automatized Naming & Rapid Alternating Stimulus Tests (RAN/RAS)

---

4. VERBAL MEMORY TESTS:

WJ-III Cognitive:	Visual-Auditory Learning (immediate & delayed-recall) Auditory Working Memory Memory for Words	Numbers Reversed Incomplete Words
NEPSY-2:	Narrative Memory Comprehension of Instructions Memory for Faces Repetition - Nonsense Words	Verbal Fluency List Learning Memory for Names Sentence Repetition
WJ-III Achievement:	Understanding Directions Story Recall (immediate and delayed-recall)	
PAL:	Note-taking Task A	Story Retell

Children's Memory Scales (CMS) - Verbal Subtests

Wide Range Assessment of Memory and Learning - 2nd Edition (WRAML-2) - Verbal Subtests

---

Table 7-10 (continued)

9 Core Areas to Assess and Examples of Instruments for Each

California Verbal Learning Test - Children's Version (CVLT-C)

Test of Memory and Learning (TOMAL) - Verbal Subtests

---

5. READING FLUENCY MEASURES:

WJ-III Achievement: Reading Fluency

Gray-Oral Reading Tests - 4th Edition (GORT-4)

Curriculum Based Measurement

DIBELS: Oral Reading Fluency

KTEA II: Word Reading Fluency
                                     Decoding Fluency
                                     Associational Fluency

Informal Reading Inventories

---

6. VISUAL SPATIAL SKILLS:

WJ-III Cognitive subtests:	Spatial Relations	Visual Matching
	Cross Out	Planning
	Picture Recognition	Pair Cancellation
NEPSY-2:	Imitating Hand Positions	Design Copy
	Visuomotor Precision	Arrows
	Geometric Puzzles	Picture Puzzles
PAL:	Receptive Coding	Copying
KABC II:	Gestalt Closure	
	Triangles	
	Block Counting	

Beery-Buktenica Developmental test of Visual-Motor Integration - 5th Edition (DTVMI-5)

Jordan Left-Right Reversal Test

Table 7-10 (continued)

9 Core Areas to Assess and Examples of Instruments for Each

Bender Visual Motor Gestalt Test-II

Rey Complex Figure Test

DKEFS   Trailmaking Test (Condition 1)   Design Fluency

Test of Visual Perceptual Skills -3

Developmental Test of Visual Perception - 2nd Edition

---

7. __ATTENTION:__

WJ-III Cognitive subtests:	Numbers Reversed	Auditory Attention
	Auditory-Working Memory	Pair Cancellation

WJ-III Achievement: Understanding Directions
                                  Story Recall (immediate and delayed-recall)

D-KEFS: Color-Word Interference (Condition 4)
                                  Trail Making Test (Condition 4)
                                  Verbal Fluency (Condition 3)
                                  Design Fluency (Condition 3)

NEPSY-2:   Auditory Attention and Response Set   Visual Attention

Conners' Continuous Performance Test - 2nd Edition (CPT-2)

Test of Everyday Attention for Children (TEA-Ch):	Selective Attention	Shifting Attention
	Sustained Attention	

KABC-II: Word Order (without color interference)
                                  Number Recall
                                  Hand Movement

Cognitive Assessment System:	Number Detection	Expressive Attention
	Receptive Attention	

Behavior Rating Scales: ACTers
                                        ADDES
                                        Brown Attention Deficit Disorders Scales
                                        Conners' Scales

Table 7-10 (continued)

9 Core Areas to Assess and Examples of Instruments for Each

8. EXECUTIVE FUNCTIONING:

WJ-III Cognitive:
Visual-Auditory Learning   Concept Formation
Auditory-Working Memory   Numbers Reversed
Auditory Attention   Pair Cancellation
Retrieval Fluency   Planning
Analysis-Synthesis

WJ-III Achievement: Understanding Directions

D-KEFS: (Every subtest on the D-KEFS)

NEPSY-2:
Auditory Attn. & Response Set   Design Fluency
Visual Attention   Verbal Fluency
Inhibition   Animal Sorting

BRIEF:
Parent & Teacher Forms (ages 8 - 18)
Self Rating Form (ages 11 - 18)

Conners' Continuous Performance Test - 2nd Edition (CPT-2)

Wisconsin Card Sorting Test (WCST)

Category Test

Stroop Test

KABC II:
Conceptual Thinking   Story Completion
Pattern Reasoning   Triangles
Rover

Porteus Maze Test

9. BACKGROUND HISTORY:

Birth History Including ANY Complications   Developmental Milestone Acquisition
Hearing Problems, Tubes, etc.   Visual Problems
Current and Prior Medications   Head Injuries or Loss of Consciousness
History of High Fevers, Seizures, etc.   Any Medical Disorders
Family Medical History   Family Educational History (esp. dyslexia)
Prior Evaluation Results   Prior Early Intervention Services
Progress Monitoring Results   Standardized Group Achievement Test Scores

Table 7-11

Examples of Instruments for School Neuropsychological Assessment

- Woodcock-Johnson - 3rd Edition (WJ-III) Tests of Cognitive Abilities
- Woodcock-Johnson - 3rd Edition (WJ-III) Tests of Achievement
- Diagnostic Supplement to WJ-III Tests of Cognitive Abilities
- Dean-Woodcock Neuropsychological Battery (DWNB) (ages 4 - 90+)
- Delis-Kaplan Executive Function System (D-KEFS) (ages 8 and up)
- Conners' Continuous Performance Test - 2nd Edition (CPT-2)
- Developmental Test of Visual Motor Integration - 5th Edition (DTVMI-5)
- NEPSY-2nd Edition (ages 3 - 16)
- Behavior Rating Inventory of Executive Functions (BRIEF)
- Children's Memory Scale (ages 5 - 16)
- Wechsler Memory Scale - 3rd Edition (WMS-III) (ages 16 & up only)
- California Verbal Learning Test-Child Version (CVLT-C) (ages 5-16)
- Wechsler Intelligence Scale for Children - 4th Edition (WISC-4) Integrated
- Wechsler Individual Achievement Test - 2nd Edition (WIAT-2)
- Test of Memory and Learning (TOMAL) (ages 5-19)
- Process Assessment of the Learner (PAL)
- Wide Range Assessment of Memory and Learning - 2nd Edition (WRAML-2) (ages 5-90)

Summary:

The field of school psychology has come a long way since the term *learning disability* was first described by Samuel Kirk. The profession is finally at a point where we have reached a pinnacle in our scientifically-based understanding of brain-behavior relationships, and our assessment technology has advanced rapidly to reflect this progress. However, school psychologists are faced with a reactionary movement in educational practice that threatens to ignore such advances and attempts to discredit psychometric assessment as a foundation for intervention. It is incumbent upon school psychologists to seek out and acquire advanced training in assessment methodology in order to integrate assessment-for-intervention into their practice of identifying and intervening with students with learning problems. It has become abundantly clear that to choose either a pure RTI model or a pure psychometric model for identifying and intervening with learning problems will inevitably lead to a disservice for a portion of children with learning problems. A marriage of these two approaches is absolutely essential in order to ensure that 'no child is left behind.' Suffice it to say, anything less may very well constitute educational malpractice.

CHAPTER 8

Two Models, Two Cases

It is now time to turn our attention to a small town in Pleasantville in order to begin a more positive discourse of the relative merits of RTI when integrated with a cognitive neuropsychological model. Pleasantville is a relatively small rural school district in Pennsylvania with an enrollment of approximately 1300 students. The district consists overwhelmingly of Caucasians with a very small population of minorities who are typically transient. The socioeconomic status of the district is predominantly lower middle-class. Prior to the 2003-04 school year, Pleasantville's core reading curriculum was a Houghton-Mifflin series that primarily emphasized a whole-language approach to reading instruction. After receipt of a Reading-First grant, the district switched to the Open Court reading series, which can best be described as a balanced approach to literacy instruction, containing both explicit instruction in phonetic principles and aspects of an experiential language arts curriculum.

Pleasantville is a district that has continued to employ the *Instructional Support Team (IST)* approach to pre-referral intervention. Consequently, two full-time Instructional Support (IS) teachers are employed by the district to coordinate the IST program. Based on individual needs for students, IST membership also includes an administrator, guidance counselor, school psychologist, Title I teachers, speech/language support teachers, and classroom teachers. In addition, the district also employs several full-time reading and math coaches with extensive experience in each respective curricular area. Table 8-1 depicts the job description of the IS teacher, while Table 8-2 illustrates a typical IST process.

Table 8-1

Instructional Support Teacher Roles

- Serve as a "coach" or mentor for regular education teacher.
- Collects baseline curriculum based measurement data on academic achievement.
- Conducts frequent classroom observations.
- Provides assistance with charting and analyzing daily curriculum based measurement data.
- Assists in linking assessment data with interventions.
- Coordinates training others to assist with intervention implementation.
- Monitors student progress.
- Schedules and coordinates IST meetings.
- Provides feedback for teachers on strategy implementation.

Table 8-2

Instructional Support Team Meeting Process

- ***Problem Identification:*** Any school staff or parent can contact the IS team to discuss a child.
- ***Problem Certification:*** The first 10 minutes of a meeting is devoted to hearing the referring team members' initial concerns.
- ***Problem Analysis:*** The next 10 minutes is devoted to brainstorming possible strategies and interventions.
- ***Goal Setting:*** The next 5 minutes involves the IS team making a determination as to which strategies should be implemented to help the student achieve behavioral and/or academic success.
- ***Plan Implementation:*** The IS teacher summarizes the choices and develops a plan of intervention for the classroom teacher or designated staff member to implement the strategies.
- ***Plan Evaluation:*** A date to reconvene and examine student progress is established. The meeting is adjourned in less than 30 minutes.

Pleasantville's current RTI approach for reading instruction consists of a three-tier system. Tier I includes the Open Court reading series in which all students are instructed for 90 minutes daily. The reading block is divided differently for students based on their rate of learning as determined by progress monitoring results. At Tier I, all students are monitored three times per year using the *Dynamic Indicators of Basic Early Literacy Skills (DIBELS)*. DIBELS consists of a set of standardized, individually-administered fluency measures of early literacy development designed to be short (one minute) and to regularly monitor the development of reading readiness skills. The specific measures include *Initial Sounds Fluency (ISF), Phonemic Segmentation Fluency (PSF), Nonsense Word Fluency (NSF),* and *Oral Reading Fluency (ORF)*. These fluency based measures are linked to one another, both psychometrically and theoretically, and have been demonstrated in research to be a good barometer of later reading proficiency.

Students identified as being at risk through these assessments receive Tier 2 interventions that involve an additional 30 minutes of reading instruction in the form of small group instruction with the classroom teacher, Title I teacher, or reading specialist. Tier 2 instruction involves participation in an increased allotment of direct instructional time that emphasizes either phonics-based skills such as word decoding skills or fluency-building activities once basic phonological skills have been established. The instruction can be delivered in either a *"pull-out"* (outside of the regular classroom) program using Title I reading teachers, or *"push-in"* support involving direct, skill-based, small-group instruction within the regular education classroom. At Tier 2, students are monitored using DIBELS results on a more frequent basis, with data collected every two to four weeks. Students who do not demonstrate adequate skill improvement on these assessments after receiving a variety of Tier 2 interventions are then recommended for Tier 3 interventions.

Tier 3 interventions consist of several options based on each student's level of need and specific area of instruction. Those students who continue to struggle with basic letter-sound correspondence can receive further increases in their direct instructional time by receiving a *double dose* of instruction. For instance, these students might participate in the Tier 2 instruction in their regular classroom, and then receive additional support in a resource classroom for further instruction. However, when a *double dose* of support is needed, this sometimes involves sacrificing the more balanced literacy instruction and comprehension-building activities in the regular classroom. Therefore, students in Tier 3 often receive direct skill instruction in basic reading that focuses on skills such as letter-sound awareness, word decoding skills, and fluency-building interventions. Hence, Tier 3 interventions are flexible, and often consist of direct small-group instruction with a reading specialist for two 30-minute blocks of time, or one 30-minute block, in addition to a 30-minute block of direct small-group instruction with the classroom teacher. Students at the most intensive levels of intervention can receive small-group instruction through nearly any combination of delivery services based on their individual areas of need as determined by progress monitoring. Oftentimes, students in Tier 3 leave their regular classroom for the entire reading and language arts instructional block in order to receive instruction at the most intensive level available. Monitoring of skills acquisition increases in frequency to a weekly basis, with the data reviewed by a diverse team consisting of the reading coaches, regular and special education teachers, Title I teachers, school psychologists, and the IST teachers. Those students who maintain appropriate progress in reading skill development are then returned back to the Tier 2 intervention level and continue to be monitored. On the other hand, students who do not make appropriate progress despite Tier 3 interventions are usually recommended for a further evaluation to determine their potential eligibility for special education services.

At this point, one must ask what strategies, supports, accommodations, or benefits are offered to children who qualify for special education services. In reality, there are three main advantages to both schools and students when qualifying for special education services under the coding of Learning Disabled. First, students are afforded specific legal rights and schools have different accountability standards when teaching a child with an educational disability. Second, schools may provide a host of accommodations and supports not otherwise afforded during the statewide standardized assessments that are required by the No Child Left Behind legislation. Lastly, most specialized instructional programs such as *Alphabetic Phonics, Horizons, Corrective Reading, Read Naturally,* etc., are scripted (see Chapter 9). Students who are found to have a specific learning disability have the right to an Individualized Educational Plan, which can alter the script and allow educators to modify and tailor already existing programs to meet the student's particular need. In other words, teachers can deviate from the predictable model of scripted interventions and proceed at their own pace using whatever materials they deem appropriate. In most cases when a student is recommended for an assessment to determine their eligibility for special education, much of the information has already been gathered along the way as part of the data collection process. This data may include informal reading inventories, statewide test results, running records, curriculum-based measurement, curricular benchmark records, classroom observations, and nationally-normed test data as well. It should be noted that within an integrated model of RTI, most evaluations occur after a child has not responded to a variety of evidence-based interventions. Furthermore, the scope and sequence of the evaluation is not necessarily to determine a child's eligibility for special education services, but to examine learning from a brain-behavioral paradigm to determine the most appropriate course of education treatment options given the student's unique profile of cognitive and academic strengths, weaknesses, and needs. The following cases attempt to illustrate this point.

Case #1: John

John began his educational career earlier than most after being identified through Pleasantville's kindergarten screening program as a student in need of further support and assistance. He qualified for the district's Jumpstart kindergarten program, a summer early entrance program designed to provide students with academic or behavioral delays an opportunity to enhance school readiness skills, prior to entry in the fall. John had displayed numerous academic and behavioral concerns, and had not been enrolled in any prior formal educational setting. His parents reported escalating behavioral problems in the home that included a variety of oppositional behaviors such as intentional enuresis when he did not get his way and even some early fire-setting behaviors. John's siblings were all much older, and his family lived in an extremely isolated area with limited opportunities for peer interaction skills. John displayed a variety of poor social interaction skills in group settings, and also exhibited great difficulty following rules, directions, and requests made by staff. For instance, on several occasions he ran away from school staff when denied his way, and was a safety risk due to his blatant disregard for school rules. One of the main goals of the school staff was to make some progress in his school readiness behaviors by including him in Jumpstart kindergarten programming.

Upon entering kindergarten, a functional behavioral intervention plan had already been developed and John received both Title I reading and math services. It should be noted that both reading and math instruction were delivered in a small group format outside of the regular classroom. Some of the behavioral interventions included basic sticker charts for appropriate classroom behaviors and peer interaction skills. Since John was observed to thrive on adult attention, his primary reward, aside from frequent verbal reinforcement and praise, was to earn 10 minutes of play time in the school gymnasium with a school staff member and peer buddy of his choice. There were significant improvements noted in his behavioral functioning over the course of John's kindergarten year. Nevertheless, his academic gains were minimal and he ended the year with marked delays compared to peers.

Both academic and behavioral interventions were maintained throughout John's first grade year. He continued to make progress in both areas, though his behavioral progress far outpaced his academic progress, and once again he ended the school year with significant delays. John's parents requested he be retained in the first grade. Initially, the school staff was hesitant to honor this request, though two key factors eased their concerns about retention. First, John was somewhat younger and physically smaller than his classmates due in part to his late birth date. Second, John was transferring to a different school the following year. His new school had a variety of reading supports and interventions beginning in 1st grade, thus there were more options for intensive academic support should he remain at this grade level. One particularly appealing intervention included participation in a new reading skill support program in his regular classroom with several additional peers.

John was retained in 1st grade, and coincidentally, the school transitioned to a different core reading series that emphasized a more balanced literacy approach involving direct phonic skills instruction integrated within the experiential literature component of the curriculum. In addition, his new school now devoted a 90-minute block of instructional time for reading and language arts instruction. At the time, John was receiving small group instruction in letter-sound correspondence and word attack skills within his regular classroom setting. He made appropriate progress in phoneme segmentation fluency (PSF) and remained above benchmark levels as determined by the DIBELS. On this assessment his PSF scores, which reflect correct phonemes identified under speeded conditions, improved from 50 to 56 to 64 correct phonemes over the fall, winter, and spring DIBELS assessments, respectively. However, John failed to demonstrate appropriate progress in the area of Nonsense Word Fluency (NWF) on the DIBELS with scores of 30, 36, and 37 correct phonemes identified over the fall, winter, and spring assessments. His Oral Reading Fluency (ORF) scores showed improvement from the winter to spring assessments, but his improvement (from 36 to 45 correct words per minute) was not as significant as most of his classroom peers.

Considering John's inconsistent progress on these reading readiness indicators, coupled with the emergence of mild concerns over his writing skills, the IST recommended that John receive a more intense and systemic intervention upon matriculating to 2nd grade. John was recommended for participation in the *Alphabetic Phonics* program (see Chapter 9), which is basically a derivative of the traditional Orton-Gillingham multi-sensory approach to reading. It is based on the assumption that 80 percent of the 30,000 most commonly used English words follow a predictable code, and are therefore phonologically consistent or regular (Uhry & Clark, 2005). *Alphabetic*

Phonics is a bottom-up or synthetic method of teaching reading, meaning the theoretical foundation of the program is hierarchically structured and sequenced based on a set of learned rules and correspondences for letters and sounds. Progress monitoring is documented by benchmark measures examining letter knowledge, alphabetizing skills, reading, spelling, and handwriting.

John had little difficulty meeting quarterly benchmark skills in the *Alphabetic Phonics* program, and continued to make steady progress throughout 2nd grade. During the final grading period, a DIBELS assessment revealed John was performing at benchmark level on Oral Reading Fluency with a reading rate of 102 correct words per minute. John also participated in a summer school reading program intended to maintain his reading fluency rates while also working on building comprehension skills. This proved successful for him because he began his third grade year with a reading rate of 99 correct words per minute on the fall DIBELS assessment. Therefore, John was able to avoid the average 10 to 20 percent decline in fluency rates that is typically observed over the summer with many students.

John's progress on the fall, winter, and spring DIBELS assessments for his 3rd grade year revealed limited gains in Oral Reading Fluency. Perhaps his earlier attainment and maintenance of benchmark-level fluency rates in the *Alphabetic Phonics* program precluded him from participating in the comprehension-building aspects of the language arts curriculum that occurred within the regular classroom. Nevertheless, his 3rd grade teacher sought IST assistance to address concerns regarding John's reading comprehension difficulties as well. The IST worked with his teacher throughout the year to develop basic positive behavior support strategies to increase on-task rates, organizational skills, and work completion rates, as well as to reduce the use of instructional methods (teaching primarily from overheads) that seemed to trigger difficulties for John and several other students.

Throughout 3rd grade, John's reading skill intervention continued to be the *Alphabetic Phonics* program, and he occasionally participated on an as-needed basis in reading skill reinforcement activities that were being delivered by a Title I teacher in his classroom. John's greatest benefit from this instruction was the acquisition of new vocabulary and language development skills specifically germane to content-oriented subjects. Certainly, a reduced level of reading skills intervention being needed was one indication of his continued progress, even though his oral reading fluency rates did not increase substantially over the course of his third grade year. A second indicator of continued progress was seen in his performance on statewide assessment tests that were administered in the latter half of his third grade year. He earned a proficient score, indicating satisfactory academic performance and a solid understanding and adequate display of both reading and math skills. Therefore, it became increasingly clear that John's progress transferred beyond his classroom, as evidenced by his ability to independently and successfully apply such skills in a variety of contexts. Furthermore, John also performed within the proficient range during his 4th grade year. This suggested that gains from earlier interventions were not only becoming increasingly evident over the course of his third grade year, but were also being maintained throughout the summer and into 4th grade. John was dismissed from the *Alphabetic Phonics* program midway through his 4th grade year.

Table 8-3

John's Woodcock-Johnson-III Achievement Test Results

	Standard Score	Percentile Rank	Range
BROAD READING	93	33rd	Average
BASIC READING SKILLS	95	36th	Average
PHON/GRAPH KNOWLEDGE	97	41st	Average
Letter-Word Identification	92	30th	Average
Reading Fluency	98	45th	Average
Passage Comprehension	93	32nd	Average
Word Attack	98	45th	Average
Spelling of Sounds	94	34th	Average

	Standard Score	Percentile Rank	Range
BROAD MATH	99	47th	Average
MATH CALC SKILLS	96	41st	Average
Calculation	96	40th	Average
Math Fluency	97	43rd	Average
Applied Problems	102	55th	Average

	Standard score	Percentile rank	Range
BROAD WRITTEN LANG	100	49th	Average
WRITTEN EXPRESSION	109	72nd	Average
Spelling	91	28th	Average
Writing Fluency	112	79th	Above Average
Writing Samples	102	54th	Average

Still, a comprehensive follow-up assessment of John was conducted with individual achievement measures before returning to Tier 1 status (regular education with no support) and closing his case with the instructional support team. The *Woodcock-Johnson Third Edition; Tests of Achievement* was administered by the IS teacher, and the following scores were obtained *(mean = 100; standard deviation = 15)*:

As evidenced from these results, John scored within the average range on all academic skill areas assessed. Since age-based norms were used to determine these scores, and John had been retained in the 1st grade, these scores actually reflected a comparison against a portion of children who were in the 5th grade. Grade-based scores were even higher than those reported above, thereby suggesting that John was not only displaying adequate skill levels for his age, but was also performing solidly within the average range among his classmates.

John is now completing the 4th grade at Pleasantville Schools. His grades have primarily consisted of A's and B's. He no longer receives a specific reading intervention, Title 1 support, or IST services. Furthermore, his behaviors are much improved compared to previous years, and his teachers attribute his newfound emotional resolve to considerably less academic frustration than he previously experienced. Perhaps the most telling sign of John's success within an RTI framework is the fact that, on most days, he can be seen reading a library book by choice as he waits for the bus to go home. Hence, RTI provided John with an opportunity to receive early intervention services without having to be identified as having a learning disability or going through a lengthy and time-consuming psychoeducational evaluation. Specific interventions in phonological development were provided at an appropriate time in the early stages of learning to read. In addition, the RTI process assisted educators in monitoring his progress through each tiered level of intervention, and adjusted his level of support when needed. Certainly, a standardized test such as the Woodcock-Johnson was helpful in validating John's progress, though it was really not a necessary component either to identify or remediate John's academic difficulties within an RTI service delivery model. Lastly, John's behavioral outbursts seemed to subside when his academic skills improved, which is so often the case among students who experience early academic frustration. Consequently, an RTI service delivery model was an effective and proactive approach to assist John in meeting his educational needs.

Case #2: Billy:

Billy weighed 7 pounds 6 ounces at birth, and was born at 39 weeks gestational age, with no medical complications reported with either the pregnancy or delivery.

According to his mother, Billy's medical and developmental history was unremarkable, as most early developmental milestones were reached within normal limits. However, he developed seizure activity by 21 months of age, as he tended to flop to one side with loss of consciousness noted. There was no regression in his skills, and there was initially good control of his seizures while initially medicated with Dilantin. Billy was eventually tapered off the medication after approximately two years but soon began experiencing seizures on a daily basis. It was reported that during his seizure activity, there was often a vacant look in his eyes, followed by five to ten minutes of behavioral activity such as chewing, pulling his eyelids, twirling his hair, putting things in his mouth, or wringing his hands. Most of his seizure activity apparently occurred during the morning hours. Billy was unresponsive to further medication including Tegretol, and eventually had an MRI which revealed a balloon dysplasia (abnormal appearance of cells) over the left frontal brain region. His increased seizure activity resulted in frequent absences from school, and often made him sleepy during class. Consequently, Billy made little educational growth while in kindergarten, and was recommended for retention the following year in 1st grade. At the time, Billy was reported as having difficulty following directions, struggled with early reading readiness skills, and easily frustrated when presented with more challenging tasks and activities.

During his 1st grade year, Billy's seizures were decreasing in frequency and duration, as he was responding favorably to Lamictal as prescribed for his seizures. A psychostimulant such as Ritalin was considered to address attentional concerns but was not medically-advised due to the tendency of such medications to lower the seizure threshold thereby making seizures more likely to occur. When his parents refused to retain Billy, he was recommended for a complete psychoeducational evaluation to determine his eligibility for further special education services. The school psychologist determined that Billy did not present the profile of a student with a learning disability since there was no discrepancy between his Full Scale IQ of 96 and his academic achievement scores. There was no indication that data from running records, current classroom performance, informal reading inventories, or curriculum-based measurement was considered when determining that Billy did not meet the eligibility criteria for special education services. The district basically determined that Billy displayed no adverse educational impact from his medical condition due to his adequate scores on the *Wechsler Individual Achievement Test: 2nd Edition* (See Table 8-4). However, given his documented medical condition, the district indicated that Billy qualified for some supports and accommodations through a Section 504 plan. These accommodations and supports primarily focused on his sleepiness in class, above average absenteeism, and a health care plan delineating a specific response for times when he experienced a seizure in school.

Table 8-4

Billy's Test Scores on the WISC IV and WIAT II

Verbal Comprehension	**SS**	**Perceptual Reasoning**	**SS**
Similarities	11	Block Design	7
Vocabulary	9	Picture Concepts	12
Comprehension	11	Matrix Reasoning	12

Working Memory Index	**SS**	**Processing Speed**	**SS**
Digit Span	8	Coding	7
Letter-Number Sequencing	11	Symbol Search	7

	COMPOSITE SCORE	**CONFIDENCE INTERVAL**	**RANGE**	**PERCENTILE RANK**
Verbal Comprehension	100	93 - 107	Average	50th
Perceptual Reasoning Index	102	94 - 109	Average	55th
Working Memory Index	97	90- 105	Average	42nd
Processing Speed Index	83	76 - 94	Below Average	13th
Full Scale Score	96	91 - 101	Average	39th

Wechsler Individual Achievement Test II

Subtest	Standard Score	Percentile Rank	Range
READING COMPOSITE	**110**	**75th**	**Above average**
Word Reading	97	42nd	Average
Reading Comprehension	90	25th	Average
Pseudoword Decoding	101	53rd	Average
MATHEMATICS COMPOSITE	**88**	**21st**	**Below average**
Numerical Operations	93	32nd	Average
Mathematics Reasoning	88	21st	Below average
WRITTEN LANG. COMPOSITE	**96**	**39th**	**Average**
Spelling	93	32nd	Average
Written Expression	98	45th	Average
ORAL LANG. COMPOSITE	**115**	**84th**	**Above average**
Listening Comprehension	109	73rd	Average
Oral Expression	117	87th	Above average

The following year, Billy transferred to the Pleasantville school district and participated in a September class-wide progress monitoring. At the time, his *Nonsense Word Fluency (NWF)* rate on the DIBELS was well above the benchmark level at 79 correct letter sounds per minute, but his *Oral Reading Fluency (ORF)* rate was 35 words per minute, which fell slightly below benchmark level rates of approximately 40 to 60 wpm. Observation data from his teacher indicated strong reading comprehension skills, though his slower reading rate appeared to be due to his tendency to attempt to sound out every word in the passage. The Instructional Support Team also reviewed his performance on group standardized achievement testing that had been performed in May of the same calendar year while he was in the 1st grade.

During progress monitoring with the DIBELS in January (winter), Billy displayed an *Oral Reading Fluency (ORF)* of 35 wpm that was identical to his rate in the September (fall) assessment. At this point, with benchmark rates for second grade students ranging from 65 to 85 words per minute, Billy clearly displayed performance that was both discrepant from his peers and representative of a complete lack of progress since he was assessed four months prior with the DIBELS. Billy was referred back to the Instructional Support Team and he began receiving additional direct instruction time for fluency-building exercises as part of a Tier 2 intervention structure. The IST also developed a list of accommodations and strategies to meet other identified needs such as increased self esteem, preferential seating to minimize the impact of his distractibility, and allowing him to add oral responses for enrichment of his typically poor written responses to tests and quizzes. By the end of his second grade year, Billy had increased his ORF to 50 words per minute (wpm). Though still behind his peers, Billy's spring ORF rate of 50 wpm did reflect progress from his prior winter and fall ORF rates of 35 wpm on each.

At the beginning of his 3rd grade year, Billy read DIBELS passages at a rate of 47 wpm which was very similar to his rate at the end of 2nd grade. It should be noted that, despite recommendations from the IST that he participate in summer programming for reading instruction, he did not; this may explain some regression that he displayed in his skills. After the next two progress monitoring assessments yielded similar scores with no apparent progress in his oral reading fluency, Billy began receiving Tier 3 interventions. This included participation in the *Read Naturally* program. *Read Naturally* focuses on building reading fluency and speed as well fostering more accurate comprehension skills. The program uses repeated exposures to modeled reading, and progress monitoring to increase overall fluency skill. It is designed for students who fall below the mean level oral fluency rates for 2nd grade (51 wpm) through 8th grade (133 wpm). At this point in time, Billy was participating in 60 minutes of direct small-group instruction with the reading specialist in the regular classroom during the reading and language arts instructional block, as well as two 30-minute intervention groups using the Read Naturally series for fluency-building. Still, Billy continued to display difficulty in developing his reading skills, and there were noted deficits with written language as well. Billy seemed to be compensating for his poor reading skills by over-relying on context and picture clues as well as his strong auditory memory skills.

Despite Billy's involvement in the most intensive Tier 3 support programming available, his progress in basic reading skills remained poor and his frustration with reading increased dramatically. There were noted increases in work-avoidant behaviors and his oral reading fluency rates, which were at this point being monitored every two weeks, actually began to steadily decrease from a high of 47 wpm in the fall, to 38 wpm in the winter, to a low of 27 wpm in the spring. Multiple meetings were held to develop further interventions addressing his increasing levels of task-avoidant and off-task behaviors. These behaviors were noted to impact his classroom performance throughout the entire day on all aspects of academic functioning. The Instructional Support Team decided that given Billy's failure to respond sufficiently to a variety of evidence-based interventions, his increasing frustration levels, and his remarkable medical history, a comprehensive psychoeducational evaluation was warranted. Fortunately, Pleasantville school district had a school-based neuropsychologist who was able to explain Billy's difficulty acquiring reading readiness skills from a brain-behavioral perspective as opposed to the flawed discrepancy model paradigm, and focused the assessment on providing a rationale for the types of interventions that may prove successful for Billy. The goal of the assessment was to provide the Instructional Support Team with additional data to make decisions regarding Billy's educational future and choose an intervention approach that best suited his particular educational needs. Table 8-5 depicts Billy's scores from the updated intellectual assessment. These scores were markedly similar to his previous intelligence test scores, though the psychologist placed more emphasis on the factor scores to explain why below average skills in working memory and processing speed may be hindering his reading fluency and comprehension skills (see Chapter six).

Table 8-5

Billy's Test Scores on the WISC IV in 3rd Grade

Verbal Comprehension	SS	Perceptual Reasoning	SS
Similarities	11	Block Design	6
Vocabulary	10	Picture Concepts	14
Comprehension	9	Matrix Reasoning	10

Working Memory Index	SS	Processing Speed	SS
Digit Span	7	Coding	6
Letter-Number Sequencing	9	Symbol Search	9

	COMPOSITE SCORE	CONFIDENCE INTERVAL	RANGE	PERCENTILE RANK
Verbal Comprehension Index/VCI	99	92 - 106	Average	47th
Perceptual Reasoning Index/PRI	100	92 - 108	Average	50th
Working Memory Index/WMI	88	81 - 97	Below Average	21st
Processing Speed Index/PSI	85	78 - 96	Below Average	16th
Full Scale IQ/FSIQ	92	87 - 97	Average	30th

READING MEASURES

Billy's Broad Reading Skills were in the *Deficient* range, and only at the 2nd percentile when compared to peers, as measured by the *Woodcock-Johnson III* Tests of Achievement (see Table 8-6). There were notable concerns with most aspects of his reading skills. For instance, he scored in the Well Below Average range on tasks requiring him to recognize sight words *(Letter-Word Identification)*, read fluently and accurately *(Reading Fluency)*, and utilize his overall passage comprehension skills *(Passage Comprehension)*.

Table 8-6

Billy's Reading Scores - WJ-III			
	Standard Score	Percentile Rank	Range
BROAD READING	**68**	**2nd**	**Deficient**
BASIC READING SKILLS	**81**	**10th**	**Below Average**
READING COMPREHENSION	**70**	**2nd**	**Well Below Average**
Letter-Word Identification	73	4th	Well Below Average
Reading Fluency	72	3rd	Well Below Average
Passage Comprehension	72	3rd	Well Below Average
Word Attack	92	29th	Average
Picture Vocabulary	113	81st	Above Average
Reading Vocabulary	78	7th	Well Below Average
Spelling of Sounds	91	28th	Average

Further observations and error analysis of his overall reading skills yielded two noteworthy findings. First, Billy demonstrated a rather inconsistent and sometimes poor effort on reading tasks, and tended to give up quickly when presented with more difficult or challenging items. Consequently, when Billy started to encounter passages with greater numbers of words that he did not quickly recognize, he often responded with *"I don't know this word"* rather than eliciting a guess. Second, Billy appeared to have little confidence in his decoding skills, and often guessed on words based on the initial letter sound rather than sounding out the entire word. This shortcut most often resulted in Billy guessing the wrong word. In summary, his difficulty in reading appeared to stem both from a skills deficit (lack of foundation skills in phonological processing) and a performance deficit (poor effort, low motivation, limited confidence).

MATH MEASURES

Billy's Broad Math Skills were in the Average range of functioning, and at the *30th* percentile when compared to peers, as measured by the *Woodcock-Johnson III* Tests of Achievement (See Table 8-7). There were few concerns noted with his overall conceptual knowledge of math *(Applied Problems)* or his ability to perform basic calculation skills involving single-digit addition, subtraction, and multiplication problems *(Math Calculation)*. However, Billy struggled during timed math tasks that required him to automatically retrieve archived information stored as facts *(Math Fluency)*.

Table 8-7

Billy's Math Scores - WJ-III			
	Standard Score	Percentile Rank	Range
BROAD MATH	**92**	**30th**	**Average**
MATH CALC SKILLS	**91**	**27th**	**Average**
MATH REASONING	**91**	**27th**	**Average**
Math Fluency	85	15th	Below Average
Applied Problems	92	30th	Average
Calculation	93	33rd	Average
Quantitative Concepts	90	26th	Average

PROCESSING MEASURES

The *Process Assessment of the Learner (PAL)* was administered to Billy in order to further examine his overall orthographic and phonological awareness skills. In addition, there are numerous items measuring rapid naming or visual-verbal retrieval skills, a key attribute underscoring reading fluency skills. Therefore, this test is a comprehensive measure for assessing the underlying components, or linguistic architecture, involved in laying the foundation for the reading and writing related processes. Scores are based on the student's grade placement and are reported as decile-based scores. A decile score indicates in which tenth of the distribution the student's performance falls in comparison to other students in the same grade. For example, a decile score of 10 indicates that 90 percent of the examinee's same age peers performed better than the examinee. Billy's overall scores are reported in Table 8-8.

Table 8-8

Billy's PAL Scores		
Subtests	Decile Scores	Descriptive Categories
Orthographic Processes		
Receptive Coding	<50	Emerging Adequate
Word Choice	<20	Deficient
Rapid Automatic Naming (RAN)		
Letters	<60	Adequate
Words	<10	Deficient
Digits	<50	Emerging Adequate
Words & Digits	<30	At Risk
Phonological Skills		
Syllables	<30	At-Risk
Phonemes	<40	At-Risk
Rimes	<10	Deficient
Word-Recognition Mechanisms		
Pseudoword Decoding	<30	At-Risk
Comprehension		
Sentence Sense	<10	Deficient
Handwriting		
Alphabet Writing	<10	Deficient
Copying (Task A & B)	<30	At-Risk

On the PAL, Billy demonstrated difficulty with most of the *phonological* tasks. This indicated deficits in critical prerequisite skill often needed for adequate reading skill development to occur. For instance, he struggled when sequencing sounds in words, made frequent sound omissions, had difficulty hearing word boundaries, and often confused similar sounds (e.g., b/p and f/v). He particularly struggled when manipulating and segmenting sounds in words (e.g. say the word "smock" without the "m"). In terms of *orthographic* processing, which involves the ability to recognize words based on the spatial contours and shapes of the letters, there were numerous deficits noted. For instance, Billy had difficulty with letter formation skills, often confused similar-looking letters, tended to reverse both letters and numbers, and experienced difficulty remembering how words "looked" when spelling.

Billy also scored in the Deficient range on numerous tasks that support the development of writing skills. For example, he struggled with the *Alphabet Writing* task, which measures automaticity in writing the lowercase letters of the alphabet in order from memory. Billy also was somewhat confused during the *Word Choice* task, which involved identifying the correct spelling of a word presented with two misspelled distracters. Lastly, he performed poorly on the *Sentence Sense* task, which measures the ability to coordinate word-recognition and sentence-comprehension processes when reading for meaning under timed conditions.

The ability to quickly and accurately tag a visual stimulus with a verbal label is a core feature of the PAL, and comprises most of the rapid naming tasks. Lower scores in these areas often correlate with poor fluency skills. Billy had difficulty with the rapid naming of words, and especially struggled when rapidly naming both words and digits combined. However, Billy tended to put forth an inconsistent effort and expressed a clear disdain for timed tasks. Given his difficulty with timed tasks, inconsistent attention and motivation, and difficulty with memory and retrieval skills, further testing of executive functioning skills appeared warranted.

***PROCESSING SUMMARY:** Billy demonstrated marked deficits in most aspects of phonological skills in words, and experienced difficulty with the manipulation and segmentation of sounds in words. He was inconsistent when asked to blend multiple sounds in sequence, had difficulty recalling letter and syllable patterns in words, and lacked much directionality when reading. In addition, he struggled with the visual-spatial appreciation of words, which is an important skill that contributes to the ability to accurately spell words. Lastly, he exhibited relatively slow visual-verbal retrieval skills, indicating a neurocognitive basis for why reading fluency might be difficult for him.*

EXECUTIVE FUNCTIONING MEASURES

The *Behavior Rating Inventory of Executive Functioning (BRIEF)* was administered to determine if Billy was displaying more global indicators of executive function deficits such as organization skills, emotional self-control, goal directed behavior, and working memory skills. All of these cognitive processes, sometimes termed *executive functions*, play a vital role in the ability to plan and execute any goal-directed, problem-solving task. A T-score of 65 or higher represents a clinically-significant score. Using his teacher as the respondent, the following scores were obtained:

Table 8-9

Score Summary-Behavior Rating Scale of Executive Functions (BRIEF)			
Scale/Index	**T-Score**	**Percentile**	**Average**
Inhibit - Assesses the ability to resist an impulse and to stop one's own behavior at the appropriate time.	55	80th	Average
Shift - Assesses the ability to move freely from one situation to another as the circumstances demand. A key aspect of shifting includes the ability to change focus from one mindset or topic to another.	55	80th	Average
Emotional Control - Assesses a child's ability to modulate emotional responses.	45	55th	Average
Behavioral Regulation Index - Represents a child's ability to modulate emotions and behavior via appropriate inhibitory control.	52	74th	Average
Initiate - Assesses behaviors relating to beginning a task or activity.	63	89th	Significant
Working Memory - Measures the capacity to hold information in mind for the purpose of completing a task. Working memory is essential to carry out multi-step activities, complete mental arithmetic, or follow complex instructions.	83	99th	Significant
Plan/Organize - Measures the child's ability to manage future-oriented task demands.	66	92nd	Significant
Organization of Materials - Measures orderliness of work, play, and storage spaces.	8	68th	Average
Monitor - Assesses work-checking habits and whether a child keeps track of the effect their behavior on others.	60	86th	Above Average
Metacognition Index - Represents the child's ability to self-manage a given task.	66	90th	Significant
Global Executive Composite - A summary score that incorporates all eight clinical scales of the BRIEF.	62	86th	Above Average

Billy's overall *Global Executive Composite (GEC)* score was in the *Above Average* range of functioning, and at the *86*[th] percentile compared to peers. This score suggested that Billy is inconsistent in his ability to regulate his behavior and organize his thoughts for successful learning to occur. There were mild concerns indicated by his score on the *Behavior Regulation Index (BRI),* which indicates some deficits in Billy's ability to modulate his emotions and behavior for successful learning to commence. Significant concerns were indicated by his score for the *Metacognition Index (MI),* as Billy was rated as displaying difficulty getting started on most assignments, having a short attention span, and often needing assistance to stay on task. There were particular difficulties suggested by his score in the area of *Working Memory,* as Billy was was rated as displaying difficulty with tasks requiring multiple steps, and tending to forget what he is doing while engaged in a task. Additional concerns were indicated by clinically-significant range scores in the area of Planning/Organization. This verified teacher reports of his observed difficulty with planning and organizing his responses on tasks in the classroom as well as his tendency to underestimate the time needed to complete many daily assignments.

Further assessment of attentional capacity and executive functioning was completed using the *Conners' Continuous Performance Test - Second Edition (CPT-2).* The CPT-2 is a norm-referenced computer-administered test of sustained visual attention and response inhibition. This task requires the child to hit a button as quickly as they can after each single white letter that appears briefly on a black computer screen. The child is instructed to do so for every letter of the alphabet EXCEPT the letter 'X'. The randomly-ordered stimulus letters are presented at varying speeds including one per second, to one every two seconds, to one every four seconds. Sophisticated analyses are then conducted on the pattern of examinee responses including such factors as reaction time, changes in reaction time based on changes in stimulus speed, numbers of omission errors (inattentive type), numbers of commission errors (impulsive type), and differences in response accuracy, consistency, etc, at various intervals of the tasks such as contrasts between performance during the first minute of the task versus the 14th minute of the task (thereby assessing sustained attention).

Billy's overall performance on the CPT-2 was significant for both omission errors and commission errors on a number of attention measures. In addition, he displayed a somewhat slower reaction time speed that varied considerably over the duration of this 14-minute task. However, his accuracy did not vary based on the spacing (1, 2, or 4-seconds) between stimuli. Thus, Billy's performance on the CPT-2 aligned with the BRIEF scale in that he displayed significant deficits with the metacognitive aspects of executive functioning. In other words, he had difficulty sustaining his attention for extended periods of time and also in adhering to task rules by inhibiting his responses in a specified manner. Billy's excessive number of omission errors on the CPT-2 also verified teacher reports that at times he has a tendency to under-focus on stimuli and therefore appears very distractible. Among the educational implications of these executive functioning deficits is that this pattern can be very problematic when reading longer passages and then being and asked to recall earlier parts of the passage. Such inconsistency of focus on stimuli can also cause individuals to miss many environmental or contextual cues (errors of omission) which could be helpful in decoding words in print or comprehending passages where a number of words are unknown.

__EXECUTIVE FUNCTIONING SUMMARY:__ Executive functioning skills refer to an array of multiple cognitive skills which allow students to form goals and objectives, devise plans of action to obtain these goals, select the cognitive skills necessary to execute the plan, as well as self-monitor their performance. Billy was described as having difficulty beginning assignments, often making careless errors, being easily distracted, and often underestimating the time needed to finish most tasks. Neuropsychological measures verified deficits corresponding to teacher reports and behavioral ratings of these deficits. This indicated that Billy displayed a neurocognitive basis for his observed difficulties in working independently on most goal-directed academic tasks, and struggled with strategy formation skills as academic tasks became more demanding.

LANGUAGE RELATED MEASURES

Billy was also administered various subtests from the *Oral and Written Language Scales (OWLS)*, in order to assess various aspects of written expression only. This assessment involved numerous items consisting of both structured and open-ended writing tasks designed to represent typical writing activities found in the classroom, thus providing a broad and extensive sample of Billy's writing skills. He earned a starndard score of *73*, which was in the Well Below Average range and at the *4th* percentile compared to peers. Billy often rushed to complete the items on this test, and this was reflected in qualitative analysis of his item responses. For instance, he often wrote incomplete sentences, inconsistently capitalized the first word in sentences, and did not always include ending punctuation. His overall written language skills appeared to be consistent with his reading skills which were significantly below grade level. Furthermore, since writing is such an "effort" based type of task, more noncompliant behaviors were observed during this activity than any other academic endeavor.

VISUAL MOTOR SKILLS

The *Beery-Buktenica Developmental Test of Visual-Motor Integration - 5th edition (DTVMI-5)* is a paper and pencil task requiring Billy to copy individual designs of increasing complexity, identify the exact match of a geometric form, and trace the stimulus forms with a pencil without going outside double-lined paths. Oftentimes, lower scores in visual-motor coordination tasks reduce paper and pencil output speed, and thus lead to difficulty with handwriting and note-taking skills. Billy's overall performance yielded a standard score of *87*, which was in the Below Average range and at the *19th* percentile compared to peers. His performance on Visual Perception subtest yielded a standard score of *101*, which was in the Average range and at the *51st* percentile compared to peers. Lastly, his performance on the Motor Coordination subtest yielded a standard score of *72*, which was in the Well Below Average range and at the *3rd* percentile compared to peers. These results suggested that Billy's visual perceptual skills were intactbut that his fine motor skills might be delayed. It was not possible to decisively conclude that his extremely low score on the Motor Coordination subtest was indicative of fine motor deficits because clinical observations revealed that Billy tended to rush through the items on this measure and he made numerous careless errors. As such, it was thought that this score might represent an underestimate of his actual fine motor skills, though the qualitative observations certainly supported assessment results that indicated impaired executive functions.

SUMMARY

Billy is a nine-year-old student currently in the 3rd grade at Pleasantville school. He has a significant history of medical conditions including a seizure disorder, a balloon dysplasia over the left frontal lobe, as well as attention deficits. He is currently medicated with Lamictal for his seizures. Ritalin was considered to address attentional deficits but was not prescribed by his doctor due to its tendency to make seizures more likely. Billy has not responded to numerous evidence based reading interventions, including the *Read Naturally* program, and has received multiple tiers of increasingly intensive reading and behavior support throughout his academic career. He particularly struggles with both reading and math fluency skills, with his overall skills significantly below grade level. Billy had previously been evaluated in 1st grade but did not qualify for special education services.

Current testing revealed his overall cognitive abilities continue to be in the Average range of functioning (FSIQ = 92) with relative weaknesses in both working memory and processing speed. In terms of his academic skills, he displayed numerous deficits in both reading and math fluency skills as well as written language skills. It should be noted that reading and math fluency both involve the rapid retrieval of over-learned archived information stored in either a numeric code (math) or verbal code (reading). There are two aspects of brain functioning to explore, beginning with the left versus right hemisphere of the brain. The left hemisphere is primarily the repository of over-learned information, while the right hemisphere is more involved in seeking novel information. Billy has a medical condition impairing his left frontal lobe, and clearly struggles with the rapid retrieval of over-learned information. Therefore, his medical condition may be hindering this particular cognitive attribute. The second relevant aspect of brain functioning worthy of exploration involves the functional difference between the frontal or anterior portions of the brain and the back or posterior portions of the brain. The frontal portions of the brain are more involved in the performance or execution of a skill (executive functioning), while the posterior or back regions are more involved with the information processing aspects of the skill. Billy's profile of scores indicated difficulties with working memory, processing speed, and executive functioning skills, all performance-based skills. Executive functioning skills refer to an array of cognitive of multiple cognitive skills that allow students to form goals and objectives, devise plans of action to obtain these goals, select the cognitive skills necessary to execute the plan, and self-monitor their performance. In other words, executive functioning modulate the processing of incoming information as well as the output of the output of information leaving the brain. Deficits with executive functioning often suggest more frontal impairment, which was consistent with the location of his dysplasia. Billy's observed and teacher-reported attentional impairments were substantiated through assessment with neuropsychological instruments and corresponded in a predictable fashion to medical evidence of an anomaly in his frontal lobes.

Further assessment driven by referral concerns over difficulty with reading skills verified marked deficits in most aspects of phonological skills in words, and had difficulty with the manipulation and segmentation of sounds in words. In addition, he also struggled with the visual-spatial appreciation of words which is an important attribute in the recognition and spelling of words. These types of deficits are more consistent with a phonologically-based learning disability which is often ascribed to more posterior regions of the brain. In summary, Billy presented the profile of a student with a significant learning disability hindering his reading and writing skills as well as global deficits in executive functioning that likely resulted from his medical condition. Thus, systematic school-based neuropsychological evaluation, coupled with progress monitoring data from a tiered intervention approach to both reading skills and behavior, yielded evidence of a clear neurocognitive basis for his academic difficulties. In addition, this assessment yielded information about related information-processing strengths and weaknesses which assisted the evaluator in determining the likely cause for his failure to respond adequately to several prior intervention techniques, and thereby assisted the evaluator in formulating recommendations for strategies that would be more likely to yield meaningful improvement in Billy's skills. At the conclusion of the evaluation process, fhe following recommendations were offered to the Instructional Support Team:

RECOMMENDATIONS

GENERAL RECOMMENDATIONS:

1. The IEP Committee should consider Billy eligible for special education services under the category *Learning Disability*. Though his marked limitations with attention and executive functioning skills may stem from his medical history, they are judged to contribute to, but not cause, Billy's difficulties in acquiring basic reading skills. Billy displays significant phonological and orthographic processing deficits consistent with a learning disability and has not responded to an increasingly intensive array of evidence-based reading interventions.

2. Billy would benefit from specially-designed instructional services to improve his reading skills a well as his overall academic skills as impacted by both reading skill deficits and attention/executive function deficits.

3. Classroom modifications such as using a behavior card to keep him focused and on-task, accompanying verbal directions with visual cues, having him work with a *study buddy* to double-check his work, and avoiding multiple-step instructions might be beneficial. Also, Billy should be asked to verbally repeat and explain directions in order to ensure that he has both heard and understood them.

4. Billy might benefit from a homework and/or organizational notebook to assist with work completion skills.

5. Billy might benefit from having lecture notes provided in advance to assist with note-taking skills.

SPECIFIC READING RECOMMENDATIONS:

6. Billy needs a more *balanced* reading program to address his constellation of both phonological processing deficits and poor executive functioning skills. The *SRA Corrective Reading* program allows students to work in a decoding program, a comprehension program, or both. *Corrective Reading*, which uses an approach called *Direct Instruction*, is a highly scripted reading program that allows teachers to work with students in small groups of up to ten students. Students are asked to respond to teacher directed questions in unison, with as many as 10 oral responses per minute required. This allows instructors to pinpoint immediately which students may be struggling with a specific sound or word pattern. *Corrective Reading* is a synthetic type of phonics program that carefully scaffolds sounds by building on previously-learned sounds and words. Long and short vowel sounds are presented in mixed order together in the scripted presentation. *Corrective Reading* may prove to be a good program for students with executive functioning difficulties and ADHA symptoms due to the structured nature and quick pace of the lessons. The scaffolding process in the introduction of sounds naturally imposes structure and organization for students who may lack the ability to self-organize decoding rules and boundaries.

7. Billy might benefit from the *"stop and start"* technique to increase comprehension skills. While reading aloud, have him stop every 30 seconds to summarize the material and respond to guided questions. Gradually increase the interval by 30 seconds at a time to enhance his comprehension skills.

8. Billy should be encouraged to read high interest materials at home each evening in order to enhance his fluency skills.

9. Billy might benefit from utilizing graphic organizers as well as answering specific questions prior to reading a passage in order to become a more directional reader and develop more consistent comprehension skills.

10. Curriculum based measurement gathering data points on a weekly basis should be built into Billy's literacy program in order to monitor the effectiveness of his reading interventions through oral word reading fluency skills. Having Billy participate in the recording of his weekly progress-monitoring scores on a wall-mounted chart in the classroom may help to build and sustain motivation for improvement and create more personal investment in his own progress.

MEMORY RECOMMENDATIONS:

11. Billy might perform better with multiple-choice tests and answer recognition format, as opposed to questions that require free recall or the organization of open-ended written responses.

12. Billy might benefit from taking tests and quizzes in an alternative setting, such as the special education classroom, to reduce distractions and aid in more effective recall.

13. Given Billy's limitations with working memory, he should be encouraged to "talk aloud" his way through multi-step or multi-sequential tasks.   Also, he may benefit from learning specific mnemonic techniques to assist with memorization of vocabulary words in his classes.

14. Billy might benefit from reading aloud as opposed to silently. Hearing his own voice might foster better retention and may also assist with comprehension.

15. Billy might learn and remember best through experiential learning such as field trips, science activities, or role playing events, as opposed to listening to verbal instructions.

WRITTEN LANGUAGE RECOMMENDATIONS:

16. Billy might benefit from learning keyboarding skills so he can effectively operate a computer and word processor to assist with written language assignments. Speeding up his mode of output will put less strain and demand on working memory systems, and should lead to more elaborative writing skills.

17. Billy would benefit from graphic organizers and semantic mapping techniques to assist him with planning and organizing more elaborate written language assignments.

18. Billy may need to be assigned a "note-taker" in class to assist with copying notes in an efficient fashion.

19. Billy may benefit from utilizing self-monitoring techniques such as the COPS strategy to provide him with a structured manner to proofread his written work for *Capitalization, Organization, Punctuation, and Spelling.*

MEDICAL RECOMMENDATIONS:

20. Data regarding Billy's academic and behavioral progress will be helpful in assisting his doctor in determining his response(s) to medication and should continue to be recorded by the school for the purpose of regularly sharing such data with his doctor. In addition, the school nurse should educate all faculty about the specific

warning signs of possible seizure activity and the proper medical precautions and responses advised by Billy's doctor.

EXECUTIVE FUNCTIONING RECOMMENDATIONS:

21. Billy requires a highly structured class setting in order to maximize his learning. Furthermore, he may benefit from a behavior incentive card rewarding task invitation as well as task completion in a timely manner.

22. Billy has difficulty modulating the amount of time necessary to complete assignments. He may benefit from a vibrating watch, which buzzes at predetermined times to let him know that it is time to move on to the next activity.

23. Billy may benefit from learning additional reading comprehension techniques by working with the *Soar to Success* program. This is a relatively fast-paced, small group instructional program, designed to accelerate reading for students in grades 3 through 6. The program mainly focuses on *top-down* strategies aimed at improving reading comprehension skills. Specific instructional strategies involve the use of graphic organizers to help students visually construct meaning from print. In addition, reciprocal teaching uses four strategies including SUMMARIZE-CLARIFY-QUESTION-and PREDICT; teachers model the use of these strategies while text is being read. Hence, the program is designed for students who lack executive strategies to derive meaning from print.

24. Billy may require extended time on math and reading tests to provide him with the additional processing time he needs to retrieve archived information from memory.

CHAPTER 9

20 Evidence-Based Interventions

The *No Child Left Behind Act of 2001, IDEA 2004,* and most federally funded grants all require educational practitioners to use "scientifically-based research" to guide not only curricular development in our schools but also the implementation of interventions for unsuccessful learners. The daunting task of sorting through the myriad of educational quick fixes, latest trends, unconventional gadgets, and disproven techniques falls on the shoulders of many school administrators with minimal scientific training. Fortunately, the wiser school officials have not fallen for most impassioned testimonials often reported with such great fanfare regarding the next magical program that will cure the ills of dyslexia or other educational disabilities. Despite the necessity of using scientific research, there needs to be a clear distinction made between "scientifically-based" interventions and "evidence-based" interventions. The vast majority of educational interventions are at best "evidence-based." Most educational research clearly lacks the scientific rigor and stringent methodology needed to demonstrate an association between a practice, strategy, curriculum, or program and student achievement. In fact, most attempts to validate a particular educational program are individual pilot studies, often conducted by publishing companies in an attempt to pitch a product to schools. It remains quite tempting to accept the results of an isolated study and immediately generalize these results to all students. Certainly, the question remains as to what specifically constitutes a scientifically based intervention from one that is merely evidence-based? Table 9-1 delineates five gold standards that the National Reading Panel (2000) has deemed necessary to validate a particular mode of treatment as being scientifically based. Unfortunately, the educational literature has a dearth of studies that actually follow these axioms, which in part led to the National Reading Panel's (2000) decision to discard the vast majority of research studies in their meta-analysis of best practices in reading. However, the following 20 interventions, listed in alphabetical order, do offer credible evidence to be successful for students who have difficulty with various aspects of reading. Most programs are described as either utilizing a cognitive strategy incorporating a *bottom-up* approach, meaning that isolated sounds are taught as a means to learn words, or *top down*, meaning a cueing system (often at the morphological or semantic level) is utilized to automatically trigger recognition. A further analysis of these reading programs follows.

Table 9-1

The "Gold Standard" for Scientific Inquiry

(National Reading Panel, 2000)

1. Studies need to utilize a *randomized control trial* that assigns students in a completely randomized fashion to an intervention group or to a control group in order to measure treatment effectiveness. Simply using a *"pre-test/post-test"* design often produces erroneous results.

2. Studies claiming that a particular intervention improves a particular outcome should report the *effect size*, as well as the statistical tests showing the unlikelihood the effect was caused by chance. Furthermore, studies should report the intervention's effect size on *all* outcomes that the study measured, and not just convenient ones for which there was a positive effect.

3. Every study needs to provide a *control group*, coupled with specific data showing there were no systematic differences between the intervention group and the control group prior to the specific intervention being implemented.

4. Few conclusions should be drawn from the effectiveness of a *singular study*. Using a conventional .05 level of statistical significance means that 1 in 20 studies will be effective due to chance alone. Therefore, meta-analyses that combine the results of individual studies will be more powerful evidence, assuming those individual studies are scientifically valid and rigorous ones themselves.

5. In order to obtain statistically significant effects, a study usually needs a relatively *large sample size*. As a rule of thumb, a sample size of 300 students, with 150 students in the treatment group and 150 students in the control group is usually required to obtain a statistical significance for an intervention to be modestly effective.

1. ALPHABETIC PHONICS:

The *Alphabetic Phonics* program is basically a derivative of the traditional Orton-Gillingham multi-sensory approach to reading. It is based on the assumption that 80 percent of the 30,000 most commonly used English words follow a predictable code, and are therefore phonologically consistent or regular (Uhry & Clark, 2005). *Alphabetic Phonics* is a **bottom-up** or synthetic method of teaching reading, meaning that the theoretical foundation of the program is hierarchically structured and sequenced based upon a set of learned rules and correspondences for letters and sounds. Progress monitoring is documented by benchmark measures examining letter knowledge, alphabetizing skills, reading, spelling, and handwriting. There is much emphasis on utilizing diacritical markers for coding the 44 phonemes and 68 graphemes in various reading situations. There are currently 14 *Alphabet Phonics* teacher training sessions in the United States. The training requires a minimum of 150 instructional hours followed by 700 hours of supervised practice with students. The structured daily lessons can take up to an hour complete, and include 11 fast paced activities including (Uhry & Clark, 2005):

Language Building (5 minutes) - warm up activity fostering language development skills.

Alphabet Recognition (5 minutes) - rapid recognition of the sequence and directionality of the alphabet.

Reading Decks (3 minutes) - drill cards to develop rapid and automatic sight word skills.

Spelling Decks (3 minutes) - students listen, echo a phoneme, say the letter names, and write the sounds in words.

New Learning (5 minutes) - a new sound is introduced through a combination of multi-sensory activities including monitoring mouth movements and using diacritical marks as visual cuing codes to auditory rules.

Reading Practice (5 minutes) - reading words, as opposed to texts or stories, which are phonetically controlled.

Handwriting Practice (5 minutes) - cursive writing taught to reinforce directionality.

Spelling Practice (10 minutes) - spelling of sounds using printed letters, as well as simultaneous oral spelling.

Verbal Expression (2-5 minutes) - use "parts of speech" cards to introduce the beginning of a lesson.

Review (5 minutes) - review index cards with learning cues about each lesson.

Reading Comprehension (5 minutes) - choose material on the student's cognitive level, not reading level, to listen and then reflect upon specific questions.

Cognitive/RTI Recommendations: Alphabetic-phonics is probably best utilized as a Tier III or Tier IV intervention for students with dysphonetic dyslexia. Despite the widespread inclusion of multi-sensory techniques as being a signature component of all Orton-Gillingham based reading strategies, there is little empirical data to validate its effectiveness (Uhry & Clark, 2005). If anything, multi-sensory techniques are wonderful strategies to vary instructional techniques and minimize boredom. There are studies to show the effectiveness of using _Alphabetic Phonics_ to improve reading gains (Hucheson, Selig, & Young, 1990), though no control groups were used to validate improved reading scores were attributed to the techniques of the program. Still, _Alphabetic Phonics_ is a comprehensive **_bottom-up_** approach to reading specifically geared toward strengthening the phonological processor or temporal-parietal regions in the brain. The emphasis on automaticity allows students to properly map sounds on to posterior brain regions in order to automatically recognize words in print. Given the fast pace of the lessons, heavy emphasis on diacritical markers, and synthetic approach toward learning phonology, _Alphabetic Phonics_ might be better suited for children with at least average cognitive abilities.

OFFSHOOT PROGRAMS: _Success for All_
Recipe for Reading

2. CORRECTIVE READING:

The _SRA Corrective Reading_ program allows students to work in a decoding program, a comprehension program, or both. Each program has four levels, and placement tests are provided so that students may enter the program at their appropriate instructional level. Both the decoding and the comprehension programs are designed for students in grades 4 through 12, as the context of the reading material is geared more for secondary level students. The first three instructional levels contain 65 lessons, with the reading levels parceled out in the following manner:

INSTRUCTIONAL LEVEL	GRADE LEVEL
LEVEL 1	2.9 or below
LEVEL 2	2.9 - 3.9
LEVEL 3	3.9 - 4.9
LEVEL 4	4.9 - 7.0

In *Corrective Reading*, daily programs can take up to 45 minutes with the goal being to accomplish one reading lesson per day. The first three levels take approximately a half-year to complete, and the fourth level takes approximately one year to complete. The program includes benchmark mastery tests as well. *Corrective Reading*, which uses an approach called *Direct Instruction*, is a highly scripted reading program that allows teachers to work with students in small groups of up to ten students. Students are asked to respond to teacher directed questions in unison, with as many as 10 oral responses per minute required. This allows instructors to immediately pinpoint which students may be struggling with a specific sound or word pattern. *Corrective Reading* is a synthetic type of phonics program that carefully scaffolds sounds by building on previously learned sounds and words. Long and short vowel sounds are presented in mixed order together in the scripted presentation. *Corrective Reading* is not a multi-sensory program and there are no diacritical markers used to assist with sound patterns. Multiple instructional tracks or strands, including phonemic awareness, auditory awareness, fluency-building and vocabulary enrichment are built into the decoding program. Reading comprehension is limited mainly to the literal and inferential levels, with the emphasis being on the student needing to decode accurately in order to comprehend.

Cognitive/RTI Recommendations: *Corrective Reading* may be a logical choice for a Tier III reading intervention given its scripted nature and utilization in a group format. It may prove to be a good program for students with executive functioning difficulties and attention deficit disorder due to the structured nature and quick pace of the lessons. The scaffolding process in the introduction of sounds naturally imposes a set of structure and organization for students who may lack the ability to self-organize decoding rules and boundaries. By drawing upon executive resources, the goal of *Corrective Reading* is to further develop the temporal-parietal regions of the brain, which are crucial to mapping sounds to print. However, the program tends to emphasize sound fluency, as opposed to printed word fluency, thereby minimizing its impact on more automatic word recognition skills. Still, the breakdown of comprehension components into various cognitive activities may assist secondary students with the planning, organization, and use of critical strategy formation skills to decipher meaning from print.

3. DISTAR:

The *Direct Instruction Model* was originally designed for disadvantaged students in the late 1960s, though it has been used to teach students with a variety of learning disabilities. This program provides instruction for reading, language, spelling, and arithmetic in grades one through six. The reading program, termed *Reading Mastery*, has six levels, with the beginning levels extending down to preschool. The lessons are very scripted, with letter sounds being taught in Level I, and letter names being taught in Level II. Diacritical markers are used extensively to teach distinctions between continuous sounds (e.g., "s", "m", "r") and closed or stop sounds (e.g., "b", "d", "t"). Reading begins when six sounds have been learned, and there is a heavy emphasis on rhyming as well to help children blend initial sounds. The *Reading Mastery* program is very much a **bottom-up** or direct phonics program, though comprehension activities are taught from the beginning. At the pre-reading level, these include interpreting pictures and ordering events in sequence. At the reading level, comprehension skills are taught first in simple sentences, and then in stories as children answer written questions about the passage. In addition, the teacher summarizes the stories and asks students to make predictions. The recommended reading time for daily lessons is 25 to 30 minutes of small group instruction, followed by 15 to 20 minutes of independent work, followed by 5 minutes of self-monitoring, and then 10 minutes of group spelling practice. There is biweekly performance monitoring using criterion referenced tests.

Cognitive/RTI Recommendations: The *DISTAR Reading Mastery Program* is best suited as a Tier III or IV intervention for elementary aged students with dysphonetic dyslexia. According to Uhry and Clark (2005), teacher training can be somewhat cumbersome, as a one-week pre-service workshop followed by an hour or two of weekly inservice trainings are recommended. In fact, skilled teachers often supervise apprentice teachers within the classroom. The National Reading Panel (2000) includes several studies indicating positive effect sizes for *DISTAR*, though more traditionally based Orton-Gillingham programs such as *Alphabetic Phonics* tend to outperform *DISTAR*. In addition, Lovett et al. (2000) noted that DISTAR used in combination with teaching direct meta-cognitive strategies was more effective in teaching reading than just utilizing *DISTAR* only. Lastly, one of the most frequent criticisms of *DISTAR* comes from teachers who feel the scripted lessons place too many restrictions on the instructor.

4. EAROBICS LITERACY LAUNCH:

The *Earobics Literacy Launch* program is a software package designed for students in pre-kindergarten through 3rd grades. It is intended for all students who need to develop early language foundation skills in order for literacy to develop. This program is especially recommended for English as a Second Language (ESL) learners. Earobics I is designed for developmental ages 4-7 and features six interactive games with over 300 levels of play. It systematically teaches the critical phonological awareness, auditory processing, and introductory phonics skills required for learning to read and spell. Earobics II software features 593 levels of play in five interactive games designed for 2nd and 3rd grade students. This program also includes teaching language comprehension skills as well. A student who utilizes Earobics 20 minutes per day, 3 days per week should be able to complete each step in a semester. There is also an additional program for adolescents and adults designed to provide foundational skills in auditory processing It is important to note there are three versions of the program. The *Earobics Home* version accommodates two students, while the *Earobics Specialist/Clinician* version accommodates 12 students. The *Earobics Classroom* version accommodates 35 students, has 10 different languages, and allows for more customized data tracking. In addition, the classroom version is combined with correlated books, tapes, and activities.

Cognitive/RTI Recommendations: *Earobics* is primarily designed as a Tier I or II level of intervention for younger students lacking basic phonological awareness skills and auditory processing abilities. The program is cleverly designed and remarkably entertaining, and may be very helpful for students with attention deficits as well as ESL learners. Play by play scoring gives students immediate feedback, and there is a color coded progress chart to monitor performance. The research studies on *Earobics* have basically consisted of pilot studies in 13 different school districts to demonstrate the effectiveness of the program. Most of these studies involved using *Earobics* in conjunction with other Tier I reading measures, such as *Open-Court* reading, and validated the effectiveness of the program by demonstrating improvement in other phonics and auditory perceptual measures (e.g., *DIBELS, PALS,* etc.).

5. FAST FORWORD:

Fast Forword is a family of computer software products based on the conceptual underpinnings developed by literacy researcher Dr. Paula Tallal. Much of Tallal's (1993) research noted that reading disabled children suffered from auditory perceptual deficits that interfered with their ability to identify rapidly changing acoustical elements embedded in speech. Reading difficulties were assumed to stem in part from the brain's inability to rapidly process consonant sounds, which are spoken at a much faster rate than vowel sounds.

Fast Forword Language Basics is designed for 4 to 6 year old children, and primarily focuses on auditory discrimination skills and sustained auditory attention. The program requires children to hold a pair of sounds or sequences of sounds in memory, and then reproduce the order of a two-sound sequence. As students work through the program, the software adapts to individual skill levels and responses targeting correct responses

80 percent of the time. Recommended usage is 30 minutes per day, five days per week, up to 6 weeks.

Fast Forword Language software is aimed at developing the cognitive skills necessary for successful reading and learning for younger children. Recommended usage is 50 minutes per day for up to 12 weeks, or 75 minutes per day for up to 10 weeks. The program focuses on the following cognitive attributes:

Memory - Children hold a statement or question in memory while retrieving picture-concept associations.

Attention - Children are required to focus to task and ignore distractions.

Processing - Children are required to quickly distinguish and discriminate among sounds.

Sequencing - Children use word order assist to comprehend sentences and identify missing parts.

The *Fast Forword Language to Reading* software exercises are similar to the *Fast Forword Language* software in terms of teaching the aforementioned cognitive skills. However, the skills also developed include word analysis, understanding English language conventions including proper word order and subject/verb agreement, remembering multi-step tasks, and building listening comprehension skills. Recommended usage is 50 minutes per day for up to 12 weeks, or 90 minutes per day for up to 8 weeks.

The *Fast Forword Middle & High School* programs focus on reinforcing and upgrading the cognitive skills critical for fluent reading. Many of the sequencing skills require the use of word order to comprehend complex statements and instructions. Recommended usage is 50 minutes per day for up to 12 weeks, or 90 minutes per day for up to 8 weeks.

The *Fast Forword Literacy Advanced* programs were designed for adolescents and young adults to build memory and improve concentration and to develop linguistic processing of orally presented words, sentences, and stories. Many of the exercises require utilization of word order to comprehend complex statements, and to understand multiple step directions. Recommended usage is 50 minutes per day for up to 12 weeks, or 90 minutes per day for up to 8 weeks.

The *Fast Forward Reading* programs consist of six products designed for students who are below grade level. Included in the program are *Progress Trackers*, which not only monitors student progress automatically, but can also provide teachers with specific recommendations for individual instruction. Recommended usage is 50 minutes per day for up to 12 weeks, or 90 minutes per day for up to 8 weeks.

Cognitive/RTI Recommendations: The emphasis of *Fast Forword* is on the development of the cognitive skills necessary for reading to commence, and not necessarily on teaching the components of how to read. The primary brain region responsible for auditory discrimination skills is *Heschl's Gyrus* in the left temporal lobe. *Fast Forword* has been severely criticized in the past due in part to its misleading claims of reading improvement, high cost, and tendency to focus on isolated skills and not reading. However, there have been more than 75 studies conducted throughout the United States illustrating the effectiveness of these programs in building phonics, fluency, listening comprehension, vocabulary, and reading comprehension skills in students from kindergarten through high school. Nevertheless, most of these studies were conducted on students in regular education or at-risk students, and not students with dyslexia. Given the relatively quick time period recommended for most of the computer programs, *Fast Forword* may prove effective as a Tier II or III intervention for students of all ages. Due to the program's emphasis on sustained auditory and visual attention, as well as enhancing other cognitive reading readiness skills such as working memory, it may also prove to be effective for students with ADHD.

6. FUNDATIONS:

A downward extension of the *Wilson Reading System is Fundations*, initially published in 2002, and designed for students in kindergarten through 3rd grades. The primary focus of *Wilson Fundations* is to develop phonemic awareness and phonology, as well as spelling rules and boundaries in young children. Similar to the *Wilson Reading System, Fundations* is a multisensory and explicit phonics model of teaching reading and spelling in a very structured and systematic approach. *Fundations* is intended to serve as a prevention program to help reduce reading and spelling failure in the general curriculum. There are 15 sequenced activities that should be rotated throughout the week for instruction. Teachers are encouraged to follow the script, though the program is flexible enough to be taught in a whole group or one-on-one setting. It is recommended that regular education teachers incorporate a 30-minute daily *Fundations* lesson into their language arts classroom instruction.

Fundations' lessons focus on carefully sequenced skills that include print knowledge, alphabet awareness, phonological awareness, phonemic awareness, decoding, vocabulary, fluency, and spelling. Critical thinking, speaking, and listening skills are practiced during storytime activities. Furthermore, targeted small group intervention is available for students in the lowest 30th percentile. In this case, students should receive additional instruction 3-5 times per week. In schools where *Fundations* is not used in the general education classrooms, a small group early intervention model is certainly appropriate. In this model, students may need to receive *Fundations* instruction for up to 40-60 minutes each day. Teacher training is minimal, as the manual and corresponding CD should be sufficient.

Cognitive/RTI Recommendations: The Florida Center for Reading Research, one of three federally funded Reading First technical centers, conducted an independent review of *Fundations* and its effectiveness. The analysis confirmed that *Fundations* addresses each of the five components required by Reading First (phonemic awareness, phonics, vocabulary, fluency and comprehension), and noted it can be incorporated into Reading First grants as a supplemental prevention or early intervention program. The emphasis of the program is to build phonemic awareness and phonics skills in young children through **bottom-up** processes, thereby stimulating the temporal-parietal regions of the brain to code sound patterns for the rapid and automatic recognition of words in print. Its best use may be as a Tier II or III intervention for younger students.

7. GREAT LEAPS READING:

Great Leaps Reading was designed as more of a supplementary reading program and requires just 10 minutes per day, for a minimum of three days per week. The program is divided into three major sections: (1) *Phonics* for developing basic sound awareness skills; (2) *Sight-Phrases* for mastering sight words skills; and (3) *Fluency*, which uses age-appropriate stories designed to build oral reading fluency and automaticity as well as to enhance student motivation. The heart and soul of the program are the strategies used to enhance fluency. *Great Leaps* argues against teaching high frequency words in isolation, and instead relies upon "sight phrases" to be mastered within the context of a story. The program is highly scaffolded, meaning that one skill mastered leads to the next. In fact, students literally "leap" to the next page once mastery on timed one minute tests is attained. The fundamental goal of *Great Leaps* is to develop fluent and independent reading skills up to a 5th grade level. There are two practical advantages to utilizing *Great Leaps* in the public school setting. First, the cost of the program is relatively inexpensive, with the K-2 Reading Package, the Middle School Reading Package, and High School Reading Package just $110.00. Second, *Great Leaps* requires little training and can be used by a teacher, parent, instructional assistant, tutor, or school volunteer. A typical training session takes about 3 hours, though most experienced teachers will find the instructions are more than adequate to begin implementation without training. There are no tape recordings or colored pictures included in the packet, as students monitor progress using a fluency chart.   *Great Leaps* now offers a math program as well building fluency skills in the basic facts.

Cognitive/RTI Recommendations: *Great Leaps* may prove to be very beneficial as a Tier II level of intervention for students who lack basic fluency skills. The program is not designed to directly enhance reading comprehension skills, though it can indirectly improve comprehension as the process of reading becomes more automatic. As previously stated, it is more of a supplementary reading program requiring little instructional time. The research literature on *Great Leaps* is not exactly robust, though the authors have published studies indicating significant student progress with learning disabled children as measured by curriculum-based assessment (Mercer et al., 2000).

8. HORIZONS FAST TRACK A-B:

There are numerous versions of the *Horizons* program including *Horizons A, Horizons B,* or *Horizons Fast Track A-B* which is an accelerated program designed to accomplish two years of reading growth in just one year. The *Horizons Fast Track A-B* program has 150 lessons, with each lesson taking approximately 50 minutes. The time is divided between 30 minutes of reading instruction, 10 minutes of spelling instruction, and 10 minutes of independent seat work. *Horizons Fast Track A-B* is a highly scripted program geared for 1st grade students, or children in grades 2 or above who are nonreaders and have weak decoding skills. There is an initial placement test as well. The initial 30 lessons of the *Fast Track* program primarily focus on phonemic awareness and learning left-to-right sequencing conventions for letters in words. During lessons 31-70, children are reading short stories up to 90 words in length, with numerous prompting taking place to call attention to various letter combinations. Spelling exercises reinforce the relationship between sounds and spelling patterns. Lessons 71-150 have no orthographic prompts in the stories, and children engage in a variety of word attack exercises. Usually, the stories are read twice, with the initial reading focusing on decoding skills, and the second reading is often a different version of the first with more emphasis on comprehension questions. Over the course of the 150 lessons, children are introduced to approximately 1600 words, and are expected to attain two years' growth.

Cognitive/RTI Recommendations: *Horizons Fast Track A-B* is a systematic and explicit ***bottom-up*** phonics program designed for younger students struggling to acquire basic sound-symbol relationships. It is probably best utilized as a Tier III or Tier IV intervention. Each lesson is divided into five parts: a) letters and sound instruction, b) word attack skills, c) oral reading of a story, d) story-based activities such as independent workbook activities, and e) letter and sentence writing, and spelling. The program is completely scripted, so teacher training is minimal, and takes just one day. *Horizons Fast Track A-B* was field tested between 1992 and 1998 and revised numerous times. It should be noted that most research on the program was conducted with regular education students, and not special education students. Tobin (2003) examined the effectiveness of *Horizons Fast Track A-B* with 1st graders, and compared them to 1st graders receiving the *Silver, Burdett, and Ginn (SBG)* reading curriculum which did not use a systemic phonics approach. Both groups of students were on approximately the same reading level at the onset of 1st grade, though students using the *Horizons Fast Track A-B* program had substantially stronger oral reading fluency and accuracy skills. Still, this study did not incorporate a control group, and there is little evidence to suggest that dyslexic students can improve two grade levels in just one year. According to the test publisher, *SRA McGraw Hill* (Engelmann et al., 1997), in comparing *Horizons Fast Track A-B* with the *Reading Mastery (DISTAR)* program, the following guidelines are recommended:

1. If children are in 1st grade and can identify letters, use of *Horizons Fast Track A- B* is appropriate. If not, then *Reading Mastery* is appropriate.

2. If children are in first or second grade and receiving special education services, *Horizons Fast Track A-B* is probably not as appropriate as *Reading Mastery*.

3. If children are in kindergarten, *Horizons Fast Track A-B* is probably not as appropriate as *Reading Mastery*.

4. If children are in grades 3 or beyond and still essential nonreaders, then both *Horizons Fast Track A-B* and *Reading Mastery* may be appropriate.

9. LADDERS TO LITERACY:

The *Ladders to Literacy* program has both a preschool and kindergarten activity book, and is designed to teach early print awareness skills, print knowledge, and oral language skills to beginning readers. The *Print Awareness* activities use a play format lesson so children can identify environmental sounds, repeat songs and nursery rhymes, and manipulate sounds. The *Print Knowledge* activities use newspapers, signs, recipes, and messages as teachers ask questions about conventions of print. The *Oral Language* section contains activities that provide conversational topics intended to facilitate language development skills. There is also a unit on *Metalinguistic Awareness* that includes activities on appropriate grammatical structures. Teachers can use the program's observational checklists to determine which tasks and teaching strategies in the lesson are developmentally appropriate for each child. Most activities are designed for larger group formats, with approximately 50 activities offered in each book.

Cognitive/RTI Recommendations: The *Ladders to Literacy* program does not have a systemic approach as most activities can be offered at any time and in any order throughout the year depending upon the child's needs.   However, differentiated instruction is offered through the teaching strategies provided in each lesson. There is professional training for *Ladders to Literacy*, consisting of a one or two-day seminar that focuses on how to incorporate the curriculum in a preschool class setting. According to the Florida Center for Reading Research, there is little empirical support documenting the effectiveness of the program. At best, *Ladders to Literacy* can be used as a Tier I or Tier II type of intervention for preschool students with varying language and cultural backgrounds. However, this is not a systemic or structured program for building phonological awareness skills, but rather serves to build early pre-literacy and print awareness skills.

10. LEXIA:

Lexia Learning Systems is a developer of software programs for both home and school to support a variety of learning skills. There are three reading programs, each targeted for a different developmental level. The *Lexia Early Readings* program is for students aged 4 to 6, and is specifically designed to increase phonological awareness. The activities in the first level of the program target phonemic awareness and include rhyming, recognizing initial and final sounds, segmenting, and blending sounds. The second level of the program focuses more on phonological processing, and includes letter knowledge, sound-symbol correspondence, consonants, short vowels, and consonant digraphs. There is a structured approach to the activities, beginning with pre-alphabetic phonological awareness types of activities. Teachers can assign program units to customize learning, and the program generates reports to monitor specific academic progress.

The *Lexia Primary Reading* program is designed for students aged 5 to 8, and targets a combination of phonics and decoding skills, vocabulary, and comprehension skills. The program gives instant feedback and adjusts automatically to each student's abilities. The primary skills reinforced include beginning and ending sounds, syllables and segmenting, sight words, decoding skills, as well as vocabulary and comprehension skills. There are five levels of varied activities that can easily correlate with curriculum standards and lesson plans.

Lastly, the *Lexia Strategies for Older Students* is designed for students aged 9 and older, and takes more of a balanced literacy approach. The skills reinforced include word attack and contextual strategies necessary for automatic word recognition, word attack strategies for multi-syllable words, and advanced strategies for recognizing Latin prefixes and suffixes, as well as vocabulary and comprehension skills. The students are encouraged to work independently in order to increase confidence in their skills. Reporting features provide tools for analyzing progress data at the student, group, or classroom level. *Lexia* is recommended for student use between 60 to 90 minutes per week, or a minimum of 15 minutes per day. There are also two computerized diagnostic reading tests to assess decoding skills, word attack strategies, reading fluency, and comprehension skills. There are graphic and tabular reports that highlight the student's needs to assist curricular programming and planning.

Cognitive/RTI Recommendations: *Lexia* is a relatively inexpensive though very comprehensive phonics program designed in accordance with the National Reading Panel's (2000) main recommendations. This is a ***bottom-up*** model of teaching reading, though the *Lexia Strategies for Older Children* does incorporate more meta-cognitive skills by relying on Latin prefixes and suffixes as word identification and semantic cues. The program is currently used in over 12,000 schools, adult education centers, tutoring centers, and correctional facilities as well as at home. *Lexia* has been the recipient of numerous awards including the *Gold Award* from the National Parenting Publications. A recent study by Macaruso, Hook, and McCabe (2006) examined the benefits of using *Lexia* to supplement the word attack skills of 1st graders already using an explicit phonics curriculum. The results indicated that *Lexia* was particularly effective for low achieving students receiving *Title I* services, as these children were able to close the reading gap with their mainstream peers. Therefore, *Lexia* may be particularly effective as a Tier II reading intervention program, especially for younger students who have difficulty with phonological processing skills.

11. Lindamood Phoneme Sequencing Program for Reading, Spelling, and Speech (LiPS):

The LiPS program, formerly known as *Auditory Discrimination in Depth (ADD)*, was developed by Charles and Patricia Lindamood, and uses a rather unique approach to systemically teaching phonemic awareness. Instead of linking sounds to letters, the program links sounds to *articulatory gestures*, or movements of the face and mouth involved in producing speech sounds. Therefore, the program is multisensory and very much a ***bottom-up*** or synthetic model of teaching reading through five developmental levels. The first level is called *Setting the Climate for Learning,* and the activities include auditory perception and sequencing sounds. The second level involves matching speech sounds with articulatory gestures based upon the shape and position of the lips, teeth, and tongue. For instance, when teaching a "b" or a "p" sound, there are photographs of a mouth position with lips pursed, and a puff of air blowing outward, to illustrate the mouth position when making these sounds. The third level teaches students to identify various sound categories by representing them with colored blocks. In other words, beginning in kindergarten, students practice representing various syllable patterns (e.g., CV, VC, CVC, etc.) in nonsense words through color-coded block representations of the sounds. The fourth level involves students associating sounds with letters printed on tiles, and there is a clear distinction made between phonologically consistent words versus phonologically inconsistent words. The last level involves spelling and decoding skills. There is a heavy emphasis on using spelling to teach reading very early in the program, and not vice-versa.

There are various other products available through the Lindamood-Bell Learning Process Center. For instance, the *Lindamood-Bell Auditory Conceptualization Test-Third Edition* was developed to assess students' ability to distinguish and manipulate speech sounds. In addition, the *Lindamood Visualizing and Verbalizing for Language Comprehension and Thinking* was developed to use concept imagery as a means to assist students with reading comprehension, critical thinking, and connecting meaning to conversation. The *Seeing Stars: Symbol Imagery for Phonemic Awareness, Sight Words and Spelling* is designed to develop symbol imagery skills in order to facilitate sight word development and comprehension of the orthography of print. The program begins by visualizing the sequence of letters for the sounds within words, and extends into multisyllabic and contextual reading and spelling. Lastly, there is also a *Math Computation & Reasoning* program, as well as an *Oral Language Comprehension and Expression* program.

Cognitive/RTI Recommendations: The *Lindamood Phoneme Sequencing Program for Reading, Spelling, and Speech (LiPS)* program is an extremely well researched and effective program that can be beneficial to most school districts as a Tier III or IV level of intervention. Interestingly, the LiPS program is more of a ***bottom-up*** method of teaching reading, while the *Visualizing and Verbalizing for Language Comprehension and Thinking* takes a ***top-down*** strategy to teach comprehension. Still, the multisensory aspect of the program and use of visual imagery, proprioceptive feedback, and color coding sounds can be especially helpful for children with disabilities ranging from dyslexia, to hyperlexia, to high functioning autistic children including Asperger's Syndrome. The heart and soul of the program is geared for dysphonetic dyslexics who struggle to properly distinguish and map out sounds in words. There are 39 Lindamood

Learning Centers across the United States and Great Britain. The *Lindamood Phoneme Sequencing* program alone requires a three-day workshop that focuses on teaching students to process sounds in words and apply phonological processing to reading, spelling, and speech. The training is highly interactive with videos and practice sessions, with the cost being approximately $679 for the entire training.

The Lindamood-Bell Learning Center reported that 2,181 students received instruction in 2005, with the majority of students being in elementary and middle-school aged. Approximately 40 percent of these students also received and speech and language therapy services as well. It should be noted that the Charles and Patricia Lindamood had backgrounds in linguistics and speech therapy, though the LiPS program is not solely designed for students with speech deficits. The results were particularly impressive for students in grades pre-kindergarten through 2nd grade, with noted gains in word attack skills, phonemic awareness, and sight word recognition abilities. Torgeson et al. (1999) also published longitudinal results using the Lindamood program with kindergarten children who had four sessions per day through 2nd grade. These children were compared to a second group of children whose treatment was more of an embedded phonics approach, a third group of children who simply received regular classroom support, and a fourth group who received no individual assistance at all. The children who received the Lindamood program produced the largest gains in word reading, with scores at the end of the treatment in the Average range.

12. PHONO-GRAPHIX:

The *Phono-Graphix* program is a systemic and multi-sensory reading program designed to teach students in kindergarten through 5th grade the underlying principals of the alphabetic code. It teaches students to segment, blend, and manipulate phonemes, and also emphasizes that sounds are represented by letters or pictures, rather than stressing that letters are represented by sounds. The program can be used by classroom teachers, reading specialists, or instructional assistants in either a small or large group format. Specific materials include the teacher's manual with scope and sequence, lesson plans, worksheets, and a white board for error correction. The instructional premise centers around four skill levels:

Level 1: One-to-one mapping of sound to print including 17 consonant sounds and 5 vowel sounds, as well as C-V-C words.

Level 2: Remaining consonants and digraphs are taught along with V-C-C, C-V-C-C, C-C-V-C, and C-C-V-C-C words.

Level 3: Teaches remaining digraphs, phonograms, spelling alternatives and irregular words as part of advanced code.

Level 4: A multi-syllabic level that teaches students to break down each phoneme and analyze it. Students develop spelling patterns through "mapping" the code.

Phono-Graphix incorporates many word building activities by moving sound picture cards into place as a word is being said. The program does not begin with phonological awareness skills, as the premise is to teach the alphabetic code using letters that are immediately transferable to reading and spelling. There is no direct teaching of fluency, vocabulary, or comprehension skills. A one-day training is recommended.

Cognitive/RTI Recommendations: *Phono-Graphix* is a highly structured **bottom-up** method of teaching reading that incorporates many multi-sensory strategies and visual cueing techniques. The program is in accordance with the National Reading Panel (2000), and has been empirically tested and shown to substantially improve word attack skills and word identification skills in students with learning disabilities (McGuinness et al., 1996). However, according to the Florida Center for Reading Research, it should be cautioned that early research on the program's effectiveness did not utilize a control group, and did not control for level of parental supervision. *Phono-Graphix* has the flexibility to be employed at a Tier I or Tier II level, depending on how it is utilized, though it is specifically recommended for younger students who have struggled with more acoustical based interventions to decipher sounds in words.

13. READ NATURALLY:

Read Naturally focuses on building reading fluency and speed as well as fostering more accurate comprehension skills. The program uses repeated exposures to modeled reading, and progress monitoring to increase overall fluency skill. It is designed for students who fall below the mean level oral fluency rates for 2nd grade (51 wpm) through 8th grade (133 wpm). There is an initial placement test that dictates the level at which each student will begin the program. Next, the student and teacher agree on a reading fluency goal, which is typically 30 to 40 words correct per minute higher than the students' current level of performance. The student must master rate, accuracy, prosody, comprehension, and retell/summary goals for at least 8 of the 24 stories in each level before moving up to the next half-grade reading level. All *Read Naturally* tasks follow a structured sequence. The student selects a story of interest, subvocalizes vocabulary terms and meanings along with a recording, and formulates a prediction about the story. The student then attempts a "cold-read" of the story, and graphs the number of words read correctly in one minute. Next, the student then reads the story aloud with the tape recording at least three times. The rate of the recorded reading level increases with each successive reading. The student then attempts a "hot read" of the passage as the teacher records errors, monitors prosody, and times the reading for one minute. A variety of comprehension questions, including main idea, details, vocabulary, drawing inferences, and a short answer question are answered either before or after the "hot read" is completed. Lastly, the student is then given 5-8 minutes to retell the story either orally or in writing. Teacher directed mini-lessons are used to address deficit areas in reading comprehension, summary writing, reading rate, and reading accuracy. *Read Naturally* is usually recommended for a minimum of 30 minutes per day, three to five days per week. Therefore, mastery of one story typically requires more than one session. Specific teacher roles involve listening to the "hot read" and assessing rate, accuracy, prosody, and appropriate phrasing. Student monitoring includes selecting stories of interest, keeping track of which step in the program has been completed, and recording and graphing data. Both "cold" and "hot" reads are recorded and graphed, along with comprehension scores and retell points.

Cognitive/RTI Recommendations: *Read Naturally* is best suited as a Tier III or IV intervention for students who have surface dyslexia, or simply lack the ability to automatically and fluently recognize words in print. There is little formal research demonstrating the program's effectiveness, save for reiterating that reading fluency is clearly noted by the National Reading Panel (2000) as being a fundamental prerequisite for the development of text comprehension. There are numerous seminars throughout the country that offer teacher training, which costs approximately $179 for the day. Furthermore, there are also opportunities to attend a *"Train the Trainer"* course, so school districts can designate an individual to train multiple educators or paraprofessionals within a school. According to Dr. Jan Hasbrouck, the curriculum director of the program, *Read Naturally* allows students the opportunity to read and then re-read the same text, as well as provides an opportunity to receive corrections and guidance if necessary. The program is founded on the principle that students who read aloud along with a model of well-paced, expressive reading and receiving specific feedback through systematic progress monitoring, will foster improved fluency skills.

14. READING RECOVERY:

The very popular *Reading Recovery* program was initially developed for low achieving children in New Zealand in the 1970s. According to its developer, Marie Clay, *Reading Recovery* was basically designed to meet the needs of the lowest performing 20 percent of kindergarteners transitioning to 1st grade. This is a one-on-one daily program, requiring 30 minutes of instruction each day, five days a week for up to 20 weeks. *Reading Recovery* emphasizes strategies for children to self-monitor their reading performance, and hopefully internalize these strategies to become independent readers. Each half-hour lesson has five structural components including: 1) rereading familiar books, 2) reading recent books while the teacher keeps a running record of specific strategies and miscues, 3) a letter-lesson based upon an error analysis of student difficulty, 4) a writing lesson based on the book, 5) introducing a new book. One noteworthy aspect of *Reading Recovery* is there are no structured or scripted sequences of reading materials, as children work their way through 20 "reading books" at different levels based upon interest and instructional needs. The primary role of the instructor is to encourage strategies and successful problem solving by drawing a student's attention to certain cues, rather than directly providing the answers.

Cognitive/RTI Recommendations: *Reading Recovery is not* a systemic and explicit phonological program for increasing reading skills, nor was it specifically designed for students with learning disabilities. Furthermore, there is no research on the success rate of *Reading Recovery* instruction for children with dyslexia (Uhry & Clark, 2005). Since the program was primarily developed for 1st graders, it does seem somewhat counterintuitive to the National Reading Panel's (2000) general conclusions stating the need for a structured phonics based program for children at this age. Most studies generally show approximately one-third of all students will not make sufficient progress using *Reading Recovery*, though approximately two-thirds of low achieving children will be able to return to regular reading groups in their classroom (Deford, Lyons, & Pinnell, 1991). Other criticisms of *Reading Recovery* include the relatively high cost, due primarily to the inability to use the program with larger groups of children, and the year-long teacher training required. In summary, *Reading Recovery* is more of a **top-down** program best suited as a Tier II or III intervention for regular education students who already have some phonological and word recognition abilities.

15. READ WELL:

The *Read Well* program is primarily designed for beginning readers in kindergarten through 3rd grade. There are 38 highly scripted programs that have the flexibility to be used in general education, Title I programs, and special education instruction. There is a placement inventory used to determine which level students should begin, and in general, the program takes from one to two years, or perhaps longer for children with dyslexia. *Read Well* is structured around a unique sound sequence that introduces high frequency sounds before low frequency sounds, and separates easily confused sounds. During the small group instruction activities, the following activities comprise a typical 30 minute lesson:

Daily decoding practice (10-15 minutes) - students initially practice hearing sounds in words, then work on sounding out words and building automaticity in letter-sound recognition skills. There is also emphasis on accuracy and fluency with word patterns, reading phonologically irregular words, and then applying these skills to multi-syllabic words.

Daily reading story (10-15 minutes) - students practice reading two types of stories: *duets* and *solos*. The *duets* involve taking turns reading with the teacher, while the *solos* are designed for building independence and fluency in reading.

Comprehension - the comprehension component involves additional instructional time, as integrated reading and writing activities are gradually introduced so students can complete story maps and guided reports. Reading comprehension is developed through discussions that focus on prediction, common text structures, summarization, and vocabulary building.

An important aspect of the *Read Well* program is the additional emphasis of individual practice. Hence, there is a homework program where students read to their parents on a regular basis, and materials are provided for additional practice as well. In fact, children with learning disabilities are often encouraged to go through the daily lessons twice, in order to obtain the additional practice. Some of the *Read Well* materials include alphabet and picture cards, decoding practice folders, sound cards, storybooks, and placement inventory and decoding assessments. Given the scripted nature of the program, most teachers will be able to learn *Read Well* through self-training. Lastly, *Read Well Plus* builds upon the *Read Well* program with 12 additional units that assist 1st grade students to become acclimated to 2nd grade benchmark standards. *Read Well Plus* teaches phonics within the context of rich and meaningful themes, including high-interest chapter trade books, as students practice reading fully decodable trade books and storybooks.

Cognitive/RTI Recommendations: *Read Well* is an explicit and systematic program for teaching phonics skills to beginning readers. The program's authors, Marilyn Sprick, Lisa Howard, and Ann Fidanque, basically validate its effectiveness due to *Read Well's* close alignment with research proven techniques put forth by the National Reading Panel (2000). Still, there is very little direct research using the actual program. However, in a pilot program conducted in Montgomery, Alabama, there were significant increases in kindergarten and 1st grade students who used *Read Well* as their core literacy program. Outcome measures were determined by assessing the percentage of students who attained benchmark literacy rates using the *DIBELS*. A much smaller pilot program conducted in Oregon revealed significant gains in kindergarteners and 1st graders using *Read Well* as part of the core curriculum (*Read Well* is not designed to be part of the core curriculum beyond 1st grade) as measured by the *Woodcock-Johnson Tests of Achievement*. There is little research literature indicating the effectiveness of Read Well with dyslexic students. In summary, *Read Well* is more of a **bottom-up** program probably most effective as a Tier III or IV intervention for younger students with decoding difficulties.

16. READ 180:

The *Read 180* program is truly a **balanced literacy** program designed to meet the needs of students who are struggling on one or more of the five pillars of reading as outlined by the National Reading Panel (2000). The 90 minute instructional model begins with teachers directing a 20-minute whole-group instruction, followed by students rotating between three smaller groups during the next 60 minutes. The first group involves small group instructional activities that allow teachers to better differentiate instruction. The second group is what makes the program unique, in that students use highly interactive and adaptive software that systemically directs the learner though the four learning zones. The *Reading Zone* includes phonics, fluency, and vocabulary instruction as students read through passages. The *Word Zone* provides systemic instruction in decoding and word recognition skills as 6000 words are defined and analyzed. The *Spelling Zone* allows students to practice spelling and receive immediate feedback, and the *Success Zone* focuses on comprehension once the other zones have been mastered. The software component of the program is highly adaptive as opportunities are provided for repeated oral reading, hearing models read with fluency, and using videos to provide background knowledge and introduce vocabulary. Based upon how the student reads, the software continually adjusts the level of instruction to adapt to the individual learner. Following the computer training, students meet for the third small group instructional activity, which involves building reading comprehension using both paperback and audiobooks. Lastly, the sessions end with a

10 minute whole group wrap-up time. The goal of *Read 180* is to develop multiple aspects of reading including the following:

Phonemic Awareness - Phonemic awareness is developed both in the context of decoding (word identification) and encoding (spelling).

Phonics - Instruction is provided through decoding tips with modeled practice in segmentation, blending, structural analysis, and correct pronunciation.

Fluency - READ 180 develops fluency through repeated reading in the software, modeled reading in the audiobooks, structured engagement techniques conducted by the teacher, and independent reading.

Text Comprehension - The software and the *rBook* instruction uses motivating videos to help students build mental models that promote text comprehension.

Vocabulary - Vocabulary development is supported through explicit instruction in the rBooks as well as the systematic introduction of content-relevant vocabulary in the software.

Spelling - Software presents spelling instruction and practice that is assessment-based and individualized for each student. Spelling errors are addressed with immediate, corrective feedback.

Writing - The *rBook* presents carefully scaffolded instruction on the key types of writing: narrative, descriptive, expository, and persuasive. Functional (technical) writing is also covered.

Cognitive/RTI Recommendations: *Read 180* is a Tier IV reading intervention that requires a strong commitment from the school district. When a district purchases *Read 180*, the company (Scholastic) will meet with district teams to develop a comprehensive, ongoing implementation and professional development plan. The two days of in-person implementation training for teachers, principals, reading and literacy specialists, and technology specialists cost $2500.00 per day. In addition, Scholastic offers the *Read 180 Seminar Series*, which consists of eight half-day seminars to provide teachers with on-going professional training.

Read 180 is designed for students from elementary through high school, though it primarily focuses on the development of fluency, vocabulary and language building, and comprehension skills. This is not an explicit phonics model of teaching reading; therefore, it may be better suited for students at the secondary level. *Read 180* uses effective meta-cognitive strategies including main idea, summarizing, sequencing, and self-monitoring to assist with comprehension, and may be particularly effective for students with executive functioning types of deficits. One of the most appealing aspects of *Read 180* is the opportunity for educators to make relevant data-based decisions using the Scholastic Achievement Manager. This provides information regarding AYP accountability requirements, and district-wide data aggregation for teachers, administrators, and technology coordinators. In the classroom, teachers can use the information generated from the Scholastic Achievement Manager to diagnose student needs and locate resources for addressing them. At the district level, administrators are able to monitor Adequate Yearly Progress and allocate resources appropriately. There are over sixty actionable reports with some specifically designed for teachers and others exclusively for administrators. *Read 180* was developed by Dr. Ted Hasselbring at Vanderbilt University and is derived from research on the use of technology for enhancing learning in students with mild disabilities. The program has been continuously researched since initially being implemented in public schools in 1999. Most results have provided initial support for the effectiveness of the program. In fact, the company website details a recent study in an Arizona school district demonstrating the effectiveness of Read 180 assisting struggling 9th and 10th graders. However, an analysis of the program by the Florida Center for Reading Research noted that some earlier findings only provide tentative support for the program due to students not being randomly assigned to treatment or control groups.

17. ROAD TO THE CODE:

The *Road to the Code* program is an 11 week program designed primarily for kindergarten and 1st grade students struggling with beginning reading and phonics skills. There are 44 developmentally sequenced lessons taught in small groups featuring three separate activities:

1. *Say-It-and-Move-It* activities teach students to segment words into phonemes by moving a small tile for each sound they say in the word.

2. *Letter Name and Sound Instruction* introduces a variety of games and activities that focus on learning 8 letter-sound correspondences often found in consonant-vowel-consonant patterns.

3. *Phonological Awareness Practice* involves sound categorization and further practice with rhyming, identifying initial sounds, and using a puppet to learn to stretch sounds.

Road to the Code is a series of scripted lessons that can be used to augment the curriculum, and can be taught by classroom teachers, resource specialists, or reading teachers. There is no professional development or training needed, as the manual is sufficient for learning the program.

Cognitive/RTI Recommendations: *Road to the Code* is an explicit and systemic phonics model of instruction, and does not focus on fluency, comprehension, or vocabulary skills. However, the program is based on the National Reading Panel's (2000) findings that teaching phonemic awareness and phonological processing in young children is essential to the establishment of strong literacy skills. The program is intended as a Tier II model of support for kindergarten and 1st grade children who struggled with the alphabetic principal. *Road to the Code* has empirical support from both an initial study completed in six kindergarten classrooms in New York (Ball & Blachman, 1988), as well as a longitudinal study with kindergartens revealing significant improvement on tests of phoneme segmentation and letter-sound knowledge at the end of kindergarten (Blachman, Ball, Black, & Tangel, 1994).

18. Systematic Instruction in Phoneme Awareness, Phonics, and Sight Words (SIPPS):

The *SIPPS Instruction* program is a three-tiered program designed by John Shefelbine for children in kindergarten through 3rd grade. There is a placement assessment that allows teachers to determine where to start children in all levels of the program. The *Beginning Level* is designed for nonreaders in either kindergarten or 1st grade and has 55 lessons, most of which are geared toward developing phonemic awareness tasks and sequencing sounds. In addition, high frequency irregular words are also taught as sight words. There is a gradual transition into decodable text, in which the majority of the words can be sounded out. The *SIPPS* program is an explicit phonics program that is highly scripted and requires choral responses by students in unison. In other words, the students are actively engaged with most teacher directed routines using visual cues and modeling to elicit group responses. This allows the instructor to readily assess student performance. The final activity of each lesson involves fluency practice, where students sit quietly at their desk and read aloud from "little books." There is a natural progression in teaching short vowels, then long vowels, as well as emphasis on using key words as well as diacritical markers to help students remember sound patterns. A typical daily lesson lasts up to 45 minutes, and consists of the following components:

- Phoneme Play
- Phonics and Decodable Words
- Sight Words
- Guided Spelling and Segmentation
- Reading a Story Chart
- Fluency Practice

The next level is the *Extension Level*, as students usually begin this level knowing at least 50 sight words and being able to read and spell simple short-vowel-pattern words. By the end of this level, students are expected to read single-syllable words with complex vowels and more than 150 high-frequency irregular words. Lastly, the *Challenge Level* focuses on *polysyllabic strategies*, as students usually begin this level having mastered much of single-syllable phonics and most high-frequency irregular sight words. With reading levels between first and third grade, these students focus on reading polysyllabic words with accuracy and increasing fluency. There is also a *SIPPS Intervention* program for students in Grades 4 through 12 that includes *SIPPS Plus*, which is basically the instructional content of the *Beginning* and *Extension* Levels with reading materials of interest to older students.

Cognitive/RTI Recommendations: *SIPPS* is primarily designed around the founding principles developed by the National Reading Panel (2000). As stated in Chapter 3, these principles involve using an explicit and systemic phonics program in the early years, though *SIPPS* has an increased emphasis on polysyllabic coding. The program is based on the premise that beginning literacy is best taught through two distinct strands, one focusing on decoding and the other on comprehension. Still, there has been very little research on *SIPPS* to validate its effectiveness, save for a two-year pilot study in California. On average, students in 1st through 6th grades gained an average of 1.6 grade equivalents in reading as measured by the *Slosson Oral Reading Test*. However, there were no control groups in the study, and these students were not dyslexic. Perhaps the most encouraging aspect of *SIPPS* is the program's success with English language learners (ELL). It should be cautioned that although the National Reading Panel (2000) determined the effectiveness of explicit phonics programs in the earlier grades, diminishing returns were observed for older students. Therefore, *SIPPS* is more of a **bottom-up** program probably most effective as a Tier II or III intervention for younger students with decoding difficulties, as well as English language learners. The quicker pace and reliance on unison responses may help keep students with attention difficulties better engaged as well.

19. SOAR TO SUCCESS:

The *Soar to Success* program is a relatively fast-paced, small group instructional program, designed to accelerate reading for students in grades 3 through 6. The program mainly focuses on ***top-down*** strategies aimed at improving reading comprehension skills. Specific instructional strategies involve the use of graphic organizers to help students visually construct meaning from print. In addition, reciprocal teaching uses four strategies including SUMMARIZE-CLARIFY-QUESTION-and PREDICT as teachers model the use of these strategies while the text is being read. There are 18 books, sequenced from simple to complex, as part of the process of scaffolding instruction. A typical 35 minute lesson often involves:

Revisiting (5 min) - students re-read alone or with a partner allowing teacher to conduct an oral reading check.

Reviewing (5 min) - students summarize the previous day's reading using graphic organizers.

Rehearsing (10 min) - teachers preview new text to be read and students make predictions, as well as construct a K-W-L chart. There is a vocabulary list developed daily, and students are requested to write a sentence with each new vocabulary word.

Reading and Reciprocal Teaching (10-15 min) - students silently read the text to verify predictions or answer questions. Next, reciprocal teaching is employed as students and teachers take turns modeling the use of four strategies: *summarize, clarify, question, predict.*

Responding/Reflecting (5 min) - students reflect on strategies, discuss, and share.

Cognitive/RTI Recommendations: The *Soar to Success* program was designed to be used in conjunction with a regular program of classroom instruction in reading and language arts, and generally can be completed in less than a year. It requires minimal teacher training, and was developed to foster effective strategies for allowing students to construct meaning from print. There is evidence to suggest its effectiveness based upon a 2-year national research study completed by Houghton-Mifflin in 1996 through 1997. The results suggested that students using *Soar to Success* performed significantly better than students from a control group on retelling, answering questions, and comprehension after 76 days of instruction. However, there is little research to suggest its effectiveness for students with dyslexia. *Soar to Success* should be utilized as a Tier ll intervention for older elementary students with weaknesses in vocabulary and reading comprehension skills.

20. WILSON READING SYSTEM:

The *Wilson Reading System* is one of the few reading programs developed specifically for adolescents and adults with dyslexia. It was developed by Barbara Wilson and is based on an Orton-Gillingham approach to reading, meaning that it is a multi-sensory and synthetic phonics approach to teaching reading for students with language based difficulties. The *Wilson Reading System* was developed for students in 3rd grade onwards and even for adults, and may also be appropriate for bilingual students who have adequate English skills, though continue to have difficulties with written language skills. The program is sequenced into 12 steps, based upon six syllable types:

Grouping of Six Syllable Types

1. Closed syllables with short vowels *(drip)*
2. Syllables with long vowels and a silent "e" *(brave)*
3. Open syllables ending in long vowels *(she)*
4. Syllables ending with the consonant "le" *(table)*
5. "R" controlled syllables *(dark)*
6. Vowel digraph/diphthong syllables *(town)*

According to Uhry and Clark (2005), there are three unique features of the *Wilson* program that can be extremely helpful for older students with dyslexia. First, there is an immediate emphasis on the six syllable types, though complex diacritical markers are not a component of the program. Instead, students create their own system of coding syllables using underlined instead of slash marks. A second feature of the program is the use of a unique finger tapping system to analyze spoken words into phonemes to assist with spelling. For example, in teaching the word "map" three lettered cards are put on the table to represent the three sounds in the word. The student is taught to say each sound while tapping a different finger to his or her thumb, as follows:

- As the student says the /m/ sound, he taps his index finger to his thumb.
- As the student says the /a/ sound, he taps his middle finger to his thumb.
- As the student says the /p/ sound, he taps his ring finger to his thumb.
- The student then says the sounds as he drags his thumb across the three fingers starting with his index finger and ending with his ring finger.

Lastly, the Sound Cards in the program are color coded, with consonants being yellow, vowels being orange, and word families green. Wilson recommends that students receive 45–90 minutes of instruction per day, and it may take more than one day to complete any given lesson. It should be noted that all steps in the program are laid out in a very structured format, with students starting at the same level. While the lessons are not scripted per se, teacher training begins with an initial 2-day overview. The 12-step plan is hierarchically arranged in the following manner:

Steps to Wilson Reading System

Sound Card Drills (2-3 min): a typical lesson begins with color coded sound cards used to introduce new sounds as well as review old ones.

Review Reading Concepts (5 min): lettered cards and finger tapping used to teach phoneme segmentation.

Word Cards (3-5 min): practice words from using sounds from sound cards.

Wordlist Reading (3-5 min): lists of both real and nonsense words are charted in terms of accuracy.

Sentence Reading (5 min): reading sentences composed of the words above charting miscues.

Quick Drill in Reverse (1-2 min): spelling is practiced as students match letters with phoneme sounds.

Review Concepts for Spelling (5 min): finger tapping sound cards to segment words.

Written Word Dictation (15 min): the student writes sounds, words, and sentences from dictation.

Passage Reading (10-15 min): the student reads a passage silently, retells the story in their own words, then reads the story aloud.

Listening Comprehension(10 min-30 min): the teacher reads aloud a passage from a higher reading level than the student's, and the student then retells the story.

Cognitive/RTI Recommendations: The *Wilson Reading Program* may be best utilized as a Tier III or IV ***bottom-up*** model of teaching reading, but its appeal toward older students stems from a ***top-down*** instructional approach towards teaching the basic structures of the English language. In other words, the program attempts to impose an organizational structure to phonological processing by emphasizing the metacognitive skills necessary to understand that words are comprised of a series of sounds that occupy a certain temporal order. Strategy formation skills such as finger tapping, color coded sound cards, and student generated diacritical markers are used instead of lower-level paired association drills between pictures and sounds. The program is carefully scaffolded to learn the regularities of the English language system. There are criterion referenced tests built into the program to allow for progress monitoring, though most of the emphasis is based on phonological development and spelling rules and boundaries, and not necessarily reading fluency. The comprehension component involves more retelling of stories and the use of visualization to assist with recall, and not necessarily metacognitive strategies to respond to specific questions about the text. The *Wilson Reading Program* has been researched with students having dyslexia (Guyer, Banks, & Guyer, 1993; Wilson, 1995), with significant gains noted for special education students.

APPENDIX I

COMPOSITE SUMMARY OF EVIDENCE-BASED READING PROGRAMS

READING PROGRAMS	ELEM.	SECONDARY	PHONEMIC AWARENESS	PHONICS	FLUENCY	COMPREHENSION	VOCABULARY	WRITING COMPONENT	MULTI-SENSORY	DIACRITICAL MARKERS	FORMAL TEACHER TRAINING
Alphabetic Phonics	X	X	X	X	X			X	X	X	X
Corrective Reading	X	X		X	X	X	X				X
DISTAR	X		X	X		X		X		X	X
Earobics	X	X	X	X			X				
Fast Forward	X	X	X	X	X	X	X				
Fundations	X		X	X	X	X	X		X	X	
Great Leaps Reading	X	X		X	X						
Horizons	X		X	X		X		X		X	X
Ladders to Literacy	X		X				X				X
LEXIA	X	X	X	X	X	X	X	X			X
LiPS	X		X	X		X		X	X	X	X
Phono-Graphix	X			X					X		X
Read Naturally	X	X		X	X	X	X	X		X	X
Reading Recovery	X			X	X	X	X			X	X
Read Well	X		X	X	X	X	X	X		X	
Read 180	X	X	X	X	X	X	X	X		X	X
Rode to Code	X		X	X						X	
SIPPS	X		X	X	X			X		X	X
Soar to Success	X	X		X		X	X	X		X	
Wilson Reading		X	X	X	X	X	X	X	X	X	X

READING PROGRAMS	PROGRESS MONITORING	SCRIPTED	DIFFERENTIATED	COMPUTERIZED	BOTTOM-UP	TOP-DOWN	TIER I	TIER II	TIER III	TIER IV
Alphabetic Phonics	X	X			X				X	X
Corrective Reading	X	X	X		X				X	X
DISTAR	X	X	X		X				X	X
Earobics	X			X	X		X	X		
Fast Forward	X			X	X	X		X	X	
Fundations	X	X	X		X			X	X	
Great Leaps Reading	X		X			X		X		
Horizons	X	X	X		X				X	X
Ladders to Literacy			X		X		X	X		
LEXIA	X		X	X	X	X		X	X	X
LiPS	X		X		X	X			X	X
Phono-Graphix	X				X		X	X	X	
Read Naturally	X		X			X			X	X
Reading Recovery	X					X		X	X	
Read Well	X	X	X		X		X		X	X
Read 180	X		X	X	X	X		X	X	X
Rode to Code		X			X			X	X	
SIPPS	X		X		X			X	X	
Soar to Success	X					X		X	X	
Wilson Reading	X		X		X	X			X	X

APPENDIX II

TEACHER CHECKLIST FOR DYSLEXIC BEHAVIORS

Make a ✓ check mark by each statement that is indicative of the student's behavior. If you have checked a total of six or more statements, the student may be dyslexic.

Characteristic Behaviors of Dysphonetic Dyslexia

The student...

____ 1. maintains a strong performance for leisure and academic activities that involve minimal listening skills.

____ 2. can comprehend more efficiently when material is read silently rather than orally.

____ 3. prefers learning from silent media (films) rather than audio media (tapes).

____ 4. has difficulty recalling everyday words in conversation.

____ 5. takes wild guesses recalling everyday words in conversation.

____ 6. has extreme difficulty blending letter sounds.

____ 7. remembers better when shown what to do than told what to do.

____ 8. experiences difficulty in remembering information (e.g., class assignments, phone messages) without making written notes.

____ 9. makes many spoonerisms ("You hissed classed today" for "you missed class today").

____ 10. does not follow oral directions well.

____ 11. omits vowels in two syllable words such as when spelling "tkn" for "taken".

____ 12. substitutes vowels, such as spelling the word "bit" for "bed".

Characteristic Behaviors of Surface Dyslexia

The student...

_____ 1. consistently uses finger or pencil to maintain place during reading.

_____ 2. has difficulty copying information (from chalkboard or paper).

_____ 3. mixes up capital and small letters when writing (e.g., dAd)

_____ 4. often fails to notice changes in the environment.

_____ 5. has difficulty reading maps.

_____ 6. has difficult time remembering directions when walking.

_____ 7. spells better aloud than in writing. Often gives the correct letters, but in the wrong sequence (e.g., "teh" for "the").

_____ 8. has difficulty describing visual characteristics of familiar people and places.

_____ 9. prefers listening to audio tapes rather than watching films.

_____ 10. experiences difficulty when copying figures and signs in mathematics.

_____ 11. omits words (and lines of words) when reading.

_____ 12. excessive vocalization during silent reading.

_____ 13. has a better memory for what is said than for what was read.

Characteristic Behaviors of Mixed Dyslexia

The student...

_____ 1. has difficulty structuring time.

_____ 2. is rigid and inflexible

_____ 3. makes frequent negative comments regarding reading tasks.

_____ 4. has a low frustration tolerance (especially during reading activities).

_____ 5. is highly distractible.

_____ 6. seems unaware of nonverbal social cues (e.g., gestures, tone of voice).

_____ 7. has difficulty making friends often due to blunt and insensitive remarks.

_____ 8. has not benefited from instruction via typical basal reading programs.

APPENDIX III

Popular Commercial Reading Program

Beginning Reading & Reading Support - Intervention Programs
1. **Open Court** - SRA/McGraw Hill
2. **Scholastic Phonic Readers & Phonic Chapter Books** - John Shefelbine
3. **Phonics for Reading** - Anita Archer et al., Curriculum Associates
4. **Reading Mastery** - SRA, Zig Engleman et al.
5. **Project READ** - http://www.projectread.com
6. **Words Their Way** - Bear et al., Merrill/Prentice Hall (1999 2nd edition)
7. **Read Well** - Sprick et al., Sopris West, www.sopriswest.com
8. **PALS Kinder, Gr. 1 & Upper Grade** (Peer Assisted Learning Strategies) - Mathes, Torgesen, et al. (1999), Available from Sonoma County SELPA
9. **Alphagram Learning Materials** - www.alphagram.com
10. **SIPPS (Systematic Instruction in Phonemic Awareness, Phonics & Sight Words)** - Developmental Studies Center
11. **Soar to Success** - Houghton-Mifflin
12. **The 6 Minute Solution** - Sopris West, www.sopriswest.com
13. **Great Leaps** - www.greatleaps.com
14. **Quick Reads** - www.pearsonlearning.com, Elfrieda "Freddy" Hiebert.
15. **Fluency Formula** - Scholastic, Wiley Blevins - www.scholastic.com

Phonemic Awareness/PreReading Phonology/Early Intervention-Prevention
1. **Phonemic Awareness in young Children** - Marilyn Adams et al., Paul Brooks pub., www.pbrookes.com
2. **Road to the Code** - Blackman et al., Paul Brooks pub., www.pbrookes.com
3. **Ladders to Literacy** - Paul Brooks pub., www.pbrookes.com
4. **Soundabet** - www.soundabet.com
5. **Lindamood/Bell- Lips** - www.lindamoodbell.com
6. **Early Reading Intervention (Project Optimize)** - Scott Forseman, www.scottforesman.com

Dictionaries for Vocabulary Work
1. **Heinle & Heinle** - nhd.heinle.com/home.aspx
2. **Longman** - www.longman.com

Motivation & Record Keeping Software
1. **Accelerated Reader/Advantage Learning Systems**
2. **Reading Counts/Scholastic Reading Inventory** - Scholastic
3. **Bookadventure.org** - www.bookadventure.org
4. **Lexile** - www.lexile.com

Phonemic Awareness
1. **Daisey's Quest and Daisey's Castle** - Great Wave Software
2. **Earobics**
3. **Waterford Early Reading Program**
4. **Fast Forward** - Scientific Learning Corp.
5. **LeapFrog School House** - www.leapfrogschoolhouse.com

Beginning Reading & Early Reading Tech Based Support Programs
1. **Scholastic Interactive Phonics Readers**
2. **Little Planet Literacy Series**
3. **Wiggleworks** - Scholastic
4. **Soliloquy** - www.soliloquylearning.com
5. **Intellitools - Balanced Literacy for Beginning Readers** - www.intellitools.com
6. **Read Naturally**
7. **Word Sort** - www.HendersonEdSoft.com
8. **Words Their Way Interactive Resource CD ROM** - Prentice Hall, www.prehall.com/bear
9. **Inspiration 7.0 & Kidspiration**
10. **Read, Write & Type** - www.readwritetype.com

Teacher Knowledge Tools

1. **CORE - The Source Book** - www.corelearn.com
2. **Bringing Words to Life: Robust Vocabulary Instruction** - Isabel Beck et al., www.guilford.com
3. **Overcoming Dyslexia** - Sally Shaywitz, Knopf publishers
4. **Speech to Print** - Louisa Moats, www.pbrookes.com
5. **Reading Instruction That Works: The Case of Balanced Teaching** - Pressley, www.guilford.com

Adapted from http://www.scoe.org/reading

REFERENCES

Adams, M. (1990). *Beginning to read: Thinking and learning about print.* Cambridge, M A : The MIT Press.

Alexander, A.W. & Slinger-Constant, A. M. (2004). Current status of treatments for dyslexia: Critical Review. *Journal of Child Neurology*, 19 (10), 744-758.

Allman, J.K., Hakeem, A., Erwin, J.M., Nimchinsky E., & Hof, P. (2001). The anterior cingulate cortex. The evolution of an interface between emotion and cognition. *Annals of the New York Academy of Science*, 935, 107-117.

Anderson, V.A., Anderson, P., Northam, E., Jacobs, R. , & Catroppa, C. (2001). Development of executive functions through late childhood and adolescence in an Australian sample, *Developmental Neuropsychology, 20* (1), 385-406.

Aylward, G.P. (1997). *Infant and early childhood neuropsychology.* New York: Plenum.

Baddeley, A. (2000). The episodic buffer: a new component of working memory. *Trends in Cognitive Science, 4* (11), 417-423.

Baddeley, A. (1998). Working memory. *C.R. Academy of Sciences III, 321* (2-3): 167-173.

Bagozzi, R. (1992). The self-regulation of attitudes, intentions, and behavior. *Social Psychology Quarterly, 55* (2), 178-204.

Bakker, D.J. (2006). Treatment of developmental dyslexia: A review. *Pediatric Rehabilitation, 9* (1), 3-13.

Ball, E.W. & Blachman, B.A. (1988). Phoneme segmentation training: Effect on reading readiness. *Annals of Dyslexia, 38,* 208-225.

Barkley, R. (2001). The executive functions and self regulation: an evolutionary neuropsychological perspective. *Neuropsychology Review, 11* (1), 1-29.

Baron, I.S. (2004). *Neuropsychological evaluation of the child.* New York: Oxford University Press.

Berninger, V.W. & Richards, T.L. (2002). *Brain literacy for educators and Psychologists.* London: Academic Press.

Blachman, B.A., Ball, E., Black, R., & Tangel, D. (1994). Kindergarten teachers develop phoneme awareness in low income inner-city classrooms. Does it make a difference? *Reading and Writing: An Interdisciplinary Journal, 6,* 1-17.

Blair, R.J. (2004). The roles of orbital frontal cortex in the modulation of antisocial behavior. *Brain and Cognition, 55,* 198-208.

Borowsky, R. Cummine, J., Owen, W.J., Friesen C.K., Shih, F., & Sarty, G.E. (2006). fMRI of ventral and dorsal processing streams in basic reading processes: Insular sensitivity to phonology. *Basic Reading Processes,* 1-22.

Borowsky, R., Owen, W.J., & Masson, M.E. (2002). Diagnostics of phonological lexical processing: pseudohomophone naming advantages, disadvantages, and base-word frequency effects. *Memory and Cognition, 30* (6), 969-987.

Bowyer-Crane, C., & Snowling, M.J. (2005). Assessing children's inference generation: What do tests of reading comprehension measure? *British Journal of Educational Psychology, 75,* 189-201.

Bremner, J.D. (2005). *Brain imaging handbook.* New York: W.W. Norton & Company.

Brosnan, M., Demetre, J., Hamill, S., Robson, K., Shepherd, H., & Cody, G. (2002). Executive functioning in adults and children with developmental dyslexia. *Neuropsychologia, 40,* 2144-2155.

Burns, M.K. (2003). Reexamining data from the national reading panel's meta-analysis: Implications for school psychology. *Psychology in the Schools, 40* (6) 605-612.

Burns, M.S. (2000). The biology of dyslexia. *Brain Connection,* Retrieved from http://www.brainconnection.com/topics/?main=col/burns00jun.

Byrnes, J. P. (2001). *Minds, brains, and learning: Understanding the psychological and educational relevance of neuroscientific research.* New York: Guilford Press.

Cain, K., & Oakhill, J. (1999). Inference making ability and its relation to comprehension failure in young children. *Reading and Writing, 11,* 489-503.

Cain, K., Oakhill, J., & Bryant, P. (2000). Phonological skills and comprehension failure: A test of the phonological processing deficit hypothesis. *Reading and Writing: An Interdisciplinary Journal, 13,* 31-56.

Cain, K., Oakhill, J.V., & Elbro, C. (2003). The ability to learn new word meanings from context by school-age children with and without language comprehension difficulties. *Journal of Child Language, 30,* 681-694.

Campbell, J.L.D., & Xue, Q. (2001). Cognitive arithmetic across cultures: *Journal of Experimental Psychology, 130* (2), 299-315.

Canter, A. (2006, February). Problem solving and RTI: New roles for school psychologists. *Communiqué, 34* (5), insert. Available: http://www.nasponline.org/advocacy/rtifactsheets.aspx

Carlin, G. (1997). *Brain droppings.* New York: Hyperion Publishers.

Carter, R. (1998). *Mapping the mind.* Berkeley: University of California Press.

Catts, H.W., Adlof, S.M., & Weismer, S.E. (2006). Language deficits in poor comprehenders: A case for the simple view of reading. *Journal of Speech, Language, and Hearing Research, 49,* 278-293.

Chall, J. (1983). *Learning to read: The great debate.* New York: McGraw-Hill.

Chow, T.W. , & Cummings, J.L. (1999). Frontal-subcortical circuits. In B.L. Miller & J. L. Cummings, *The human frontal lobes: functions and disorder,* (p.4), New York: Guilford Publications.

Cicerone, K. (2002). The enigma of executive functioning: Theoretical contributions to therapeutic interventions. In P.J. Eslinger (Ed.), *Neuropsychological Interventions: Clinical research and practice.* New York: Guilford Press.

Cunningham, J.W. (2001). Book review of the Report of the National Reading Panel: Teaching children to read: An evidence-based assessment of the scientific research literature on reading and its implications for reading instruction. *Reading Research Quarterly, 36,* 326-335.

Deford, D.E., Lyons, C.A., & Pinnell, G. S. (1991). *Bridges to literacy: Learning from reading recovery.* Portsmouth, NH: Heinemann.

Della Toffalo, D.A. (2006). *Neuropsychology and RTI: The odd couple?* Workshop presented at the 2006 Annual Fall Conference of the Association of School Psychologists of Pennsylvania. State College, PA. October 18, 2006.

Demb, J.B., Boynton, G.M., & Heeger, D.J. (1998). Psychophysical evidence for a magnocellular deficit in dyslexics. *Vision Research, 38,* 15555-15559.

Dolan, R.J. (1999). On the neurology of morals. *Nature Neuroscience, 2* (11), 927-929.

Duara, R., Kushch, A., Gross-Glenn, K., Barker, W.W., Jallad, B., Pascal, S., Loewenstein, D.A., Sheldon, J., Rabin, M., Levin, B., & Lubs, H. (1991). Neuroanatomical differences between dyslexic and normal readers on magnetic resonance imaging scans. *Archives of Neurology, 48,* 410-416.

Engelmann S., Engelmann, O., & Davis, K. L.S. (1997). *Horizons learning to read: Fast track A-B teacher's guide.* Columbus, Ohio: SRA/McGraw-Hill.

Feifer, S.G., & DeFina, P.D. (2000). *The Neuropsychology of Reading Disorders: Diagnosis and Intervention.* Middletown, MD: School Neuropsych Press.

Feifer, S.G., & DeFina, P.D. (2002). *The Neuropsychology of Written Language Disorders: Diagnosis and Intervention.* Middletown, MD: School Neuropsych Press.

Fiorello, C.E., Hale, J.B., & Snyder, L.E. (2006). Cognitive hypothesis testing and response to intervention for children with reading problems. *Psychology in the Schools, 43* (8), 835-853.

Florida Center for Reading Research, 277 N. Bronough St., Suite 7250, Tallahassee, FL 32301 http://www.fcrr.org.

Francils, D.J., Fletcher, J.M., Catts, H.W., & Tomblin, J.B. (2005). Dimensions affecting the assessment of reading comprehension. In S.A. Stahl & S.G. Paris (Eds.), *Children's reading comprehension and assessment* (p. 369-394). Mahwah, N.J.: Erlbaum.

Fuchs, L.S. (1998). Computer applications to address implementation difficulties associated with curriculum-based measurement. In M. R. Shinn (Ed.), *Advanced applications of curriculum-based measurement* (pp. 89-112). New York: Guilford.

Fuchs, D., Mock, D. Morgan, P.L.,& Young, C.L. (2003). Responsiveness-to-intervention: Definitions, evidence, and implications for the learning disabilities construct. *Learning Disabilities Research & Practice, 18*, 157-171.

Galaburda, A.M. (1989). Ordinary and extraordinary brain development: Anatomical variation in developmental dyslexia: *Annals of Dyslexia, 39*, 67-80.

Galaburda, A.M. (1993). Neuroanatomical basis of developmental dyslexia. *Neurological Clinic, 11*, 161-173.

Galabruda, A.M. & Cestnick, L. (2003). Developmental dyslexia. *Review of Neurology, 36*, (S. 3-9).

Giancola, P. (1995). Evidence for dorsolateral and orbital prefrontal cortical involvement in the expression of aggressive behavior. *Aggressive Behavior, 21*, 431-450.

Goldberg, E. (1989). Gradiental approach to neocortical functional organization. *Journal of Clinical and Experimental Neuropsychology, 11*(4), 489-517.

Goldberg, E. (2001). *The executive brain: Frontal lobes and the civilized mind.* New York: Oxford University Press.

Goldberg, E. (2005). *The wisdom paradox.* New York: Gotham Books.

Gough, P.B., Hoover, W.A., & Peterson, C.L. (1996). Some observations on a simple view of reading. In C. Cornoldi & J. Oakhill (Eds.), *Reading comprehension difficulties: Processes and intervention* (p.1-13). Mahwah, N.J.: Erlbaum.

Guyer, B.P., Banks, S.R., & Guyer, K.E. (1993). Spelling improvement by college students who are dyslexic. *Annals of Dyslexia, 43*, 186-193.

Golestani, N., Molko, N., Dehaene, S., Lebihan, D., & Pallier, C. (2006). Brain structure predicts the learning of foreign speech sounds. *Cerebral Cortex, 7.*

Hale, J.B. (2006). Implementing IDEA 2004 with a three-tier model that includes response to intervention and cognitive assessment methods. *School Psychology Forum, 1*(1). Bethesda, MD: National Association of School Psychologists. Retrieved from www.nasponline.org/publications/spf/index.aspx.

Hale, J.B. & Fiorello, C.A. (2004). *School neuropsychology: A practitioner's handbook.* New York: Guilford Press.

Hale, J.B., Kaufman, A., Naglieri, J.A., & Kavale, K.A. (2006). Implementation of IDEA: Integrating response to intervention and cognitive assessment methods. *Psychology in the Schools, 43* (7), 753-770.

Heim, S. & Keil, A. (2004). Large-scale neural correlates of developmental dyslexia. *European Child & Adolescent Psychiatry, 13*, 125-40.

Holtmaat, A., Wilbrecht, L., Knott, G.W., Welker, E., & Syoboda, K. (2006). Experience dependent and cell-type-specific spine growth in the neocortex. *Nature, 441*(7096), 979-983.

Hopko, D.R., Ashcraft, M.H., & Gute, J. (1998). Mathematics anxiety and working memory: Support for the existence of a deficient inhibition mechanism. *Journal of Anxiety Disorders,12* (4), 343-355.

Hubel, D.H., & Wiesel, T.N. (1970). The period of susceptibility to the effects of unilateral eye closure in kittens. *Journal of Physiology, 206* (2), 419-436.

Hucheson, L., Selig, H., & Young, N. (1990). A success story: A large urban district offers a working model for implementing multi-sensory teaching into the resource and regular classroom. *Annals of Dyslexia, 40,* 79-96.

Huitt, W. (1999). Conation as an important factor of mind. *Educational Psychology Interactive.* Valdosta, GA: Valdosta State University. Retrieved from http://chiron.valdosta.edu/whuitt/col/regys/conation.html.

Hynd, G.W., Hall, J., Novey, E.S., Eliopulos, D., Black, K., Gonzalez, J.J., Edmonds, J.E., Riccio, C., & Cohen, M. (1995). Dyslexia and corpus callosum morphology. *Archives of Neurology, 52,* 32-28.

International Dyslexia Association (IDA) (2003). *Finding the answers (pamphlet).* Baltimore, MD: Author.

Kaufman, A.S. (1994). *Intelligent testing with the WISC III.* New York: John Wiley & Sons.

Kavale, K.A., & Forness, S.R. (2000). What definitions of learning disability say and don't say. *Journal of Learning Disabilities, 33* (3), 239-256.

Klorman, R., Hazel-Fernandez, L.A., Shaywitz, S.E., Fletcher, J.M., Marchione, K.E., Holahan, J.M., Stuebing, K.K., & Shaywitz, B.A. (1999). Executive functioning deficits in attention-deficit hyperactivity disorder children are independent of oppositional defiant or reading disorder. *Journal of the American Academy of Child and Adolescent Psychiatry, 27,* 163-170.

Kotulak, R. (1996). *Inside the brain: Revolutionary discoveries of how the mind works.* Kansas City: Andrews McMeel Publishing.

Kovaleski, J.F. (2002). *Best practices in operating pre-referral intervention teams in Pennsylvania.* In A. Thomas & J. Grimes (Eds), *Best practices in school psychology IV* (pp 645-655) Bethesda, MD: NASP.

Kraly, F.S. (2006). *Brain science and psychological disorders.* New York: W.W. Norton & Company.

Kratochwill, T.R., Albers, C.A., & Shernoff, E.S. (2004). School-based interventions. *Child and Adolescent Psychiatric Clinics of North America, 13,* 885-903.

Learning Disabilities Roundtable, U.S. Department of Education (2002). *Specific learning disabilities: Finding common ground.* Washington DC: U.S. Department of Education, Office of Special Education Programs. Office of Innovation and Development.

LeDoux, J. (1996). *The emotional brain.* Simon & Schuster: New York.

Levine, M.D., & Reed, M. (1999). *Developmental variation and learning disorders.* Massachusetts: Educators Publishing Services, Inc.

Lezak, M.D. (1995). *Neuropsychological assessment: Third edition.* New York: Oxford University Press.

Lezak, M.D., Howieson, D.B., & Loring, D.W. (2004). *Neuropsychological assessment: Fourth edition.* New York: Oxford University Press.

Livingstone, M.S., Rosen, G.D., Drislane, F.W., & Galaburda, A.M. (1991). *Proceedings Of the National Academy of Science, USA, 88,* 7943-7947.

Lovett, M., Lacerenza, L., Borden, S.L., Frijters, J.C., Steinbach, K.A., & DePalma, M. (2000). Components of effective remediation for developmental reading disabilities: Combining phonological and strategy-based instruction to improve outcomes. *Journal of Educational Psychology, 92,* 263-283.

Luria, A., (1970). The functional organization of the brain. *Scientific American, 222,* 66-78.

Macaruso, P., Hook, P.E., & McCabe, R. (2006). The efficacy of computer-based supplementary phonics programs for advancing reading skills in at-risk elementary students. *Journal of Research in Reading, 29* (2), 162-172.

Malloy, P. F., & Richardson, E.D. (1994). Assessment of frontal lobe functions. *Journal of Neuropsychiatry Clinical Neuroscience, 6,* 399-410.

McCandliss, B.D., Cohen, L., & Dehaene, S. (2003). The visual word form area: Expertise for reading in the fusiform gyrus. *Trends in Cognitive Sciences, 7* (7), 293-299.

McCandliss, B.D. & Noble, K.G. (2003). The development of reading impairment: A cognitive neuroscience model. *Mental Retardation and Developmental Disabilities, 9,* 196-205.

McCook, J.E. (2006). *The RTI guide: Developing and implementing a model in your schools.* Horsham, Pennsylvania: LRP Publications.

McGuinness, C., McGuinness, D., & McGuiness, G. (1996). Phono-graphix: A new method for remediation reading difficulties. *Annals of Dyslexia, 46,* 73-96.

Mega, M.S. , & Cummings, J.L. (1994). Frontal-subcortical circuits and neuropsychiatric disorders. *Journal of Neuropsychiatry Clinical Neuroscience, 6,* 358-370.

Mercer, C.D., Campbell, K.U., Miller, M.D., Mercer, K.D., & Lane, H.B. (2000). Effects of reading fluency intervention for middle schoolers with specific learning disabilities. *Learning Disabilities Research and Practice, 15* (4), 179-189.

Mirsa, M., Katzir, T., Wolf, M., & Poldrack, R.A. (2004). Neural systems for rapid automatized naming (RAN) in skilled readers: Unraveling the RAN-reading relationship. *Science Study of Reading, 8,* 241-256.

Moats, L. (2004). Relevance of neuroscience to effective education for students with reading and other learning disabilities. *Journal of Child Neurology, 19* (10), 840-845.

Moffitt, T.E., & Henry, B. (1989). Neuropsychological assessment of executive functions in self-reported delinquents. *Developmental Psycholopathology, 1,* 105-118.

Morgan, A.B., & Lilienfeld, S.O. (2000). A meta-analytic review of the relation between antisocial behavior and neuropsychological measures of executive functions. *Clinical Psychology Review, 20* (1), 113-136.

Nagy, W., Osborn, J., Winsor, P., & O'Flahavan, J. (1994). Structural analysis: Some Guidelines for instruction. In F. Lehr & J. Osborn (Eds.), *Reading, language, and literacy* (p.45-58). Hillsdale, N.J.: Erlbaum.

Nation, K., Clarke, P., Marshall, C.M., & Durand, M. (2004). Hidden language impairments in children: Parallels between poor reading comprehension and specific language impairments? *Journal of Speech, Language, and Hearing Research, 47,* 199-211.

Nation, K., Clarke, P., & Snowling, M.J. (2002). General cognitive ability in children with reading comprehension difficulties. *British Journal of Educational Psychology, 72,* 549-560.

Nation, K., & Snowling, M. (1997). Assessing reading difficulties: The validity and utility of current measures of reading skill. *British Journal of Educational Psychology, 67,* 359-370.

Nation, K., & Snowling, M.J. (1998). Individual differences in contextual facilitation: Evidence from dyslexia and poor reading comprehension. *Child Development, 69,* 994-1009.

National Association of State Directors of Special Education. (May, 2006). *Myths about response to intervention (Rtl) implementation.* Retrieved February 24, 2007, from http://nasdse.org/documents/Myths%20about%20Rtl.pdf

National Reading Panel (2000). *Teaching Children to Read: An Evidenced Based Assessment of the Scientific Research Literature on Reading and its Implications for Reading Instruction.* Washington, D.C.: National Institutes of Child Health and Human Development.

Noble, K.G., & McCandliss, B.D. (2005). Reading development and impairment: Behavioral, social, and neurobiological factors. *Developmental and Behavioral Pediatrics, 26* (5), 370-376.

Owen, W.J., Borowsky, R., & Sarty, G.E. (2004). FMRI of two measures of phonological processing in visual word recognition: Ecological validity matters. *Brain and Language, 90,* 40-46.

Paulesu, E., Frith, U., Snowlilng, M., Gallagher, A., Morton, J., Frackowiak, R. S. J., & Frith, C. (1996). Is developmental dyslexia a disconnection syndrome? *Brain, 119,* 143-157.

Paulesu, E., Demonet, J.F., Fazio, F., McCrory, E., Chanoine, V., Brunswick, N., Cappa, S.F., Cossu, G., Habib, M., Frith, C.D., & Frith, U. (2001). Dyslexia: Cultural diversity and biological unity. *Science, 291,* 2165-2167.

Pinker, S. (2000). *The language instinct.* New York: Harper-Collins Publisher.

Pokorni, J., Worthington, C., & Jamison, P. (2004). Phonological awareness intervention: Comparison of Fast ForWord, earobics, and LiPS. *Journal of Educational Resources, 97,* 147-157.

Posner, M.I., & Raichle, M.E. (1994). *Images of mind.* New York: W.H. Freeman and Company.

Pugh, K.R., Mencl, W.E., Jenner, A.R., Katz, L., Frost, S.J., Lee, J.R., Shaywitz, S.E., & Shaywitz, B.A. (2000). Functional neuroimaging studies of reading and reading disability (developmental dyslexia). *Mental Retardation and Developmental Disabilities Research Reviews, 6,* 207-213.

Ratey, J.J. (2001). *A user's guide to the brain: Perception, attention, and the four theatres of the brain.* New York: Pantheon Books.

Rechsly, R.J. (2003). *What if LD identification changed to reflect research findings?* Paper presented at the National Research Center on Learning Disabilities Responsiveness-to-Intervention Symposium, Kansas City, MO.

Reiter, A., Tucha, O., & Lange, K.W. (2004). Executive functions in children with dyslexia. *Dyslexia, 11,* 116-131.

Restak, R. (2001). *Mozart's brain and the fighter pilot: Unleashing your brain's potential.* New York: Harmony Books.

Richards, T.L., Aylward, E.H., Field, K.M., Grimme, A.C., Raskind, W., Richards, A., Nagy, W., Eckert, M., Leonard, C., Abbott, R.D., & Berninger, V.W. (2006). Converging evidence for triple word form theory in children with dyslexia. *Developmental Neuropsychology, 30* (1), 547-589.

Ritter, S., Gunter, H.D., Specht, H.J., & Rupp, A. (2005). Neuromagnetic responses reflect the temporal pitch change of regular interval of sounds. *Neuroimage, 27* (3), 533-543.

Rolls, E.T. (1997). The orbitofrontal cortex. *Philosophical Transactions of the Royal Society B, 351,* 1433-1443.

Rourke, B.P. (1995). *Syndrome of nonverbal learning disabilities; Neurodevelopmental manifestations.* New York: Guilford Press.

Rourke, B.P., van der Vlugt, H., & Rourke, S. B. (2002). *Practice of child-clinical neuropsychology: An introduction.* The Netherlands: Swets & Zeitlinger.

Rumsey, J.M. (1996). *Neuroimaging in developmental dyslexia.* In G.R. Lyon & J.M. Rumsey (Eds.), *Neuroimaging: A window to the neurological foundations of learning and behavior in children.* (p. 57-77). Baltimore: Paul H. Brookes.

Sagan, C. (1997). *The demon-haunted world: Science as a candle in the dark.* New York: Ballantine Books.

Sandak, R., Mencl, W.E., Frost, S. ., Rueckl, J.G., Katz, L., Moore, D.L., Mason, S.A., Fulbright, R.K., Constable, R.T., & Pugh, K.R., (2004). The neurobiology of adaptive learning in reading: A contrast of different training conditions. *Cognitive, Affective, & Behavioral Neuroscience, 4* (1), 67-88.

Sattler, J. (1988). *Assessment of children.* Jerome M. Sattler Publisher: San Diego.

Schatschneider, C., & Torgeson, J.K. (2004). Using our current understanding of dyslexia to support early identification and intervention. *Journal of Child Neurology, 19,* 759-765.

Semrud-Clikeman, M. (2005). Neuropsychological aspects for evaluating learning disabilities. *Journal of Learning Disabilities, 38,* 563-568.

Shastry, B.S. (2007). Developmental dyslexia: An update. *Human Genetics, 52* (2), 104-109.

Shaywitz, S. (1998). Dyslexia. *The New England Journal of Medicine, 338* (5), 307-311.

Shaywitz, S. (2004). *Overcoming dyslexia.* New York: Random House.

Shaywitz, S., & Shaywitz, B. (2005). Dyslexia: Specific reading disability. *Biological Psychiatry, 57,* 1301-1309.

Shaywitz, S.E., Shaywitz, B.A., & Fulbright, R.K. (2003). Neural systems for compensation and persistence. Young adult outcome of childhood reading disability. *Biological Psychiatry, 54,* 25-33.

Shaywitz, B.A., Shaywitz, S.E., Pugh, K.R., Mencl, W.E., Fullbright, R.K., Skudlarski, P. (2002). Disruption of posterior brain systems for reading in children with developmental dyslexia. *Biological Psychiatry, 52,* 101-110.

Shinn, M.R. (2002). Best practices in using curriculum-based measurement in a problem-solving model. In A. Thomas & J. Grimes (Eds.), *Best practices in school psychology IV* (pp. 671-697). Bethesda, MD: National Association of School Psychologists.

Siegel, D. J. (2006). *The developing mind: Toward a neurobiology of interpersonal experience.* New York: The Guilford Press.

Smythe, I., Everatt, J., & Salter, R. (Eds.). (2004). *The international book of dyslexia: A guide to practice and resources.* West Sussex, England: John Wiley & Sons.

Snow, C.E., Burns, M.S., & Griffin, P. (Eds.). (1998). *Preventing reading difficulties in young children.* Washington D.C.: National Academy Press.

Spafford, C.A. & Grosser, G.S. (2005). *Dyslexia and reading difficulties: Research and resource guide for working with all struggling readers.* Boston, MA: Pearson Education, Inc.

Spreen, O., Risser, A.H. & Edgell, D. (1995). *Developmental neuropsychology.* New York: Oxford University Press.

Stahl, S.M. (2000). *Essential psychopharmacology.* New York: Cambridge University Press.

Stahl, S.A., & Nagy, W.E. (2006). *Teaching word meanings.* Mahwah, N. J.: Erlbaum.

Stein, J. (2000). The neurobiology of reading. *Prostaglandins, Leukotrienes and Essential Fatty Acids, 63* (1/2), 109-116.

Tallal, P., Miller, S., & Fitch, R.H. (1993). Neurobiological basis of speech. A case for the preeminence of temporal speech. *Annals of the New York Academy of Science, 682,* 27-47.

Temple, E. (2002). Brain mechanisms in normal and dyslexic readers. *Current Opinion in Neurobiology, 12,* 178-193.

Tobin, K.G. (2003). The effects of Horizons reading program and prior phonological awareness training on the reading skills of first graders. *Journal of Direct Instruction, (3),* 1-16.

Torgeson, J.K., Rashotte, C.A., & Alexander, A. (2003). Progress towards Understanding the instructional conditions necessary for remediating reading difficulties in older children. In B.R. Forman (Ed.), *Preventing and Remediating Reading Difficulties: Bringing Science to Scale.* Timonium, MD: York Press.

Torgeson, J., Wagner, R., Rashotte, C., Rose, E., Lindamood, P., & Conway, T., & Garvan, C. (1999). Preventing reading failure in young children with phonological processing disabilities: Group and individual responses to instruction. *Journal of Educational Psychology, 91,* 579-593.

Tunmer W., & Chapman, J. (2003). The reading recovery approach to preventive early intervention: As good as it gets? *Read Psychology, 24,* 405-428.

Uhry, J. K. & Clark, D. B. (2005). *Dyslexia: Theory and practice of instruction.* Baltimore MD: York

Vargo, F.E., Grosser, G.S., & Spafford, C.S. (1995). Digit span and other WISC-R scores in the diagnosis of dyslexia in children. *Perceptual and Motor Skills, 80,* 1219-1229.

Vellutino, F.R., Scanlon, D.M., & Lyon, G.R. (2000). Differentiating between difficult-to-remediate and readily remediate poor readers: More evidence against the IQ-achievement discrepancy definition of reading disability. *Journal of Learning Disabilities, 33* (3), 223-238.

Weingartner, H. (2000). Metaphors and models of executive functioning: comment on Giancola (2000). *Experimental and Clinical Psychopharmacology, 8* (4), 609-611.

Willcutt, E.G., Olson, R.K., Pennington, B.F., Boada, R., Ogline, J.S., Tunick, R.A., & Chabildas, N.A. (2001). Comparison of the cognitive deficits in reading disability and attention deficit hyperactivity disorder. *Journal of Abnormal Psychology, 110,* 157-172.

Wilson, B.A. (1995). *Wilson reading system: MSLE research report.* Unpublished report from Wilson Language Training, 162 West Main Street, Millbury, MA 01527.

Wolf, M. (1999). What time may tell: Towards a new conceptualization of developmental dyslexia. *Annals of Dyslexia, 49,* 3-23.

Wolf, M., & Bowers, P.G. (1999). The double deficit hypothesis for the developmental dyslexias. *Journal of Educational Psychology, 91,* 415-438.

ABOUT THE AUTHORS

Dr. Steven G. Feifer, D. Ed., NCSP, ABSNP is a nationally renowned speaker in the field of learning disabilities and has conducted numerous seminars and trainings for educators and psychologists throughout the United States and Canada. He is dually trained as both a nationally certified school psychologist from James Madison University, and is also board certified by the American Board of School Neuropsychology. His doctorate work was conducted at Indiana University of Pennsylvania, with research stints at the National Institute of Health (NIH) in Bethesda, MD. Dr. Feifer has co-authored five books on learning disorders and remediation strategies for children. His first book, ***The Neuropsychology of Reading Disorders: Diagnosis and Intervention*** was voted *"neuropsychology publication of the year"* for 2001 by the National Association of School Psychologists. Dr. Feifer currently works as a school psychologist in Frederick, MD, is a course instructor in the ABSNP neuropsychology training program, and consults with numerous school districts throughout the country. His hobbies include playing golf poorly, playing drums even worse, and spending as much time as possible with his beloved wife and three children.

Douglas A. Della Toffalo, Ph.D. ABSNP is a nationally-certified school psychologist and licensed psychologist in Pennsylvania who currently works as a school psychologist in a small rural school district in PA. His active private practice in multiple locations throughout Western PA consists primarily of conducting and supervising pediatric neuropsychological evaluations for diagnostic clarification and intervention planning as well as teen and adult neuropsychological evaluations for transition planning and vocational rehabilitation purposes. Dr. Della Toffalo contracts with school districts and advocacy organizations regarding legal disputes and due process hearings. He has conducted numerous trainings and seminars for psychologists, educators, and counselors on topics such as neuropsychological assessment, Response to Intervention (RtI), Transition planning, and a variety of low-incidence disorders. He has participated in the design and standardization of several neuropsychological measures and authored publications on topics such as outcomes in community-based mental health treatment, diagnostic decisions regarding emotional disturbance, and executive functions.

Dr. Della Toffalo completed his doctoral work in School Psychology at Penn State University, and he completed post-graduate training in clinical neuropsychology through the Fielding Institute. Dr. Della Toffalo is board certified by the American Board of School Neuropsychology.

Notes

NOTES

NOTES